THE BDD FAMILY

COPING WITH BODY DYSMORPHIC DISORDER IN A PEER SUPPORT GROUP

EVA FISHER, PhD

FEAR TO COURAGE, LLC

The BDD Family: Coping with Body Dysmorphic Disorder in a Peer Support Group

Published by Fear to Courage, LLC
Denver, CO

ISBN: 979-8-218-02154-2

PSYCHOLOGY / Mental Health

Cover design by NZ Graphics, copyright owned by Eva Fisher

Photography by Bryan Grant

The peer support, advice, opinions, and personal experiences shared by the author and BDD forum members are provided for educational and informational purposes only. The content in the book is not intended to be a substitute for consultation with health care providers. Each individual's health concerns should be evaluated by a qualified professional.

QUANTITY PURCHASES: Schools, companies, professional groups, clubs, and other organizations may qualify for special terms when ordering quantities of this title. For information, email Eva@FeartoCourage.com.

This book is dedicated to everyone who is battling BDD, and to their friends, family members, and loved ones.

CONTENTS

Preface   ix

PART ONE
MY BDD EXPERIENCES

1. MY ROAD TO RECOVERY   3
   Childhood Trauma   3
   Hating My Appearance   5
   Gaining Insight   6
   Seeking Treatment   7
   Recovery from BDD   8

2. LEARNING ABOUT BDD   11
   A Secret Disorder   12
   My BDD Symptoms   14
   What Caused My BDD?   15
   Diagnosing Myself   16
   Finding the BDD Forum   17
   Forum Members and Messages   18

PART TWO
THE BDD FORUM FAMILY

3. BDD PEER SUPPORT   23
   Why Peer Support Is Valuable   23
   Disclosing BDD Experiences   26
   Asking Questions about BDD   28
   Sharing Personal Stories   29
   Having Conversations: "Thank you for your replies"   31

4. SEEKING AND PROVIDING SUPPORT   35
   Seeking Support: "I need someone to help me"   35
   Providing Support: "Get treatment"   37
   Helping Family Members and Friends   38

5. BDD FORUM LEADERS 41
    Forum Leaders and Roles 41
    Roger: Greeter and Information Giver 42
    Kathy: Advocate and Mediator 45
    Mia: Encourager and Opinion Giver 47
    Janet: Cheerleader and Opinion Giver 50
    Fran: Encourager and Forum Critic 52

PART THREE
BATTLING BDD SYMPTOMS

6. LOOKING FOR CAUSES 61
    Childhood Bullying and Abuse 61
    Family's Focus on Appearance 63
    Abnormal Brain Functioning 65

7. PAINFUL APPEARANCE OBSESSIONS 67
    Feeling Ugly: "I'm ugly and weird looking" 67
    Distorted Body Image: "My body looks odd now" 73
    Negative Emotions: "I feel like nothing" 77
    Suicidality: "I feel too ugly to live" 80

8. BDD-RELATED BEHAVIORS 87
    Seeking Cosmetic Procedures (Surgery) 87
    Mirror Checking/Avoidance 91
    Hiding Flaws (Camouflaging) 93
    Taking Selfies (Photos and Videos) 95
    Seeking Reassurance: "I know she's lying" 99
    Social Comparison: "My closest friend is beautiful" 104

9. IMPACT ON RELATIONSHIPS AND CAREER 109
    Avoiding Social Gatherings 109
    Dating and Relationships 111
    Parenting with BDD 115
    Changing Career Ambitions 117

PART FOUR
OVERCOMING BDD

10. GETTING DIAGNOSED 123
    Diagnosis by Self, Friends, and Family 123
    Clinical Diagnosis: "Am I in the right place?" 127
    Diagnosis on the Forum: "Do I have BDD?" 130

11. TREATMENT EXPERIENCES 133
    Clinical Treatment 133
    Barriers to Treatment 140
    Treatment Resources and Information 149

12. COPING WITH BDD SYMPTOMS 153
    Self-Acceptance/Accepting Flaws 153
    Hobbies/Music/Exercise/Nature 156
    Posting to the Forum 158
    Positive Reappraisal 160

13. RECOVERY STORIES 163
    From Recovery to Advocacy 163
    Beating BDD Story 164

PART FIVE
SUPPORTIVE ONLINE COMMUNITY

14. EMOTIONAL SUPPORT 171
    Forum Leaders 171
    Members and Moderators 176

15. NETWORK SUPPORT 185
    Forum Leaders: "We are always here" 185
    Moderators and Members: "Welcome to the forum" 190

16. CONFLICTS BETWEEN MEMBERS 195
    The Forum Flamer 196
    Trolling on the Forum 199
    Beauty or the Beast? 201
    Fran and Roger Collide 203
    Roger Targets the Forum Flamer 205

PART SIX
CONCLUSION

17. SUPPORT GROUP PROS AND CONS   209
    Benefits   209
    Drawbacks   214

18. MOVING BEYOND BDD   223

APPENDIX A: BDD RESOURCES   227
A1: Organizations and Websites   227
A2: Suicide Prevention Resources   228
A3: BDD Clinics and Therapists   229
A4: Self-Diagnosis Information   232
A5: Books about BDD   232

APPENDIX B: MESSAGES (FULL TEXT)   235
B1: Fran's Story/Introduction Post   235
B2: Coping with Suicidal Thoughts   239
B3: Grandmother Caused BDD   241
B4: The Most Beautiful Woman   243
B5: How to Cope with a Bad Day   245
B6: Recovery to Advocacy Story   248
B7: Beating BDD Story   252
B8: Feeling Too Ugly to Live   258
B9: Fran Leaving Forum   263
B10: Roger (Moderator) Updated Rules   269

APPENDIX C: RESEARCH RESULTS   273
Personal Disclosure   274
Social Support   274

ENDNOTES   277
Bibliography   285
Acknowledgments   291
About the Author   293
Become Part of the Global BDD Family   295

PREFACE

What do you want to accomplish in life? What are your goals, hopes, and dreams?

Writing a book for people with body dysmorphic disorder (BDD) has been one of my goals since recovering from the disorder nearly twenty years ago. I am grateful that therapy and medication enabled me to overcome body dysmorphic disorder when I was thirty-six years old. As a result, I found myself reflecting on my recovery and wondering what I could do to help others before my fortieth birthday. I wanted individuals with BDD to get the treatment they needed to recover. I wanted them to live a life free from the shame and depression I had experienced for nearly 15 years. But what could I do to help others diagnose themselves and get the treatment they needed?

That was the question I pondered a week before my fortieth birthday. I knew BDD was not well known, even by many therapists. I had read *The Broken Mirror* and learned BDD is a serious and devastating, yet underrecognized, mental health condition. According to the author, Dr. Katharine Phillips, we all need to know it exists, how to identify it, and what treatments work. That was my call to action. Only a handful of other books had been written about BDD at the time. So perhaps writing a book about my recovery could help?

I knew my personal story was one of many. Millions of men and women suffer from this disorder. Significantly less get the support they need to recover. Everyone's story is different and important. I wanted to learn how other people were coping with and overcoming BDD. Doing more research on the topic seemed like the best way to accomplish that goal.

I decided to combine my desire to get a PhD in communication with my goal of raising awareness about BDD. In 2008, I joined the first cohort of graduate students in the Colorado State University PhD program for public communication and technology. The focus for my dissertation research was analyzing personal disclosure and social support messages posted to an online BDD public forum. After graduating, I shared my recovery story on the International OCD Foundation website. That was the first step I took to raise awareness about BDD and spread hope that recovery is possible.

In 2020, the global pandemic increased mental stress and anguish for millions of people in the United States and around the world. The pandemic exacerbated symptoms of depression, anxiety, and other mental health disorders, including BDD. As a result, I started an online peer support group for individuals suffering from BDD in spring 2021.

Multiple BDD peer support groups meet via web conferencing in the United States and the United Kingdom. More books are being written by individuals with BDD and by therapists who treat the condition. Organizations such as the International OCD Foundation and the BDD Foundation provide valuable information about diagnosis and treatment.

The condition is no longer as underrecognized as it was when I started my dissertation research. However, many people still suffer in silence and feel ugly, alone, depressed, and suicidal, unaware they have a treatable mental health condition. But there is help for people with BDD. Peer support groups offer access to information, advice, and empathy from others who understand. These groups supplement support from family members, friends, partners, and treatment specialists. I gained a deep respect and appreciation for the value of peer support while studying the messages posted to the BDD forum.

RELEASE OF FEAR / SHAME

Many participants viewed the forum as a place where they could share their deepest fears with other members and get help. New members often described their symptoms and then asked others if they had BDD or were truly ugly. The answer is not an easy or simple one. People with BDD feel ugly and disfigured even though they often appear normal or attractive to others.

Some members wanted to get a professional diagnosis but were unwilling to share their appearance concerns outside the forum. Self-stigma and shame prevented them from getting a diagnosis from therapists. Even after people received a clinical BDD diagnosis, they remained skeptical, convinced what they saw in the mirror was real.

One poster asked others why believing they were ugly caused them such distress. The answers ranged from fear of being an outcast to feeling unwanted, unlovable, and rejected by others. People with BDD may know their fears are irrational, but they cannot stop these thoughts from controlling their lives. One member replied to the question this way:

> I feel like because I'm ugly I have no importance in this world and that I won't be successful. Yet at the same time, the rational part of me knows that isn't true. Looks aren't everything. Ugly or beautiful, everyone is important and beautiful in their own way.
>
> I think a lot of people with BDD, including myself just think that in order to be happy, we have to be beautiful. it's a vicious cycle. ☹

People with BDD have negative thoughts about their appearance and believe if they looked better, their lives would improve. The truth is, only when they overcome BDD can their lives get better. When I had BDD, I believed feeling ugly kept me from being successful and happy. After I self-diagnosed myself with BDD, the stigma of feeling ugly was replaced with the stigma of having a mental health disorder. My desire to get better gave me the courage to seek and find clinical and pharmacological treatment. Getting help enabled me to overcome the disorder. I no longer hate my nose and now appreciate the positive aspects of my appearance.

This book contains excerpts from hundreds of members who posted messages to the BDD forum over the course of one year (2012). These messages are still relevant since they describe in detail many of the same thoughts, feelings, and behaviors individuals have today. My personal experiences with BDD are included, along with information from researchers and clinicians, to educate those unfamiliar with the disorder. Additional resources are provided in the Appendix with contact information for treatment centers, specialists, and organizations that offer help for people with BDD, along with their family members and friends.

One of my favorite poems is attributed to Ralph Waldo Emerson. Emerson lived in Concord, Massachusetts, where I often spent time while living and working in Boston. His "What Is Success" poem has always been inspirational for me:

What Is Success?
To laugh often and much;
To win the respect of intelligent people
and the affection of children;
To earn the appreciation of honest critics
and endure the betrayal of false friends;
To appreciate beauty;
To find the best in others;
To leave the world a bit better, whether by
a healthy child, a garden patch
or a redeemed social condition;
To know even one life has breathed
easier because you have lived;
This is to have succeeded.

I hope this book raises awareness about BDD and the suffering the condition causes millions of people in the United States and around the world. I also want to encourage those who have BDD, or who recognize themselves in the stories here, that recovery is possible. Please reach out to your peers, loved ones, and qualified therapists to get the treatment and support you need to recover. Thank you for reading, and please be kind and compassionate with yourself and others, along your journey of coping with and recovery from BDD.

PART ONE
MY BDD EXPERIENCES

My Road to Recovery

I shall be telling this with a sigh
Somewhere ages and ages hence:
Two roads diverged in a wood, and I—
I took the one less traveled by,
And that has made all the difference.

(from "The Road Not Taken" by Robert Frost)

Childhood Trauma

"Stop behaving like your father!" I remember my mother scolding me after one of my emotional outbursts when I was young. My father would often yell and raise his voice when he was upset about something my mother, my brother, or I had done. My mother's admonition to not act like him came from comparing his temper to my emotional outbursts.

After many years together, my parents had become adept at pushing each other's emotional buttons. There were days when my father would come home from work and sit quietly in front of the television, smoking his pipe, and ignoring the family. Other days, if his workday did not go well, he would vent his anger toward my mother, my brother, and me. He usually calmed down after we had retreated to our rooms to escape his anger. My father was never physically abusive, but he had a temper fueled by neuroticism and by his mother's emotional disengagement during his childhood.

When my brother and I were teenagers, my mother refused to be trapped in the house during my father's tantrums. She would leave for hours and drive somewhere until he had calmed down and it was safe to return home. During these times, my father would turn his anger toward my brother and me. He would tell us it was my mother's fault we did not love him, and he blamed her for turning us against him. Of course, he never seemed to realize (until I confronted him toward the end of his life) that his arguments with my mother alienated us from him.

Their arguments sometimes deteriorated into throwing objects; a glass ashtray went flying past my father's head at one point. The breaking point for my mother came after my father retired and he was around the house ALL the time. He rarely moved from the living room chair during the day. He would sit there making negative observations about activities taking place around him. I remember my mother vacuuming the rug around his feet. She filed for divorce six months later.

The contempt my parents expressed for one another during their yelling matches was palpable. Their hostility made a lasting impression on me as a child. I was also constantly teased at school by my classmates. As a result, I would come home in tears, having endured another stressful day at school. My emotional outbursts became too much for my mother to bear. After divorcing my father, she wanted peace and quiet at home. I remember the day she reprimanded me for acting like my father. She warned me if I did, I would suffer the same fate. I would make others around me miserable and have no chance of being in a loving relationship.

I took those words to heart. Instead of getting visibly upset, I turned my negative emotions inward toward myself. Self-hatred was easier to bear than maternal disapproval. I internalized another unintended message from my mother; if I was behaving like my father, and she hated my father, she was also rejecting me. On some deep level, I felt unlovable and genetically flawed. Yet my mother continued to be my best friend during my twenties. Our bond remained strong despite my fear of not fulfilling her expectations.

Hating My Appearance

I remember starting to stare at myself in the mirror when I was sixteen years old. Before then, I had spent most of my free time walking and reading outdoors, watching television, writing, or playing with my friends and pets. Then, after I turned sixteen, I became increasingly aware of my appearance, especially my face. I started wearing makeup, reading fashion magazines, and comparing my appearance to my peers and models in the magazines. As a result, I found my appearance and facial features sadly lacking. My eyes were too small and close together, my nose too large, my forehead too short, and my chin too long. Also, though I was slender, my hips and thighs looked out of proportion to the rest of my body. I identified my body as "pear-shaped" according to the fashion magazines I read.

It was not until I turned eighteen, during the summer before my freshman year at college, that I confessed to my mother how much I hated my appearance, especially my nose. I told her that I didn't want to get married and have children, in case they ended up having my fat, ugly nose. I also told my mother I had thoughts about committing suicide due to the fear of passing my defect on to my children. Her response was to pay for plastic surgery (rhinoplasty) to have my nose "corrected" by making it thinner.

After the surgery, I was horrified by the facial swelling and black eyes. My mother had to cover all the mirrors in the house while my nose healed. However, soon after the swelling went down, I realized I still hated my nose. My profile looked odd to me now. I never mentioned my displeasure with the results to my mother. She clearly felt the surgery had been successful and was pleased with my altered appearance. I felt terrible, still hated my appearance, and now felt guilty because the surgery had not made me feel better about myself.

I was a good student throughout college, even though I struggled with low self-esteem and depression. My grades enabled me to graduate cum laude, though I would have preferred summa or magna. After college, I managed an art gallery in Boston and found it extremely stressful being on my own for the first time. Soon after breaking up with my boyfriend, the stress and feelings of emotional abandonment caused my symptoms to worsen. I spent hours in the morning and evening staring at my face in the mirror, looking at the pores in my nose, and picking at my skin. At one point, the picking caused a small facial scar. I remember collapsing on a stairway in tears later that day, devastated by the terrible mark I had caused, convinced it would never go away.

GAINING INSIGHT

After I turned thirty, I decided to move from Boston to Boulder, Colorado, where my brother and best friend lived. My mother, having been diagnosed with breast cancer at the age of sixty-one, soon followed. She wanted to be close to her son and daughter during her illness. I went back to school to become a website designer, while my brother earned a law degree, got married, and settled down in Denver. My best friend became an ultra-runner and introduced me to the sport of long-distance running. Trail running and hiking in the Rocky Mountains helped relieve the stress and anxiety I often felt upon waking. My appearance still preoccupied me, so being outdoors alleviated my symptoms for a while. If I was not able to look at my face, I didn't obsess about my nose.

Meanwhile, my mother was struggling with the effects of a second mastectomy and chemotherapy. She became depressed, and her doctor prescribed Prozac for the symptoms. The Prozac helped to relieve her depression, and she became much more optimistic about her chances of survival. Her attention then turned to me and my depression, though she didn't know its cause. I had never again confessed to her how much I hated my appearance or about the related symptoms of skin picking, comparison with others, or the preoccupation with my nose. It surprised me that she noticed I was depressed. I had become so familiar

with the constant state of anxiety about my appearance that it 〉
longer apparent to me.

My mother suggested I get a prescription for Prozac since it had helped relieve her symptoms. I disliked the idea of taking prescription medication, and so I resisted her suggestions. Also, since I believed I truly was ugly, I felt my negative feelings were justified. Then, one day while waiting in line at the grocery store, a magazine cover caught my attention. On the cover of *Shape* magazine was a beautiful blond model in a bright blue bikini. As I scanned the headlines surrounding the model, I noticed an article titled "Hate your looks? What it means when your mirror lies." The title caught my attention because my friends, past boyfriends, and family members had always insisted I looked fine to them, which contradicted what the mirror told me.

Inside the magazine was an article about BDD by Liz Brody.[1] The article described the symptoms, possible causes, and treatment for the disorder. There was a five-item self-diagnosis questionnaire and a list of ten common symptoms of the disorder from the book by Katharine Phillips, *The Broken Mirror: Understanding and Treating Body Dysmorphic Disorder*. The article discussed effective treatments, both pharmacological and clinical, and noted that cosmetic surgery is often ineffective in treating symptoms of the disorder. Sufferers described feelings of shame and embarrassment that were incredibly familiar to me. Also, I was relieved to read that people with the disorder are often considered to be quite attractive, even while believing they are ugly. This reassured me that my friends and family members were telling me the truth rather than just trying to make me feel better by saying I looked fine to them.

SEEKING TREATMENT

That article changed my life. Now I had a name for my symptoms. Now I knew Prozac could help me. I felt empowered by the information, and for the first time in fifteen years, I had hope I was not as ugly as I imagined myself to be. That article provided me with the insight and information I needed to diagnose myself with the disorder. However, the realization I was not seeing myself in the same way that I appeared to others was shocking at first. I was both relieved and dismayed by the possibility that what I saw in the mirror was not what others saw when they looked at me. The stigma about having a mental health condition was less important to me than the stigma and shame I felt about my perceived appearance defects. As a result, I referred myself for treatment.

The psychiatrist at the health maintenance organization (HMO) was not familiar with BDD, so she diagnosed me with depression. She agreed to put me on Prozac, which, fortunately, is one of the medications shown to reduce symptoms of the disorder. I also entered therapy with a clinical psychologist at the HMO. The medication started to take effect after a few weeks, and my anxiety and preoccupation with my appearance slowly started to diminish. My mother was the first to notice the change in my demeanor. She was delighted to see me smile and told me I was becoming the young woman she always imagined I could be. Sadly, my mother passed away shortly after I started treatment.

After being on Prozac and in clinical treatment for two years, my symptoms improved. My anxiety about my ugliness dissipated and became manageable. I was no longer obsessing about my appearance and staring at my face in the mirror for hours every day. However, the psychiatrist at the HMO was convinced I was a "lifer" and would be on Prozac for the rest of my life. I did not want to be on prescription medication long term due to the side effects of Prozac. As a result, I started practicing meditation and was able to slowly stop taking prescription medication to treat the BDD symptoms.

RECOVERY FROM BDD

Now, twenty-five years after diagnosing myself with BDD, I consider myself to be recovered from the disorder. I no longer agonize about my appearance, and most of the time, I am at peace with how I look. My relationship with my body has improved. I enjoy my physical self and appreciate what I can do with my body, rather than only worrying about how it appears to others. I also understand that my self-worth is not dependent upon how I look. My psychological treatment involved coming to terms with my childhood fears of abandonment and loss of love. Now I recognize that my feelings about my appearance originate inside me. That makes them manageable.

There are still difficult times when I struggle with symptoms, especially when I am stressed or anxious. I have adopted coping mechanisms to keep my symptoms under control, such as limiting the number of mirrors in my house. Also, I keep the lights dimmed when getting ready for bed at night. That way, I don't focus on small details when I am tired and need to sleep. I still dislike my profile and probably will never like my nose. I have accepted that. That's okay. I am not my nose.

After recovering from BDD, the quality of my life has improved dramatically. I now appreciate myself in ways that were impossible when I was obsessed with hating my appearance. The focus of my life revolves around my family and friends, my relationship, and my passion for helping people cope with the disorder. Please contact me to learn more about peer support groups, overcoming symptoms, and getting treatment.

I AM NOT MY NOSE!

Learning about BDD

Think about the difference between your body and your body image and focus on changing the latter. If you think you are ugly, it doesn't mean other people see you the same way. And having your body surgically altered might not change the way you feel about it. "Usually, BDD patients think all they have to do is change their appearance. We teach them what needs to change is how they see themselves." (Dr. Sabine Wilhelm, quoted in "When the Mirror Lies"[1])

I wanted to educate myself and learn more about BDD after recovering. I bought *The Broken Mirror* by Katharine Phillips and other books by BDD researchers and clinicians, including *Feeling Good About the Way You Look* by Sabine Wilhelm. *The Broken Mirror* contains information about BDD symptoms, causes, and treatment options, along with stories from patients, and diagnostic tools like the Body Dysmorphic Disorder Questionnaire (BDDQ). I also read hundreds of academic studies published by BDD researchers while pursuing my dissertation research. Many of the articles and books are listed in the bibliography. I encourage readers who want more information about BDD to review the resources in Appendix A. Educating yourself about the disorder is the first step in defeating your personal BDD bully.

A SECRET DISORDER

I never told my parents about undergoing treatment for depression and BDD. I was worried they would either be ashamed of me for having a mental health disorder or would agree my appearance flaws were real and needed to be fixed. I did share my BDD diagnosis with my best friend and running companion, Stephanie, who was kind and supportive and kept my secret. The only other people who knew about my BDD symptoms were the psychologist and psychiatrist at the medical center (HMO) where I was treated for depression, and my counselor who helped me resolve core issues related to childhood trauma.

I kept my condition a secret because part of me was convinced my nose was still deformed, even after the surgery. When I had BDD, my insight level was absent/delusional. Delusional means I fully believed the image that stared back at me in the mirror was real. However, with BDD, the mirror *does* lie because many people with BDD are considered attractive by family members, friends, and significant others.[2] This is one of the ironies involved with BDD; even as people struggle to deal with perceived ugliness, others admire them for their appearance.

BDD is a devastating, debilitating disorder, and one that needs to be better recognized so more people can recover. Unfortunately, BDD is often underrecognized by friends, family members, and even therapists due to the embarrassment, guilt, and shame that individuals feel about their appearance concerns.[3] Many people with BDD are unwilling to share their symptoms with others, since doing so could elicit a negative response, such as being accused of being vain or selfish.

As a result, individuals with BDD often feel alone and isolated, unaware that millions of other people in the United States and around the world suffer from this underrecognized disorder. Studies have found that BDD impacts from 1.7 percent to 2.9 percent of adults in the United States,[4] with the disorder affecting about 2.5 percent of women and 2.2 percent of men.[5] This makes BDD more prevalent than obsessive-compulsive disorder (OCD), which has lifetime prevalence rates of 1.5 percent of women and 1.0 percent of men.[6] BDD affects more women and men in the United States than bulimia or anorexia:

bulimia is seen in roughly 1.5 percent of women and 0.5 percent of men, and anorexia in 0.35 percent of women and 0.1 percent of men.[7]

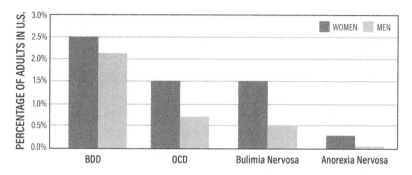

PREVALENCE OF BDD COMPARED TO OTHER DISORDERS

Figure 1: Prevalence of BDD in the United States Compared to Other Disorders[8]

BDD affects women and men at an approximately equal rate, with slightly higher occurrences in females.[9] When I explain to people that BDD affects men and women almost equally, they are often surprised. Body image insecurities are usually attributed to girls and women due to the emphasis placed on them to be pretty and attractive, especially during adolescence.[10] However, BDD does not discriminate, as shown by the common themes of hating one's nose, hair, face, and body in messages posted to the BDD forum (Chapter 7).

When I had BDD, I was convinced being depressed about my appearance was normal since I felt ugly. Major depressive disorder is the most common comorbid disorder in people with BDD, followed by social phobia and OCD.[11] Comorbid disorders coexist in one individual, which can make diagnosing BDD difficult. Other disorders that can coexist with BDD include bipolar disorder, eating disorders, personality disorders, and substance abuse disorders. If you diagnose yourself with BDD, it is important to follow up with a knowledgeable psychiatrist or psychologist to ensure your treatment options are tailored to your symptoms.

My BDD Symptoms

I remember obsessing about the shape and size of my nose for hours every day, convinced others were judging me negatively based on my nose. I could not have a conversation with anyone, including family members, friends, and boyfriends, without my attention being diverted to thoughts about my nose. Whenever I had the chance, I would check my nose and face in the mirror, wishing the rhinoplasty had been more successful.

My symptoms were similar to those of other people who suffer from body dysmorphic disorder. About one-third of people with BDD think about their perceived flaws for one to three hours a day, nearly 40 percent for three to eight hours a day, and about a quarter for more than eight hours a day. Most people with BDD realize they spend too much time thinking about their appearance, but others believe everyone worries about their appearance for hours every day.[12]

I believed my appearance concerns were justified because my mother, friends, and society put so much importance on being beautiful and attractive to others. Being unhappy with one's appearance is commonplace in modern society. Studies have shown that more than half of women and almost half of men are dissatisfied with their overall appearance, and even more are dissatisfied with particular body areas. So how is body dysmorphic disorder different from normal appearance concerns? Dr. Phillips and other researchers speculate that body dissatisfaction spans a continuum from mild to moderate to severe and disabling. BDD is on the severe/disabling end of this continuum.[13]

BDD symptoms are further complicated by the behaviors that individuals with the disorder undertake. These behaviors can become rituals and are therefore considered compulsive. They include (from most to least common) camouflaging the perceived defect(s); comparing one's appearance to others (social comparison); checking one's appearance in mirrors and other reflective surfaces; seeking cosmetic treatments such as surgery and dermatology; engaging in excessive grooming; questioning others about the perceived flaw or convincing others it is unattractive (reassurance seeking); touching the perceived flaw; excessively changing clothes; dieting; skin picking to improve appearance; tanning to improve the perceived flaw; and engaging in excessive exercise, including excessive weight lifting.[14]

Social comparison with other women was a never-ending occupation for me. It was like being in a beauty contest with every woman who was younger, prettier, or thinner than I was. I envied them and agonized over why I didn't have the beautiful nose, legs, eyes, face, or body they had. Facial symmetry was important to me; I wanted to have a high forehead, larger eyes, slender nose, strong jawline, and smaller chin. I was looking at other women through rose-colored glasses and seeing myself through gray goggles. Having plastic surgery on my nose did not help and made my symptoms worse. I continued to agonize over my appearance and felt guilty that I was not happy with the outcome. This is common for people with BDD who undergo cosmetic surgery procedures; they are rarely pleased with the results and often feel worse after the procedures.[15]

My mother agreed to the rhinoplasty after I revealed my suicidal thoughts to her. I am fortunate that my suicide ideation did not lead to a suicide attempt. For me, living with my appearance flaws was better than not being alive at all. Tragically, many people with BDD think about killing themselves, and others succeed. Available evidence indicates approximately 80 percent of individuals with BDD experience lifetime suicidal ideation, and 24 to 28 percent have attempted suicide.[16] Often, they are young men and women who feel so hopeless about their perceived appearance defects that suicide seems like the only way to end their suffering.

WHAT CAUSED MY BDD?

I have attributed multiple causes to the onset of my symptoms. They include a genetic predisposition for mental health disorders, childhood trauma, teasing, and being obsessed with the beauty ideal promoted by the media. My father seemed to have neurotic personality traits, and my maternal grandmother suffered from depression. In addition, I was extremely shy and introverted as a child, hypersensitive to criticism, and a perfectionist. Common personality traits among people with BDD are perfectionism along with shyness, social anxiety, low self-esteem, and sensitivity to rejection and criticism.[17]

Despite these negative influences, I have reasons to be thankful for the visual acuity I inherited from my parents. My parents were both artists; my mother had a fine arts degree from New York University, and my father had a graphic design degree from the University of Vienna. I remember my mother's combined art studio and bedroom, where she painted floral still lifes and portraits throughout my childhood.

My father was an art director for a greeting card company, where he designed wrapping paper and holiday decor. I followed in my parents' artistic footsteps by becoming an art history/art studio major, managing an art gallery in Boston after college and taking painting classes as an adult. In addition, I worked as a website designer for ten years and taught college classes in website and graphic design.

Researchers have found a high percentage of patients with BDD (about 20 percent) also have a lifetime job or education in art and design.[18] People with BDD may be superior at appreciating art and beauty due to focusing on small, visual details that are imperceptible to others.[19] Thus, BDD traits could facilitate artistic creativity by heightening one's ability to appreciate beauty. I know being surrounded by beauty in art and nature brings joy into my life.

DIAGNOSING MYSELF

Standing in line at a grocery store in Colorado was not how I expected to diagnose myself with BDD. However, when I spotted the beautiful blond model on the magazine cover at the checkout, my attention was riveted. I envied her gorgeous hair, blue eyes, strong jawline, smooth skin, and slender body. My constant need to compare myself with models in fashion magazines led me to discover I had BDD. The article titled "Hate your looks? What it means when your mirror lies"[20] caught my eye. I definitely disliked my looks when comparing myself to the blond model on the magazine cover.

I skimmed the article about BDD in the magazine, amazed at how similar patients' experiences were to mine. I answered yes to three of the questions that psychiatrists use to determine whether a person suffers from BDD. First, "Are you very concerned about the appearance of some part or parts of your body you consider especially unattractive?" Second, "Do these concerns preoccupy you for at least an hour a day?" And third, "Have your feelings about your looks caused you distress, pain, or torment?" In addition, I checked yes to two clues a person could have BDD: "You avoid mirrors because you don't like how you look" and "You frequently compare yourself to others and often think you look worse than they do." After reading the article and doing more research, I was convinced I had BDD.

The psychiatrist at the medical center where I went for treatment did not share my conviction, since she was not aware of the disorder. Instead, she diagnosed me with depression and prescribed Prozac, a medication that is also effective in treating BDD. I worked with a psychologist to combat the feelings of depression and anxiety caused by my appearance concerns. Fortunately, both the medication and therapy were effective in reducing my negative feelings and compulsive behaviors. Two years after I started treatment, my BDD symptoms diminished and became manageable.

Finding the BDD Forum

I was first introduced to BDD support forums while reading Sabine Wilhelm's book *Feeling Good about the Way You Look*.[21] In the resources section, she referred readers to the BDD Central website. BDD Central was founded in 2002 by Britney Brimhall and contained multiple resources, including general education about BDD, a list of BDD treatment specialists, peer support forums, and links to BDD-related websites and blogs. The forums had a wide variety of topics, such as BDD and Relationships, BDD and Family, BDD and Dating, Success Stories, Research Studies, an Off Topic thread, and an Ask the Therapist thread moderated by clinician James Claiborn. BDD Central was one of the most popular websites for BDD-related information and peer support from 2002 to 2012.

I had initially planned on making BDD Central the focus of my dissertation research. Unfortunately, shortly after starting my research proposal, BDD Central ceased to exist. I still remember the day in

September 2012 when I walked into my advisor's office for a meeting. His first words to me were, "Where is the BDD Central site?" I told him perhaps it was temporarily down. Then I looked at his computer screen and knew the site was more than down—it was gone. I was shocked and dismayed that the popular website was no longer available. I could not imagine how the many BDD Central members would cope with its loss.

As a result, I chose the second-most popular BDD forum in 2012 for my research, based on the number of threads, posts, and members.[22] I had never posted to an online forum or support group while recovering from the disorder. Social media and online communication were not as popular in the late 1990s as they are today. Facebook started in 2004 and Twitter in 2006. During my research, I discovered a message thread started by former BDD Central members asking about the defunct website (Chapter 15). Their dismay at its loss and concern for one another demonstrated the power of peer support. Like disaster victims sharing a similar fate, finding others from BDD Central made them feel less alone.

FORUM MEMBERS AND MESSAGES

I read hundreds of messages by forum members for my dissertation research.[23] Five members stood out as the most active posters; they replied first or second in message threads and were the most prolific providers of supportive comments. I renamed the young man Roger and the four women Kathy, Mia, Janet, and Fran to protect their forum usernames. Roger posted more than one hundred messages during the year, and the four women each posted more than forty-five messages. These five members became the _emergent leaders_[24] since they provided almost as much social support (43 percent) as the other 218 members combined. Most members (the less frequent posters) posted only one to two messages, primarily seeking support. The two moderators (renamed Anna and Rose) provided support to other members, yet each posted fewer than thirty messages.[25]

Message excerpts from the less frequent posters are labeled with the person's gender identity (Female, Male, Undetermined) and with "Initial Post" or "Reply." When more than one reply is provided, they are labeled as 1, 2, 3, etc., to identify the order in which replies appeared in the thread. Moderator posts are labeled with the moderator's name and (Moderator). When the original poster replied to other members, OP is used to indicate the reply is from the person who posted the initial message. Almost all initial posts on the BDD forum received one or more replies (98 percent), with the median number being three replies.[26] Message excerpts have been edited for grammar and spelling (where needed) to improve readability.

The poster's gender identity was determined using multiple context clues, including the username, the gender identity disclosed by the person, and information revealed within a person's initial posts or replies to other members. More women than men posted to the forum: ninety-nine (44 percent) were identified as female, seventy-four (33 percent) were identified as male, and for fifty-two members (23 percent), their gender could not be determined. Members visited the site from multiple countries, including the United States, Canada, the United Kingdom, Ireland, India, and Malaysia. Forum members ranged in age from fifteen to fifty-three years old. Most members were in their early twenties to mid-forties.[27]

Reading and coding the forum posts (close to a thousand entries) was an emotional roller coaster. Both initial posts and replies contained detailed accounts of intense emotional and mental suffering. Members who responded often empathized with the original posters and shared similar experiences with emotional trauma and mental pain, including suicidal thoughts and feelings. Others recounted childhood memories of physical, emotional, and sexual abuse; rape; and parental neglect. The worst part was reading posts from people who wanted to end their lives: "I feel like I am falling down a pit and screaming but no one can hear me. I hate my body so much ... I don't want to be in it anymore. I want this pain to end. I just want to die."

Thankfully, forum members responded to these posts by providing compassion, sympathy, hope, and advice to seek professional help. The support offered on the forum provided emotional relief and lightened the dark cloud of depression that descended upon me as I read through the messages. My warning to readers suffering from BDD symptoms is that some messages may contain content that could be triggering.

However, member replies contain helpful advice and emotional support, including coping strategies, treatment options, and recovery stories.

Even while writing this book, reviewing these posts caused me to become emotionally distraught due to the intense suffering people with BDD endure. I am grateful more BDD resources are now available, including treatment centers, online support groups, and organizations such as the International OCD Foundation (United States) and the BDD Foundation (United Kingdom). There is no need to suffer in silence and every reason to get the help you need to recover.

PART TWO
THE BDD FORUM
FAMILY

BDD Peer Support

Roger-Reply: Congratulations on posting by the way, it can be hard for people to discuss these kind of things and you've come to the right place the people on this forum are fantastic.

Female-Initial Post: I've never written on any forum before. Guess I thought I would never be able to connect with anonymous usernames giving me advice over the web. But I don't really know where to turn anymore and my state in life is really wearing me down.

Why Peer Support Is Valuable

Individuals suffering from mental health disorders need a network of people who can provide empathy, encouragement, assistance, and advice. They want to know others understand their struggles so they feel less alone. Support can be found in both primary and secondary groups. Primary groups (family members, relatives, and friends) tend to be smaller, more informal, intimate, and enduring. Secondary groups tend to be larger, and interactions are guided by rules and regulations. Work, volunteer, and religious organizations are examples of secondary groups.[1]

People who perceive greater support from family members, friends, and significant others experience less severe BDD symptoms.[2] This is because social support can provide buffer effects on stress as well as direct effects on individual well-being.[3] Supportive relationships can aid recovery from illness, protect against clinical depression, reduce the risk of suicide, encourage behavioral commitment to prescribed medical regimens, and promote the use of community health services.[4]

For Roger (the most frequent poster), the BDD forum served as his extended family. He felt a kinship with people who were undergoing similar struggles with the disorder. The BDD forum enabled him and other members to feel less alone by connecting with fellow sufferers around the world. Roger believed everyone who lived with, was affected by, or sought to overcome the disorder was a member of his global BDD family:

> **Roger-Initial Post:** Please do realize you are not alone in this fight. Every person with BDD is a brother and sister in a battle to rid yourself of your own personal bully. It's a fight you can win but one that is easier with people standing behind you all the way. A common cause that unites all of us from all around the globe into a group of people determined to make a difference. We are the BDD family.

Online peer support groups, such as the BDD forum, can supplement the support provided by primary group members, face-to-face groups, and clinical treatment specialists. Rather than replacing other forms of support, peer support groups provide additional resources for people whose lives are crippled by this debilitating and underrecognized disorder. I have met many therapists, researchers, and advocates who are committed to helping people with body dysmorphic disorder. They are all part of the worldwide BDD community dedicated to supporting people with the disorder, providing effective treatment, and raising public awareness.

Peer support groups have existed for hundreds of years in fraternal organizations, such as Freemasonry, but flourished in the middle of the twentieth century with Alcoholics Anonymous and other twelve-step programs. These programs demonstrate that group support is essential in helping people recover from stressful situations.[5] The essence of support in a mutual aid group are the responses a person receives and provides to other members. [6, 7]

There are advantages to participating in online groups compared to relying on family members and friends for support: more candor (both less harsh and more forthright responses to problems), less negative judgment, reduced obligation to reciprocate support, more immediate ability to seek support, greater expertise, stigma management, ease of access, more expressive communication, and anonymity.[8] Peer support groups have similar empowerment outcomes for active participants (posters) and for lurkers (people who read messages without posting). They are better informed, more confident about treatment, have enhanced self-esteem, and feel increased optimism and control.[9]

Online support forums offer members twenty-four-hour availability, selective participation in posting and responding to messages, privacy, immediate or delayed responding, and having messages available for an extended period. Online resources are not restricted by temporal and geographic limitations.[10] Most online forums work via asynchronous communication; participants post messages that are stored online for others to read, and individuals can log on and respond at different times.[11]

BDD forum members could join the group anonymously and have access to worldwide peer support day or night. Many individuals with BDD do not disclose their personal experiences to family members and friends because of the pervasive shame that fuels their symptoms. Those who do reveal their thoughts and feelings often find others either do not believe them or cannot comprehend their experiences.[12]

I find that participants in my online support groups appreciate the easy access to getting help. They can join and leave the group at their discretion without feeling obligated to provide support on an ongoing basis. This is different from asking primary group members for support, where relationships are usually ongoing, require reciprocal sharing, and are not easy to leave.

DISCLOSING BDD EXPERIENCES

The BDD forum enabled members to disclose detailed descriptions of their personal experiences in an anonymous setting. Personal disclosure (self-disclosure) is an interaction between at least two individuals where one person deliberately divulges something personal to another.[13] Self-disclosure in support groups can be high in both depth and breadth,[14] meaning people share a lot of personal information when meeting others online. This was evident when new forum members openly shared personal details about themselves in their introductions, such as their sexual orientation or having gender dysphoria (being transgender).

A twenty-two-year-old gay man joined the BDD forum because he wanted to share his experiences with body dysmorphic disorder:

> **Male-Initial Post:** I have finally decided to join to share my story and see if others out there are feeling the same as me, and can help. Or I can help others?

> I obsess and spend hours in the mirror at times trying to sort out my looks, I hate it if my hair is out of place, I also dye my hair A LOT, any roots showing makes me feel even worse. I have a problem with my nose, my forehead and skin such as it being shiny. I look in the worst lighted room with the big mirrors in my house and I think this doesn't help, but it is a ritual.

> I am gay and have a very supportive boyfriend, but sometimes I take my anxiety out on him and I wish i did not do that. I know he says I am not ugly, but like we all know it doesn't matter what others feel, it's in my own head. I want to stop looking in the mirrors and thinking I should be under a bridge and out living my life again.

A transgender male wanted to know if he could have gender dysphoria and BDD. He posted his diagnosis in his introduction and described the pain he felt at not being supported by his mother:

Male-Initial Post: All my life, I've been a boy, until I realized that I didn't have a male body when I was 11-12. Obviously, as you can imagine, it severely upset me and I was always depressed. It started to make sense why guys wouldn't be my friend and why everyone was calling me a girl and why I was always put in groups with girls. I hated it. (I'm 17 right now.) I have a therapist who specializes in transgender patients and she would let me start hormones if my mom would let me, but my mom doesn't support me at all.

Several introductions were extensive (more than a thousand words) and contained personal information about one's BDD struggles, relationships, and career goals (see Fran's introduction in Appendix B1). Alternatively, other self-introductions could be brief, such as when a member introduced herself and her social anxiety symptoms before going on to describe her current struggles with BDD:

Female-Initial Post: So some background about myself—I've been suffering very bad anxiety since 15. I am 22 now. It never really bothered me because my safety zone was home—my anxiety symptoms usually disappeared when I was at home. Okay, so moving on to problems I am having now!

Personal disclosures in message replies were often used to display empathy with others' experiences. One woman replied to another and empathized with her feelings of ugliness:

Female-Reply: hi i am sooooo tired of being ugly too. so very tired of it. and it's hard a lot of times, when i have to look in a mirror or see a picture of myself and i just really don't want to look at it (my image) anymore. i feel like my soul belongs in a different body, a pretty one.

Another man shared his personal struggles and suicidal thoughts in his initial post. In response, a woman expressed sympathy, offered information about BDD, and disclosed her problems:

The shame intensifies under stress
bc BDD reappears and no one gets it, everything

hidda make seen verein ok fake but thats at the pid

Female-Reply: I'm sorry to hear you are going through such an awful time. BDD can go dormant for years and then reappear or it can be constant...For me BDD died down in my early 20's but has now come back with a vengeance. I'm 27 and have had BDD since I was 17. I also suffer from depression and body focused repetitive behaviours. I find stress does make it worse as well. I'm going through a particularly tough point in my life and it's really worsened my BDD.

Members also provided personal examples in their replies to explain why the advice they received was or was not helpful. One man disagreed that reading books about BDD would comfort him:

Male-Reply: I have both the books you mentioned and it didn't do much to comfort me other than show me all the other types of bdd that are out there. I did read the book "At Face Value" which was pretty good as it dealt with a guy that had facially disfiguring cancer and I could relate more to it. The best I can do I guess is just try to not give a $#%^ about what other people think. I hope someday, I have the emotional strength it takes to be that kind of guy.

Replies to other members primarily contained supportive comments. However, responses often morphed into sharing one's personal struggles with BDD and seeking support from others.

ASKING QUESTIONS ABOUT BDD

Forum members wanted to learn about others' experiences with BDD. These queries could be direct (by asking questions) or indirect (by expressing uncertainty, doubt, or curiosity). Direct questions were used to solicit similar experiences: "Anyone else here have people using or walking over you because of your insecurities (or because you are scared of not being liked)?" Replies to these questions often contained empathy followed by similar experiences, advice, and opinions.

One man discussed his hair loss obsession and concluded his narrative by asking for advice: "If anyone has gone through this obsession before, your advice would be very much appreciated." One of the respondents empathized with his hair loss obsession and advised him to get treatment:

> **Male-Reply:** Right here, friend. I had really bad BDD related to hair loss for about 10 years now... I have tried everything over the past 10 years to treat this myself and nothing worked. Only getting help from my doctor and a psychologist has worked. And not just a little bit, I feel like my life has been transformed. Go to a doctor, tell them you have BDD. It's not easy to do but you will never regret it once you finally take that step.

A common communication strategy, primarily used by new members, was sharing personal experiences and then asking if anyone had similar experiences: "I'm totally new to this forum. I found it through google searches on BDD and thought it would be a good way to contact others who suffer from this disorder. I guess I just really would love to hear some of your stories, personal experiences, and habits all related to BBD." Some members cast themselves as protagonists and other people as antagonists when sharing their BDD experiences. These messages became stories with a plot; characters; and a beginning, middle, and end.

Sharing Personal Stories

The most notable example of sharing personal stories occurred when a young woman replied to a female poster about the struggles she faced with her boyfriend. She empathized with the original poster about wanting to be "the most beautiful woman in the world" for her boyfriend (Appendix B4):

> **Female-Reply:** Your text really struck a chord with me, because you've expressed very well what it's like. Isn't it weird how a person, probably on the other side of the world, can express exactly how you feel yourself?

I have the same problem in my relationship right now (it's my first and I'm 24). With wanting to be the most beautiful girl in the world for my boyfriend, completely crashing down as soon as you see a beautiful woman leaving you feeling completely worthless, and the porn thing. The problem is my boyfriend is quite a good looking guy with lots of money, who's had a model ex (6ft tall, blonde, skinny) and who once told me that my body wasn't up to scratch (weighing 114 pounds).

The young woman then described her most recent issue with her boyfriend. She had asked him to give her compliments, but he refused, and so they got into a "big fight." Her boyfriend also liked to watch porn. This was a problem because it impacted her self-esteem:

And then the porn thing, I sorta get it, I really do, when it applies to other people. I would never tell another woman that it's because there is something wrong with her, for him it's probably just a form of foreplay. But when my boyfriend does it makes me feel so $#%^ about myself.

Because the women in those movies are not beautiful, they're trashy and usually not even fit. But then again, he has cheated on me with a prostitute once (as I know of, could be many more times). Even though, at that time, I had sex with him up to 6 times a day whenever we met, all just to please him and make him not stray (my father destroyed my family and left me after having cheated on my mother, and after that didn't want any contact with me).

She ended her story by complimenting the previous poster on her ability to express herself, because she valued intelligence in other people but did not value her own intelligence. This self-deprecating comment concluded her narrative about herself and her adulterous boyfriend:

I don't really know what to say to you, just that you're obviously very intelligent being able to express yourself the way you've done. And I know that it seems that in this world that counts for nothing, but for some people it does. For me it does. Just not when it comes to myself.

Constructing personal stories is a natural human process that helps people understand their experiences and organize events in a coherent fashion.[15] This process gives individuals a sense of predictability and control over their lives, since once an experience has structure and meaning, the emotional effects of that experience become more manageable. The stories told on the BDD forum enabled members to solicit support and empathy from others who understood their struggles.

Having Conversations: "Thank you for your replies"

BDD forum members appreciated having others respond to their messages. Doing so created a conversation between the original poster and other members. These conversations wove the diverse message threads into a supportive online community. Conversations between the original poster and forum members took place in almost 40 percent of the message threads (within the first three replies).[16]

Most replies were by female members (sixty-four females, thirty-four males, nine undetermined gender) who answered others' questions or disclosed their BDD experiences. Sometimes the original poster continued the conversation by asking a follow-up question or expressing gratitude to those who responded. In thirty-one of the message replies (27.4 percent), the original poster thanked other members, as shown in the following example:

> **Undetermined-Reply (OP):** Thank you so much! Logically I know I should go to a doctor about it, I have a lot of symptoms of hypochondriasis that my friends are telling me to see someone about as well, so I suppose I can talk about both when I'm there. I meant to do it today when I was at the doctor for something different, but I got too nervous!

Other times, the original posters acknowledged the advice they received, then asked for more advice on a different topic. In the following message, the female poster thanked another member for her advice, then wanted to know how to deal with her boyfriend's comments:

Female-Reply (OP): Thanks for responding to my post. I will mention it to my therapist next time I go, since this really is a big time waster for me.

I have a question. What do you do if people in your life are unknowingly making you feel bad/self-conscious about your looks? I have dark blond hair, and even when I was younger I remember wishing to be a brunette like the majority of my family. So since I think brown hair is prettier, I already was dabbling in dyeing my hair and stuff. But then I started dating my boyfriend, and he says he thinks brunettes are hotter than blondes. Even though he's said I'm not blond (I disagree, my hair is too light to classify as brown), I still feel like I'm not the girl he'd like to have and I'm not pretty enough for him. I'd like to tell him to not say things like that, but I'll just sound oversensitive. So what do I do about stuff like that?

Most replies were received in a positive manner by the original posters. However, some members disagreed with the opinions and advice they received, especially related to their appearance concerns. The male poster below took issue with another person's assessment that his nose obsession was caused by neurological defects in his brain:

Male-Reply 2 (OP): thanks for your comment again.

I agree with most of what you are saying. Defect in visual processing does take a large part in BDD but it seems that there is indeed a mild deformation of my nose. I don't think what I am seeing is unrealistic. I could understand that you guys may really have the neurological part in it but for me it would be very tiny to even non-existent.

Conversations also took place when the original poster asked a question other members wanted to answer. For example, a young woman wanted to know if she had BDD because she was missing school, hated her pale skin, and constantly wore fake tan: "I just want to know if any of you think i have bdd and if there's anything i can do to get better because i really do want to be normal again." One of the moderators (Rose) answered first. Rose asked her if she had received a BDD diagnosis, suggested she get help from a therapist, and advised her to use blush to improve her complexion. The original poster confirmed she was in treatment for her BDD symptoms and thanked Rose for her reply:

> **Female-Reply 2 (OP):** I've asked my therapist and she thinks its bdd as well and she wants to do this thing called cbt- Cognitive behavioral therapy, I think it is the products I'm wearing but I'm going to see a dermatologist soon anyway and see what they say. I'm still missing a lot of school but they've said it might be better if i have a home tutor instead. thanks for the reply. think i will try using different make up that goes better with my natural skin color hopefully things will get better soon!

Rose continued the conversation by replying and encouraged her to try cognitive behavioral therapy (CBT): "Hey, I've heard good things about CBT! I hope it'll help you, keep me posted about how you're doing if you want.😊" The thread ended with no further responses from the original poster. This was not uncommon, since half of the message threads had fewer than three replies. I appreciated reading extended conversations between members when they occurred. Replies often contained advice, support, and information about BDD. These conversations enabled the BDD forum to become a supportive online community.

Conversations sometimes continued via private messages (PMs). Members offered to connect via PM or indicated they had conversations via PM. A young woman from Canada found the forum after diagnosing herself with the disorder and wanted to find new friends: "I would love to meet some nice and interesting people who I can talk to and relate to. Please don't hesitate to PM me or chat with me on here!"

Another woman thanked Janet for conversing with her via PM when she needed encouragement (Chapter 15): "I would love to say a huge thank you to Janet. She pm me and has kept a steady convo with me, giving me the most encouraging thoughts I could ask for. You're the best, and it's nice to have you to vent to a little each day. SO MUCH APPRECIATED."

Seeking and
Providing Support

Male-Initial Post: First off it is great to find a community like this and others that support sufferers of this condition. In fact if it wasn't for this wonderful thing we call the Internet; I would never have 1. discovered what my bizarre obsessions were related to. 2. Gathered the mental strength to smash this condition on the head.

Seeking Support: "I need someone to help me"

Individuals on the BDD forum primarily sought and shared information (advice and opinions) about treatment, diagnosis, coping, and recovery. They usually asked for help either before or after disclosing their BDD symptoms in initial posts. A common question on the forum was about how to cope with BDD symptoms: "Should I see a professional? Speak to family? Or is there another self-help way of approaching this?" Most requests seeking support were direct; individuals disclosed their BDD symptoms and asked for help:

Male-Initial Post: I don't even know why I'm writing this. I just don't know what to do anymore. I need someone to help me. I need someone to talk to honestly about my problems so I can perhaps see the whole thing from a different angle. I don't want this to take over my life, I want to be the old me once again; the happy, enthusiastic, ambitious and sweet boy who made everyone laugh.

When inquiries were indirect, posters expressed uncertainty or doubt about their options: "I can't decide if I should just take medication or just attempt to get counselling without the meds."

The most striking example of seeking opinions on the forum was when individuals asked about their perceived appearance flaws. Members asked others for reassurance despite being unable to post personal images on the site. The site's policy was summarized by one of the moderators in the directions for all members to follow: "Due to the potentially triggering nature, sharing personal pictures is not allowed on this forum. We hope this will help you concentrate less on your physical appearance and more on your behavior and feelings, assisting your recovery."

The visual anonymity offered by the BDD forum did not prevent individuals from asking others about whether their perceived appearance flaws were real. In the following post, a female member wanted to know if her hands were too small for her body. In order to overcome not being able to post a picture, she instead included the size of her hands and her height:

Female-Initial Post: Hey everyone, I'm new here, but to make a long story short, for several years now I have had this complex about my hands. I have received the occasional comment about how small my hands are. I know they are small, but I am also a petite woman at 5'1. I measured my hand and it is about 6 inches. That is an inch shorter than the average woman's hand in America, but I am below average height.

After introducing herself to forum members and sharing her hand and body proportions, she asked others if her hands were in the "normal" range, based on the measurements provided:

So I'm wondering... are my hands in the "normal" range of small, or are they... freakish? I feel so depressed over it, I have been suicidal and I just can't face living life feeling like I have "midget hands" or something I guess I can't attach a picture, which would be helpful, but hopefully you can get an idea from the measurement I gave.

Members often asked others for their opinions about whether they had BDD or were truly ugly. For example, one poster shared her appearance-related problems such as being bullied in school. She concluded her post by asking others if they thought she had BDD: "Do I have BDD? Or am I just a truly ugly girl who can't accept that she's ugly?"

PROVIDING SUPPORT: "GET TREATMENT"

When members asked if they had BDD, others primarily advised them to get professional diagnosis and treatment. In response to the question about having BDD or being ugly, one of the moderators offered advice to get therapy:

> **Anna (Moderator)-Reply:** It sounds a bit like BDD because it just keeps moving from one area to the next, but maybe you've just had really bad luck with bullying. The same happened to me and it was awful...But if it's BDD or traits, you do need to have therapy to help you deal with it. How are you doing?

Many members appreciated the helpful advice provided in forum messages: "I would like to say that this is the first time I have tried seeking advice/help from total strangers. I discovered this forum while browsing another website and was astonished by just how big and helpful this community is."

Members primarily offered advice and information in their replies. For example, one man responded to another's appearance concerns by advising the person to get clinical treatment: "Get treatment. Even if you don't believe me about the way you look, you still recognize that you have a disorder and the distress caused by BDD is unbearable. At least get that distress dealt with. There is no reason you need to suffer through that."

Responding to others' requests by providing support can have positive effects on the provider's health, such as feelings of belongingness, reduced stress and mortality, and the empowerment that comes from being useful to others.[1] While helping others, individuals engage in self-reflection by reappraising their own problems objectively. In turn, they learn new coping skills and shift their perspective to a more positive light, which can lead to a reduction in their emotional distress.[2]

HELPING FAMILY MEMBERS AND FRIENDS

Two men whose girlfriends had BDD sought advice from forum members about how to help them. They both wanted to be supportive and understanding. One man's girlfriend had recently ended their relationship and later confessed she felt like a "crazy" person due to her BDD symptoms:

> **Male-Initial Post:** My girlfriend has been recently diagnosed with BDD. She has recently started thinking that she is no good for me from what I understand about 4/5 days ago she broke up with me for no reason. Just out of the blue after calming her down and discussing it with her I found out the above reason she thought I could do better and didn't want to go out with a 'crazy', 'mad' woman etc. ... Tonight she broke up with me again this led me to google (wikipedia was no help) but i did find this forum. How can i comfort her and make her understand how much I love her and want to be with her?

A female forum member empathized with his girlfriend and confessed she also felt like a "crazy mad woman" who would never let anyone get close to her:

> **Female-Reply:** I thought I'd tell you what it's like for me and maybe that will give you some insight as to how your girlfriend is feeling.

I constantly think about how unattractive I am, how worthless I am and it doesn't matter how many times people try to tell me differently, I don't believe them. I think they are just saying it because they feel bad for me.

When I look in the mirror it makes me want to scream, and cry. You said crazy mad woman, that's also how i feel! And I can't ever imagine anyone wanting to be with me, I never let anyone get close.

Roger replied to the other boyfriend's post and disclosed his girlfriend had left him when he shared his BDD symptoms with her. Roger advised him to read *The Broken Mirror* so he could learn more about BDD relationships:

Roger-Reply: BDD relationships can definitely work, you'll be tested but the best things in life test you they really do. If you want some info on BDD I suggest reading 'the broken mirror' if i remember rightly there's a section on being the partner of a BDD sufferer that might be helpful to you.

Most of us on this forum are BDD sufferers in some form or another so we can empathise with your girlfriend and our best wishes go out there to you and her.

The Broken Mirror[3] offers family members, spouses, and friends suggestions for supporting loved ones with BDD. Dr. Phillips urges family members to take loved ones' symptoms seriously, encourage psychiatric treatment, focus on the suffering caused by the disorder (when loved ones are reluctant to get treatment), don't focus on the perceived defect, create a supportive home environment, don't give reassurance, encourage participation in family events, give praise for small gains, get immediate help for loved ones who are suicidal, take time for yourself, don't blame yourself, remember that you are not alone, and maintain hope!

If your friend, spouse, or family member refuses to get treatment (or if finding effective treatment is difficult), then it's important to help yourself by joining a support group so you can feel less alone. Also, consider getting therapy to learn about CBT techniques and coping strategies to alleviate stress and anxiety.[4] Please refer to the resources provided in Appendix A for more information on support groups, websites, and books about BDD.

Forum members served primarily as support seekers or support providers, based on their level of participation and knowledge about BDD. Members who posted frequently and had greater insight about BDD were primarily the support providers. Less frequent posters (those who posted only one to two messages during the year) were primarily support seekers. However, these roles were fluid and not mutually exclusive since the same person could engage in both activities. Both roles were essential to the successful functioning of the BDD forum.

BDD Forum Leaders

Roger-Initial Post: *The road to freeing yourself from the clutches of Body Dysmorphia can be a long and arduous path, in it we sometimes forget the little victories we achieve on the way.*

I want this to be a thread about the victories we do have, no matter how little, no matter how big, i want it to reach 1,000 and be here to remind us what we are truly capable of.

Forum Leaders and Roles

Roger, Kathy, Mia, Janet, and Fran (the most active members) became the emergent leaders of the BDD forum. They made the forum a more welcoming place by frequently responding to members' painful BDD experiences with kindness and compassion. I particularly felt a kinship with Roger because he believed everyone who suffered from BDD was part of his global "BDD family" (Chapter 3).

Many of us have supportive roles to play within our families, social groups, and communities. I serve as a peer group facilitator, writer, and advocate by raising awareness about the disorder and providing hope that recovery is possible. The five forum leaders each took on supportive roles within the BDD forum (Table 1). All of them shared the roles of information/opinion giver and cheerleader/encourager. Other roles, like advocate and greeter, were specific to Roger and Kathy. The following forum leader roles and profiles were compiled from messages they posted during the year.

Table 1

Group Roles Performed by the Five Forum Leaders

Group Roles	Forum Leaders	Examples
Advocate Promoted the value of the forum	Roger, Kathy	The forum is great, I love it!
Cheerleader/Encourager Offered praise, understanding, and acceptance to members	Roger, Kathy, Mia, Janet, Fran	Omg that's incredible! im so happy for you. I hope you get a job at the end too.
Evaluator/Critic Pointed out problems and needed improvements on the forum	Kathy, Fran	To be honest I don't understand why the moderators haven't done anything about this!
Greeter Welcomed new members	Roger, Kathy	Welcome to the forum.
Information/Opinion Giver Provided advice and opinions meant to help solve others' problems	Roger, Kathy, Mia, Janet, Fran	You should make an appointment with your GP and discuss it with him/her.
Mediator/Harmonizer Intervened in disputes between members	Kathy	I'm not sure what your aim was in posting it, maybe you could clarify this?

ROGER: GREETER AND INFORMATION GIVER

Roger became a BDD forum member in March 2012 and was also a BDD Central member. He did not post a self-introduction message and instead shared his personal experiences in replies to other members. Roger was twenty-three years old and lived in Great Britain. He had to drop out of university due to his BDD symptoms and was committed to overcoming the disorder using CBT.

Roger could be considered the primary information/opinion giver on the BDD forum due to posting more comments containing advice and information than other members. The *information giver* offers facts and relates his own experience to others' problems.[1] He also served as the primary forum *greeter* and *advocate*. Roger believed members were like his extended family, so he reached out to new members, welcomed them to the forum, and encouraged them to keep posting. Roger also advised members to get clinical treatment and assured them recovery from BDD was possible.

He replied to a female member who was writing a college paper about the effects of having BDD. She wanted to know how it had impacted others' lives. Roger replied to her post by describing how it had impacted his life and his determination to get better:

> **Roger-Reply:** My story isn't really much, i started having image issues around the time most people do, late teenage years. Odd comments here and there from people would stick in my mind then rattle around my head like a ping pong ball.
>
> It never seriously affected me though until about the second year in college where things were starting to have an effect on my social life, love life etc. By the time i had dropped out of uni about a year later it had embedded itself in my brain and now aged 23 it's a constant fight to even want to do anything.
>
> Nothing matters to me anymore, i am singular in my goal and that is to beat this disorder, this problem, this issue. If i do manage it i have no idea how i would spend the rest of my life. Maybe it is my life and beating it is my personal meaning. Hopefully one day i will get to find out.

Roger's appearance obsessions were primarily related to his facial hair, nose, and skin:

Roger-Reply: As for my story i'll make it as brief as i can, had BDD since i was about 14, 15 or 16 although i didn't know about it until i was about 20 (i'm 23 now). My problem areas are nose, skin and hair which are all the top 3 areas of concern although my hair concern is probably more around facial hair than anything else.

My treatment at the moment is Cognitive behavioural therapy and sheer bloody determination which at times i seriously lack but i'm doing ok for the most part.

Roger-Reply: My nose is my biggest issue and so i often find myself turning towards the sun when i'm talking to people rather than having the sun at either side of me cos i hate it when it lights up half of my face so don't worry you are far from alone.

Roger started a thread encouraging forum members to share their favorite color, music, movies, songs, hobbies, and character traits. He started the thread by posting a list of his interests as an example to others. His favorite color was blue, his favorite films were *Ace Ventura Pet Detective*, *Aliens*, *Jurassic Park*, *Minority Report*, and *Prometheus*; his favorite music genres included Ambient, Dark Wave, Indie, New Wave, and Trance; and his favorite musicians included Above & Beyond, Echo & The Bunnymen, Empire of the Sun, and The Presets. For his hobbies and interests, Roger liked: "football (soccer for the Americans ☺) and badminton, basketball and bike riding." He described himself as "a little moody at times" due to the BDD but for the most part, he liked a good laugh, loved taking part in childish pranks, and was "very honest, compassionate and expressive."

Roger greeted new members, exchanged supportive messages with existing members, and frequently provided BDD information and advice in alignment with treatment professionals. There were only a few times when his responses contained criticism and sarcasm; these were primarily aimed at the forum flamer. Both he and Kathy were protective of the forum and wanted to defend the community against anyone who did not have others' best interests at heart (Chapter 16).

Kathy: Advocate and Mediator

Kathy was the second most frequent poster to the forum after Roger; she posted more than fifty messages during the year. Kathy joined the BDD forum in June 2011, almost a year before Roger. She was a twenty-year-old (almost twenty-one) British university student who disclosed her symptoms when replying to other members:

> **Kathy-Reply:** I get headaches like that too, also at the sides like my temples get very sore too. I get this when I have to go out and I'm around other people.

> **Kathy-Reply:** I hate my skin to, I have disgusting spots which I pick and make worse 😞 by judgment do you mean from other people or yourself, or both? I don't smoke pot, I've tried it a few times but it just didn't stick. Self harming is my method of coping.

Kathy served as a forum *greeter* and *advocate* by welcoming new members and praising the forum as a supportive community. She served as *mediator* when disputes arose between Fran and Roger and tried to moderate the negative comments made by the forum flamer. She, like Roger, did not appreciate when others posted nasty comments on the forum; they both cared about making the forum a supportive place for those suffering from BDD.

Kathy frequently replied to Roger's posts and disclosed personal information in response to his inquiries. In one post, Roger provided some characteristics of perfectionism (in red text) and disclosed he had perfectionist traits. Kathy also considered herself a perfectionist:

> **Kathy-Reply:** Very interesting Roger, I also strive for perfection and I can relate to each of the red phrases! I guess there's a link between being a perfectionist and having BDD, I think it comes down to our self esteem. My self esteem is extremely low therefore I think I can't do anything well so I have to work hard to prove myself to others but nothing is ever good enough. People point out to me a lot at uni that

I'm a perfectionist and I'm to hard on my self but I've always thought it to be good until I read your post, it's not healthy at all to be like this.

Kathy revealed that her favorite color was teal or pink, and her favorite films were *Titanic, Alien, Bridget Jones's Diary, Parent Trap,* and *Coco Avant Chanel.* She had no idea what types of music she liked, but her favorite groups/musicians included Kings of Leon, Taylor Swift, The Fray, Sara McLachlan, Alex Clare, and Beyonce. She declined to describe her character traits. Her hobbies were spending time with her boyfriend and doing creative activities:

> I like reading and drawing, watching films, I love spending time with my boyfriend and talking to him on the phone, I like to make clothes etc too, but I'm a fashion student so in my free time I tend not to do it as much. I like cooking and baking, going for walks, I love to be in the middle of nowhere, I like photography, i love animals, I love looking at the stars and I like to day dream 😃 lol.

Kathy replied to Fran's post asking to what extent feeling ugly had impacted members' goals and ambitions. Kathy had given up her dream of being a dancer due to her appearance concerns. Instead, she chose a career in fashion design. She doubted she could accomplish her career goals, deal with her BDD, and become a mother:

> **Kathy-Reply**: The problem I have now is that I'm studying fashion, and I think it's such a looks ruled industry I don't know how I will cope! It's a battle for me everyday because I don't think I'm good enough, I don't think I'm capable to do what I want! I'm also an ambitious person but the way I feel about myself completely holds me back. I just hope it doesn't stop me from doing what i love!
>
> What you are saying about children I have thought about, I think it's so hard for a woman to have a career and be a mum! That's what scares me I think I'm running out of time to do everything I want! I want a successful career, I want to travel the world and one day I also want children! But I'm 21 in a couple of months, I don't graduate until I'm

23 so I think by the time I get my career in line and I do everything I want to do I think it will be to late for children 😕 and like you if I were to ever have kids I'd want to be with my child not constantly working. I just can't decide what I want most because I really don't think I can have it all 😕

Kathy and Fran shared similar traits and characteristics. They both had career ambitions, supportive boyfriends, were creative and artistic, enjoyed being outdoors, cared about animals, and wanted to be mothers one day. I could relate to both Kathy and Fran, given that I had a career in art and design, loved animals, enjoyed being outdoors, and had supportive boyfriends in my twenties, despite struggling with BDD symptoms. The difference was I did not want to have children in my twenties. Despite having the rhinoplasty, I still hated my nose and feared my children would inherit my original ugly nose.

Mia: Encourager and Opinion Giver

Mia posted more than forty-five messages to the forum during the year. She became a forum member in November 2011, four months after Kathy. Mia both sought and provided support on the BDD forum. She was twenty-two years old, lived in Canada, and was in therapy due to her appearance-related obsessions. Mia was convinced she had a bump on her nose. She took multiple selfies and touched it repeatedly. She started a message thread trying to find others who shared her problem:

Mia-Initial Post: Oh man...I've got a serious problem with my nose. Does anybody else?

I want to feel better about it, and my counsellor says I'm pretty and I know most people think I am, but I don't. I almost don't want to not think its ugly because I feel like I'd be tricking myself because I know I have a bump on my nose when I turn to the side. Even if it was a little bit smaller I'd be happy.

It's getting to the point where I touch it so much that scabs have formed, I take soo many pictures of myself just to get the right angle. I'm SOO happy I wear glasses, I was offered laser eye surgery for my birthday and I turned it down because of my nose.

It makes me SOOOOOO sad that I don't even like being around pretty girls anymore.

Anyways, I'm just wondering if anyone else out there has a problem with their nose like I do? It's beginning to drive me nuts a little bit. *sigh*

Mia served as an information/opinion giver and cheerleader/ encourager when responding to other members. The *encourager* praises, agrees with, and accepts the contributions of other members.[2] Mia served as an information/opinion giver when she provided advice and opinions about others' experiences with BDD.

Mia primarily disclosed her personal experiences and feelings about herself in replies to other members to express empathy and understanding:

Mia-Reply: YUP..I KNOW HOW YOU FEEL!!!!!!!!!!! every person in the world could say im pretty...but i know ill never be the prettiest and i know ill never think im pretty on the outside...it f***ing sucks. but you know what??? one day when you're old...you'll look back and think...man i was pretty (i bet or at least i hope)

In another post, Mia described her appearance changing in mirrors, cameras, and videos and wanted to know what she really looked like. She sought reassurance by entering her image in a contest to see if others judged her as attractive:

Mia-Initial Post: Anyways I was just thinking that I'm overall just confused about how i look. if you asked me to describe how I look, I wouldn't really be able to. I look different in mirrors, cameras, videos etc...i just like can't comprehend how i look.

Sometimes I think it's because I prefer facts over imagination and I feel like a person's looks are sooo subjective that I'm just overall confused. I just get confused that to one person i may be good looking while to another one I'm not at all, and to myself...i don't even know how i look.

then to top it all off, i entered a contest where you had to send a picture in (yes i enter contests as a hobby, if you want info on how u can just message me 😄) and there was like a top 10 people and I wasn't in it......which I thought I was going to get very sad about but I didn't, i more or less just don't care, but it confuses me even more because the girls that got chosen are not attractive to me!!!!

I wish there was one answer to the question "am i good looking", i guess all that matters is if I think im good looking...but I defintely don't....i dont even know what i look like!!!!!!!!!!!!!!!!!!!!

Mia replied to Janet and revealed she also used marijuana (weed) to self-medicate. Both were in therapy due to their BDD symptoms. They communicated with each other on and off the forum using private messaging and by connecting on Facebook.

Mia-Reply: I smoke a lot of weed too. like a lot lol. I don't know if it makes my BDD any better or worse.

I certainly don't care about much except for food or sleeping when I'm high and I get very paranoid when I walk alone at night and stuff. Well maybe it makes it worse in the sense that I hate being in public high.

Lol..man if I'm high and I see my eyebrows though. I go insane, I've lost an hour to waxing/ plucking those badboys before without even noticing it.

Like Mia, my BDD was focused on the shape and size of my nose. Janet and I both used meditation and mindfulness techniques during treatment for our BDD symptoms. However, unlike Mia and Janet, I did not use drugs or marijuana to self-medicate.

JANET: CHEERLEADER AND OPINION GIVER

Janet posted more than forty-five messages after becoming a member in March 2012, the same month Roger joined the forum. Janet served as a BDD forum cheerleader/encourager and information/opinion giver. She was in therapy for the disorder and used marijuana to self-medicate:

> **Janet-Initial Post:** I finally plucked up the courage to join this forum. Baby steps baby steps. . . I have the worst skin in the world. With far too much hair. Its so disgusting that if anyone sees it, they are likely to recoil in disgust and possibly throw up.
>
> I do rely heavily on marijuana to soothe me through the day, and tend to deny the fact I'm addicted. I'm determined to make progress with the help of my psychologist. Anyone else in this limbo stage? I'm getting help but the BDD is my world.

Janet believed mindfulness training, along with CBT, could cure her BDD symptoms. She refused to take prescription medications (SSRIs) and like Roger, wanted to battle BDD using only CBT. Her favorite quotation came from Louise L. Hay: "You are not a helpless victim of your own thoughts, but rather a master of your own mind." She strongly believed changing her thoughts could change her life:

> **Janet-Reply:** I am lucky enough to have a therapist basically an expert in BDD. I'm very much beginning to understand my BDD and change it, it's a beautiful thing. It's difficult for me to read some of the things posted here because I used to think the same way. We have to bring it into the present moment. Get into the now, operate from your options available today. We are actually fully capable of changing our thought. Change your thoughts, change your life! Is a powerful thought I use every day. I am constantly observing the crazy thoughts my BDD come up with. I write them down and edit them to what I

would like the thought the be, essentially I aim for neutral, because to me neutral = space. In thought form it's something like "I'm not ugly, I'm not beautiful, I'm in between the two and that's ok"

Janet opposed the idea that BDD could not be cured. She encouraged others to help themselves so they could recover:

Whoa- no cure? I keep hearing this? I put it down to fear. And I don't believe that most have already forsaken the chance to practice mindfulness. It's free. It's a choice. You gotta choose life and all its pitfalls. Bottom line, you can overcome BDD. It is not incurable. Saying there is no cure for this simply perpetuates the vicious cycle that most people with BDD are in, and that is something I simply do not agree with. If someone had told me a few years ago that BDD was incurable I would have believed them and not bothered to help myself. I'm so glad I never stumbled across that opinion in my quest for health and happiness.

Overall, Janet was optimistic about overcoming her BDD symptoms using CBT and mindfulness techniques, since she was actively engaged in the healing process:

I'm in CBT about 2 months in. My therapist is an expert in BDD, and she knows that she can try to help me all day long but it actually REQUIRES my active participation or CBT would just be a waste of time.

Ironic huh? All this suffering, turns out we have the tools to change it, if we actively participate in our own healing. Which is so encouraging I think.

Janet replied to Roger's post about perfectionism and realized she, too, tried to be perfect. She and her therapist had come to this realization together during her recent session:

Janet-Reply: Great post. This just came in my therapy last week. I was saying something and she asked if I felt I was striving for perfection. Amazingly, I realized that yes, looking back I've been hiding my perfectionism from everyone. Never before have I looked at my actions and realized I'm looking for a goal, an end point of perfection that, as you can plainly see - does not exist. It's quite a relief to realise this about myself. No wonder I'm never satisfied, I'm unconsciously trying to be perfect, and it doesn't exist!

Using positive coping strategies (such as mindfulness and meditation) were helpful in alleviating my BDD symptoms and enabled me to transition off medication. Like Roger, Kathy, and Janet, I am a perfectionist and strive to achieve a high level of quality in my creative and work endeavors. However, I have stopped letting perfectionism get in the way of my goals. Perfection is impossible to achieve because it "doesn't exist" in life or in one's physical appearance.

FRAN: ENCOURAGER AND FORUM CRITIC

Fran was a twenty-eight-year-old medical student who joined the BDD forum in October 2012. She posted more than forty-five messages in the last three months of the year. Fran's posts were extensive in both breadth and depth; her self-introduction was approximately 1,200 words (Appendix B1). Like Mia and Janet, Fran both sought and provided support on the forum. She served as an encourager/cheerleader when she offered praise, empathy, and compliments to members who were struggling with BDD symptoms.

Fran also provided information and advice about coping with BDD, such as recommending *The Broken Mirror* to other members (Chapter 11). She became an evaluator/critic of the BDD forum when her positive messages were not reciprocated (Chapter 17). The *evaluator* provides feedback on the group's rules and functioning.[3] Fran described herself as an intelligent, ambitious medical student with a fantastic boyfriend. However, she constantly wore makeup to conceal her perceived ugliness from him, herself, and from other people:

Fran-Initial Post: I am 28. I have a very demanding life which had made me come to the very top of all my frustrations. I am a medical student in my last year. I have managed until now in a way i don't understand how it was possible.

I think I am ugly, since I can remember. Not in the way that i have a big nose or ears or so, but i think its the mix of them all, my father's eyes, the eyebrows that are long gone (little left), and all the little small things that together just created a nasty reflection in the mirror. I wear makeup ALL THE TIME. Also when I sleep. I wake up, first thing i do is check the mirror to know what the day will have in store for me. It is almost always a big disappointment, sometimes a smaller disappointment which may be corrected if lucky. Every morning, looking with fear and some hope into that mirror, as if i wait for my face to have changed all of the sudden over the night.

Fran believed she was a great person who could accomplish anything. However, her appearance did not match her good qualities. There was a striking contrast between Fran's positive self-image and the ugly person she saw in the mirror every morning:

Psychologists may want to relate this ugly-feeling to a deeper personal insecurity, but I really must disagree, at least in my case. I am a very talented woman, on my "good days" i am the most social and fun person, and there is nothing I cannot do, I am VERY good at most sports, smart and intelligent in my studies, inventive, handy, loving and caring of humans and animals, and I think I am really a great person that can accomplish anything. I just wish my face would match all this. I just wish to be looking ok, to be able to fulfill my life. And my lovely boyfriend's life.

Fran diagnosed herself with dermatillomania (compulsive skin picking disorder) after reading another member's post. About a third of people with BDD pick at their acne bumps, blackheads, and other skin imperfections, which can cause scarring and further damage.[4] Fran described her symptoms in detail, which included picking at her scabs and those of her boyfriend:

Fran-Reply: Omg, I had never heard of dermatillomania before, so when I looked it up now I realize I also have a degree of it! I'm amazed that there it is an actual disorder.

I am so sure its linked to my BDD, because I just CANNOT STAND irregularities of my skin (or my boyfriends'!) and pick and pick away anything sticking out. Especially when I am alone I do this because I don't care how my makeup is getting ruined. My poor boyfriend has been a bit upset with me many times because I just can't strike his back gently without just HAVING to pick (pain!), scrub off or squeeze his little pimples or crusts.

This was really an eye-opener for me, I knew I was too obsessed with this picking because it is irresistible to me to feel an irregularity and leave it alone. Takes huge effort.

Always when I am alone for a longer period I end up with facial sores because I have to remove all pimples, then their serum crusts, then blood crusts. Luckily I haven't deformed my face yet. Now that I know it's part of my disorder I will think extra when having the need to do this destructive habit!

Fran had good days and bad days. On her bad days, she could become depressed to the point of feeling suicidal, but on her good days, she felt beautiful and self-confident. She posted a message after having a fantastic day filled with many positive experiences:

Fran-Initial Post: Sorry didn't mean to start a whole thread about this, but I just wanted to scream out that I had the most fantastic day today!! I left home feeling beautiful this morning, had school all day and got the appreciation i deserved!!

Chairs pulled out for me. Winks from guys. Respect, doors opened. Flirting!! Made a new friend.

People listened, I was social, I was joking and spontaneously humorous like I didn't think I could be anymore, I was happy, I was smiling! I was the star of the day and I rocked it!

And no time during the day did I feel less beautiful, and as I go home (the final test) I see myself in the elevator mirror, and there was....beautiful!

This is one in a year experience so I just wanted to say that to everybody lol

It's all related to me feeling beautiful, and getting treated like the person I feel inside. I felt like: THIS is what I deserve.

I'm going to come in here and read this post in the other 364 days of the year in which are not like this lol, and get reminded that good/perfect days exists.

But again people, another proof that it is linked completely to beauty. I really have no other insecurities about anything. My day was perfect.

WOHOOO!!!!!

Only one person replied to her post, and he both praised her and expressed envy at her success: "I'm delighted for you, and (I don't know whether this is a feeling you'll recognise) a little bit jealous." Fran replied by agreeing with his feelings of envy, since she was also envious of her own success. She planned to keep re-reading the post as a reminder that good days were possible.

She replied to Roger's post and shared her favorite colors, movies, music, hobbies, and character traits. Fran's favorite colors were pink, white, and aquamarine. She listed nineteen films she enjoyed and noted there were "many more" because she had no favorite one. She loved comedies a lot but also dramas and some action films. Fran's favorite music included "ambient, oriental tunes, butt-shaking music and also some old classics" from her "fantastic youth."

Fran had many hobbies and interests, including drawing, sewing, home decorating, gymnastics, dancing, watching movies with her boyfriend, running/jogging, weightlifting, volleyball, soccer, track and field, writing novels and poems, and teaching her cat tricks: "She knows to sit, to lay down, to do tunnel under my legs, to go up and down from thing on demand, to come and give me a kiss on my mouth etc etc." Finally, Fran described herself as kind and generous, energetic and inventive, with an enormous love for animals, especially homeless cats:

> One of my biggest traits is my enormous love for animals. I cannot stand an animal in suffering, it gives me great anguish. I have had to accept that I cannot save all animals in suffering. Although I every day feed and give water to about 9 homeless cats outdoors.

Fran decided to change her focus from being a surgeon to becoming a psychiatrist and potentially helping people with BDD: "I will continue on my thesis on BDD, it is very exciting and who knows, maybe one day I will choose to specialize within psychiatry. Some of your stories have indeed fascinated me."

Fran's desire to help people with BDD by becoming a psychiatrist was admirable, along with her enthusiasm for the forum, positive feedback to members, and embracing both her good days and bad days. She was open, honest, intelligent, and caring (just some of the good traits she listed about herself), and enjoyed the outdoors, running, and being with her boyfriend. On the flip side, her constant focus on herself and her symptoms, and the overly optimistic tone in her messages, seemed to lack empathy for other people's problems.

To her credit, Fran realized her effusive praise for herself could have given members the wrong impression about her battle with BDD. This was especially true because she could become suicidal on her "bad days." Like the other forum leaders, Fran dedicated much time and effort to helping members with the disorder. Unlike the other leaders, Fran's concerns were frequently about herself, her triumphs, and her struggles with the disorder.

Fran was seeking friendships on the forum, but like someone who bursts into a party and starts introducing herself to everyone there, she seemed to come across a little strong. She frequently reached out to other members, then became discouraged when they failed to respond in kind. Even though I admired her efforts, Fran's love/hate relationship with the forum was disconcerting. Her interactions with Roger and the other forum leaders could be supportive or combative (Chapter 16). Fran "really wanted to help" spread some optimism and cheer to counter the negative emotions expressed by most members.

I hope all the emergent leaders were able to overcome their BDD symptoms. Their communication with other members made the BDD forum a supportive online community. Most members came to the forum seeking support and posted one to two messages. These messages offer valuable insights into the daily struggles people with BDD endure. The anonymity offered by the forum enabled members to openly share their inner torment with others who could understand.

PART THREE
BATTLING BDD SYMPTOMS

LOOKING FOR CAUSES

Male-Initial Post: My visual perception seems to be extremely distorted to the point where I sometimes feel like I am hallucinating, I think about how my hair looks for hours, and hours, and hours every day. I constantly feel physical symptoms of anxiety, I constantly think people are looking at my hair, and all of this despite the fact that no one I have asked agrees that my hair looks thin in any way, even myself most days.

CHILDHOOD BULLYING AND ABUSE

The participants on the BDD forum primarily attributed childhood bullying, teasing, abuse, critical remarks from parents, and family trauma to the onset of their BDD symptoms. The exact cause for BDD is unknown.[1] However, some possible developmental causes include childhood bullying,[2] childhood teasing about appearance and competency,[3] childhood maltreatment and trauma,[4] growing up in a family with an emphasis on appearance,[5] perfectionist standards concerning appearance, and exposure to high ideals of attractiveness and beauty in the mass media.[6]

Childhood bullying was the reason given for one man's low self-esteem and BDD symptoms: "Being bullied has a terrible effect on many people, I myself received many put downs, called names, ridiculed, etc about my appearance." Another man attributed his traumatic childhood experiences to his BDD symptoms. He was beaten by his mother and teased about his weight by his family:

Male-Initial Post: I have had a tough childhood. My parents were always arguing and once they divorced my mom became addicted to xanax and caused her to beat me and my twin sis. My family used to always tease me on my weight but it a bad way like insulting. I started getting worse in high school because I felt everyone looked at me the same way my family did.

One woman recalled childhood teasing about her freckles and her uncle's comment about her eyes being "too big" for her face. She attributed these comments to believing she was ugly:

Female-Initial Post: More factors that make me ugly, judging not from my own perceptions but by comments from others, include the freckles that faded over time but were very pronounced in childhood. I would be ribbed (by adults!) about having the measles, or asked if I'd been staring out the screen door. In addition, I have to be very careful to remove facial hair, in the form of mustache and unibrow. If I don't, I've been teased about that too. My eyes are large and green, which generally gets compliments, but an uncle told me they were TOO big for my face. So there goes that.

A female poster recounted childhood abuse by her father, being teased by classmates, and being raped by a stranger. She believed childhood trauma was the cause of multiple mental health problems:

Female-Initial Post: I have had depression and anxiety all my life and am on anti-depressants, have been since I was in third grade. My dad was very emotionally, verbally, and physically abusive and I was the victim of a rape by a man when I was only 17 years old and he raped me several times and threatened me if I ever told so I wonder if maybe all these things have made it worse. I was teased all the time in school and was never a popular kid. I would go to school and get picked on then go home and be beaten by my father. My whole childhood was traumatic. I have come a very long way and have gotten over my social anxiety and am recovered from OCD and trichotillomania and skin picking which I did REALLY bad for years and years.

Research has found that childhood maltreatment and trauma (emotional abuse, physical neglect, and emotional neglect) are more prevalent in people with BDD than in those without the disorder. More severe childhood maltreatment is linked to a greater severity of BDD symptoms, anxiety, and suicide ideation.[7]

FAMILY'S FOCUS ON APPEARANCE

A female forum member revealed her mother was diagnosed with borderline personality disorder and was extremely beautiful. She believed her mother's mental health disorder and focus on beauty contributed to her BDD symptoms:

Female-Initial Post: I don't know how much of my BDD is genetic or as a result of my upbringing, probably both. My mother was diagnosed with Borderline Personality Disorder when I was little and also kind of displayed fears about her appearance, much like I do. She was also very beautiful and had very high standards about how I should look. I was a very beautiful child and was put into beauty pageants and modeled for several toy companies but, for some reason, when I turned 13 my face completely changed and people started telling me I was ugly.

One young woman attributed the onset of her body image disorder to her grandmother's comments about her appearance when she was a child. She was upset when her grandmother later made the same negative remarks about her niece's appearance (Appendix B3):

Female-Initial Post: Long story short, I was diagnosed with BDD a couple years ago, have been suffering with it almost all my life. Work with my therapist made it pretty clear to understand that a lot of my body issues started as a result of my Nana's constant comment and judgement of my looks when I was a child. She was extremely loving, but also, always telling me to suck in, "suck in that gut" etc. when I was a kid, despite the fact that I was very scrawny as a child (underweight, by doctors). Twenty-some years later I'm still hearing her commentary in my mind, but I've done a lot of work to make a lot of improvements.

I realize that Nana's thinking on bodies and figures is as distorted as some of us; she's an extreme perfectionist and expects perfection is other people's physiques, to the point of being completely irrational. But just like me when I was a child, my niece doesn't know this, so she'll think that what Nana says is truth. What can I do to break the cycle?

Another man blamed his father for his hair loss obsession. Ten years later, he clearly remembered the insensitive comment his father made when he was sixteen years old: "I had really bad BDD related to hair loss for about ten years now. My dad told me I was going bald when I was sixteen and I never was able to shake that moment. Of course that is nearly unheard of and I have the same amount of hair today, which is the same amount I have always had, so my dad is an idiot but that didn't stop me from losing my mind."

Childhood trauma and teasing about appearance can be a potent mixture of precipitating factors for the onset of BDD symptoms. The negative emotions from being teased can easily be internalized and interpreted as fact without parental intervention.[8] Studies have found that nearly 80 percent of people with BDD reported a history of childhood maltreatment such as bullying, abuse, or neglect.[9]

Abnormal Brain Functioning

Another possible cause for BDD symptoms is abnormal brain functioning. Neurobiological factors include dysregulation of the serotonin system in the brain,[10] inherited genetic nervous system imbalances,[11] and related personality disorders (avoidant, dependent, OCD, paranoid, neuroticism).[12] Researchers theorize that a combination of developmental, psychosocial, cognitive, behavioral, and neurobiological factors may contribute to the onset of BDD symptoms.[13]

Two forum members attributed abnormal brain functioning to their BDD symptoms. They had received treatment for BDD so perhaps learned about neurobiological causes from their clinicians or by doing additional research. One man who was in therapy for his balding obsession explained how the amygdala affects visual processing in people with BDD:

> **Male-Reply:** Research has shown that aspect of BDD is due to neurological abnormalities. The human visual system has links to a structure in the brain called the amygdala. The amygdala is responsible for processing fear responses. The link to the visual system allows us to tell when something we are seeing is a threat. The problem with those of us who have BDD is that whole system is overactive. We process too much visual information as threatening and since we are fixated on our looks, everything we see in the mirror or in photos of ourselves, seems frightening, even when it objectively isn't. That is why we can see extremely minor details and feel that they are overwhelmingly horrible.

The amygdala is a small, almond-shaped structure in the brain used for processing visual stimuli.[14] For people with BDD, minor appearance flaws take on enormous proportions. This would be similar to a person viewing one's body in a fun-house mirror or face in a magnifying mirror, resulting in a distorted image.

The same man continued his explanation about neurological causes for BDD by comparing abnormal visual processing to hearing voices in schizophrenia:

Male-Reply: This condition is so tricky and so deeply ingrained and so severe that it really is impossible for most of us to see ourselves accurately, even for a brief moment. Your perception of your own reflection, just like mine, and just like everyone else here is probably completely f***ed up. The reason is neurological. Your brain is lying to you. This is the case with all of us. Virtually everyone with BDD has abnormal visual processing in the brain. In many ways it is completely different from people without the condition. Just as the brain of someone with schizophrenia perceives voices that aren't there, the brains of people with BDD perceive deformities that aren't there.

BDD shares similarities with other mental health disorders, including eating disorders, OCD, and social anxiety disorder (SAD). Both BDD and eating disorders, such as anorexia nervosa (AN) and bulimia nervosa (BN), involve distorted body image and dissatisfaction with one's appearance.[15] Another neurobiological cause for BDD includes discrepancies in visual processing that cause imbalances in visuospatial information processing.[16]

This means people with BDD see the details in their appearance rather than viewing their body as a whole (seeing the trees rather than the forest). They pay more attention to local, visual details than to processing visual stimuli holistically.[17] As an artist, I equate this perception to viewing an Impressionist painting. Small, colorful brushstrokes fill the canvas at close range, obscuring the landscape. Step back further, and the scenery comes into focus. For people with BDD, tiny appearance flaws take on monumental proportions. And the closer they look, the more distorted and hideous their appearance becomes.

Painful Appearance Obsessions

Female-Reply: Omg this is me. I love nighttime or dimmed lights and I am most comfortable at my own house lighting. If people turn up lights I freak bc I'm starting to age at 41. I used to be this way my whole life but now it's getting so bad I only leave my house if I have to. I can't look at people either I feel ugly. I used to be a swimsuit model but pimples and wrinkles is all I see. I weigh 120 and I'm 5 7 with blonde hair but I hide like a monster. I know I'm getting uglier as I get older. Lighting makes it so much worse.

Feeling Ugly: "I'm ugly and weird looking"

Many individuals who posted to the forum were extremely preoccupied with perceived defects or flaws in their physical appearance. Forum members disclosed feeling ugly and expressed dislike or hatred either toward their overall appearance, their face or body, or particular features. The most common appearance-related concerns, in order of prevalence, were about one's face, facial features (head, skin, nose, jaw, teeth, and hair), feeling ugly, and issues with body shape and size.

For example, one young woman from London believed she was ugly and would never have a boyfriend. She was obsessed with looking in mirrors and wanted to change her appearance because she felt inadequate. These negative thoughts resulted in her feeling sick and depressed:

> **Female-Initial Post:** Hello everyone i suffer with BDD. I am a very ugly looking person and feel that I will never have a boyfriend as i look so horrible. I am a young person from London.
>
> I always feel inadequate and whatever i do is not good enough and i always have to keep looking at mirrors etc not because i am happy with my image it is that i am unhappy and want to change myself all of the time. I just feel so sick with these thoughts.

These obsessive thoughts are characteristic of BDD and do not have to be focused on specific facial features or body parts.[1] The perceptions of ugliness can be all-consuming and result in hatred for one's overall physical appearance. Some female members, including Fran, were depressed because they felt trapped in an ugly body. One woman wanted to end it all since she was convinced these feelings would never go away:

> **Female-Initial Post:** Have you had those days where all you do is cry? Cry about how deformed and weird you look... And although you try and try to think about something different, to think about happy thoughts or all the things you have to be thankful for, that shadow just comes creeping back saying how malformed and ugly you are, how everyone must secretly agree with this, how you will never just look NORMAL no matter how hard you try. How unfortunate your body is, chained to this earth, imprisoned in such an ugly shell. How pathetic you must be to think, to CARE about all this.
>
> THAT is when I fantasize about ending it all. I feel like the opinions I have about my body will never change. I don't know if this is something relatable. I'm just starting to wonder (more like DOUBT) if there will ever be a way to get over all of this!

One male poster was socially isolated and believed he was "short, fat, and weird looking." He compared himself to a Hobbit, the mythical creatures created by J.R.R. Tolkien in *The Hobbit* and *The Lord of the Rings*:

Male-Initial Post: I am a 5ft5 male with 70kg in weigh. My nose looks like a pig nose and my face is not clearly defined and out of proportion. I am as fat as a pig and as short as a Hobbit. Have been depressed for many years. For so many years, there has never been someone who is interested in me, even the not-so-attractive ones. The second eyes i could get so far are out of humiliations. I could manage to make myself feel better by not going out at all. But as soon as the holidays end, i would have to get out of the shell again which means that I would be seeing all sorts of attractive women on the street while feeling very inadequate about myself. I could not quit thinking about it. I am dying for genuine attractions from women but i am short, fat and weird looking. How could I be able to get out of the loop and stop thinking about it? How could I re-start a normal social life and have enough confidence to ask women out? 😳

One woman responded by reciprocating his feelings of being ugly and alone. She could not name any one thing she hated about herself, since she hated everything, and listed all her perceived flaws. The parts of her body she wanted to fix could change from week to week. This illustrates how persistent and pervasive BDD thoughts can be. As a result, she felt life had "passed her by" and she had nothing to look forward to:

Female-Reply: For me I hate everything about myself. I'm ugly and weird looking. I couldn't even begin to list everything I would change it really is everything. I do get more obsessive about certain parts but it can shift and change week on week. For me I hate my nose. It's wonky and to the side. I hate my hairline, it's too high and weird. I would like a hair transplant. I would like laser on my skin as it's awful with spots and broken veins. I would like an eyebrow lift as I don't like my eyebrows. I'd like filler in my eyebags, round my mouth and in my lips.

I'd also like lipo on my jaw and a chin implant. At my most extreme point I also wanted jaw implants and cheek implants but I've got past this now. I hate my boobs as my nipples are too low so I'd want an uplift. I would like liposuction on my legs as well. I hate my legs, i have broken veins, stretch marks and short fat legs. I'm absolutely obsessed with wrinkles around my eyes and as I'm getting older i'm petrified of ageing. I currently have 7 eye creams that I use numerous times a day. I'm afraid of smiling and am obsessed with lighting. I can't even watch certain programmes on tv as it triggers my obsessions. I feel life has passed me by and there is nothing to look forward to.

Other posters were not convinced they were ugly but believed people judged them negatively based on their appearance. In the following example, a female poster was convinced people were calling her ugly in public. She asked others on the forum if they had similar experiences and wanted them to explain why this occurred:

Female-Initial Post: Does this happen to you where people will say you are ugly in public? It has happened to me several times in my life. I don't even find myself that ugly, why would this happen to me? The thing that upsets me the most is when little kids say it because I know they really mean it. Adults say it to me too and sometimes pretty girls will laugh at me like they feel bad for me. I get so angry but that makes people even happier. Does this happen to anyone else? Does anyone have any idea as to why this would happen to someone? Trust me, I'm not THAT ugly. It has taken its toll on my self-esteem and my gender life - but that's another story.

The uncertainty about why people were calling her ugly prompted her to seek reassurance. She wanted to find others who could empathize or explain why it was happening. Asking questions and disclosing personal experiences in initial posts were commonly used to encourage others to share similar experiences. New members wanted to feel less alone and to reduce uncertainty about their situation.

One male poster was curious why the thought of being ugly distressed people on the forum so much. Participants' reasons ranged from fear of rejection, being an outcast, wanting to be happy, and wanting to be loved and accepted by other people:

> **Male-Initial Post:** I am interested to hear what it is about being ugly that distresses people so much. I am not saying anyone here is ugly, but that is what we fear. What is it about being ugly that distresses you so much?

> **Male-Reply 1:** The fear of being embarrassed or outcast, I think the fear of somebody seeing your flaws which you try to hide, that would be the worst kind of distress.

> **Female-Reply 2:** i am trying to figure that out as well. being ugly to me, means being un wanted, unloveable. For me, I put so much emphasis on looks, and my looks put all the weight on my worth. I feel like because I'm ugly I have no importance in this world and that I won't be successful. Yet at the same time, the rational part of me knows that isn't true. Looks aren't everything. Ugly or beautiful, everyone is important and beautiful in their own way. 😔

> I think a lot of people with BDD, including myself just think that in order to be happy, we have to be beautiful. it's a vicious cycle.

> **Undetermined-Reply 3:** OK, well my BDD was spurred by very chronic bullying which started about 5 or 6 years ago (i'm 15 now). I suppose the prospect of being ugly distresses me so much simply because of the fear of rejection, (like the bullying).

Many individuals on the forum feared rejection due to their perceived ugliness and appearance flaws. People with BDD often have negative core beliefs about their appearance and believe they need to be attractive to be loved, accepted, and successful. Other core beliefs include "If I looked better, my whole life would be better" and "Happiness comes from looking good."[2] These beliefs remind me of a famous *Saturday Night Live* comedy sketch by Billy Crystal, where he provides his impersonation of actor Fernando Lamas. He suavely tells audience members "It is better to look good than to feel good." People with BDD believe *looking good* will result in *feeling good* about themselves.

Forum members had varying levels of insight related to their appearance concerns and BDD symptoms. The forum leaders had good insight and realized their appearance obsessions and behaviors were caused by having BDD. However, other members seemed to have poor to delusional levels of insight. One man learned he had BDD but still believed he was genuinely ugly: "In the past couple of weeks i've discovered that i have BDD, clinical depression and social anxiety disorder. I know I have BDD, but I AM genuinely UGLY."

Another member knew his thoughts about balding were irrational but was unable to extinguish them. He was in therapy for BDD, so he was aware his perceptions were not true, yet he was still worried about losing his hair. He believed the reflection he saw in the mirror was accurate:

> **Male-Reply:** My BDD involves hair loss. This has been going on since I was 15 years old, I'm 25 now. Even though hair loss in one's mid-teens is extremely rare, even though my hair hasn't seemed to change at all in the past decade, even though everyone I know says that I am not going bald, even though I have been to a doctor who said I show no signs of hair loss, even though I have been diagnosed with BDD and told that I have severe perceptual distortions, it is still hard for me to believe that I am not losing my hair most days. Because what I see in the mirror is reality. How can it not be? I know what I see, the mirror can't lie.

Thoughts about losing his hair consumed him, even though he and others could not perceive his appearance had changed. Learning about the disorder can help individuals move from delusional beliefs to having good or fair insight, meaning they realize their thoughts are caused by having BDD. However, gaining insight about BDD does not by itself diminish one's negative thoughts. Treatment using SSRIs and CBT can be effective at increasing insight levels and overcoming symptoms.[3]

People with BDD must accept they have a mental health condition that causes cognitive distortions in visual processing (Chapter 6). This was difficult for me to accept since I am artistic and wanted to believe what I was seeing was accurate. Once I accepted that the mirror *does* lie to people with BDD, I was able to take steps to combat my negative thoughts. For example, I reminded myself others did not see what I saw, since I tended to exaggerate my imperfections. These cognitive distortions can make individuals with BDD feel disfigured, even when they appear normal to others.

DISTORTED BODY IMAGE: "MY BODY LOOKS ODD NOW"

Body image obsessions afflict both men and women with BDD.[4] Individuals may feel they are too short or may be concerned about looking too thin. One male poster lost weight and felt better about himself but believed his head now looked too large for his body. He wanted to know if others had similar experiences and how they coped:

Male-Initial Post: The problem is, even if I feel better about myself and think my body looks better, I don't feel like everything adds up. I feel very weird now when I look at myself and like something is wrong. I don't know if this is just because it takes time to get used to it? One thing I've been thinking is that my head vs my body looks odd now, I have a pretty big head and so I feel it looks weird on a smaller frame than when I was bigger overall.

I want to know if other people here have been through some similar experience when losing weight and how it turned out for you, was it a temporary issue with getting used to your new looks or has it caused problems for you ever since? How did you cope with it?

Another female poster lost weight and had a "perfect BMI" yet was still obsessed about her appearance. She received lots of compliments about her body but felt anxious because she still had terrible self-confidence. As a result, she constantly talked about her concerns with her friends, family members, and her boyfriend. This caused her more anxiety because she was afraid they thought she was looking for attention. She started her post by asking others to share their stories and experiences related to BDD:

> **Female-Initial Post:** I guess I just really would love to hear some of your stories, personal experiences, and habits all related to BDD.
>
> I'm a 20 year old girl who really has nothing she should be complaining about at all (and this just makes me feel even more selfish for feeling so terrible at times). I guess I should start by saying I was bullied throughout all of my school years for my weight. After leaving school, I lost it all.
>
> Now I have a perfect BMI, receive many compliments from people, yet I still have... just plain awful self-confidence. . . I can't go five minutes without thinking about my weight, I always talk about it to my friends, family and boyfriend (this causes me more anxiety sometimes just because I'm afraid they don't understand and think I'm looking for attention), I feel severe guilt for eating anything I deem as bad food and I work out obsessively.

Individuals on the forum were afraid family members and friends would think they were vain and seeking attention if they continually talked about their appearance concerns. People with BDD may fear that seeking reassurance will be mistaken for vanity and thus fail to disclose their concerns to family and friends.[5] Disclosing their fears on the forum was preferable since other members could understand their concerns and provide support. However, even forum members confused their body image concerns with vanity or narcissism. Whereas vanity is driven by adoration of one's appearance, reassurance seeking in BDD is driven by concerns about how distorted or ugly one's body or features appear to others.

BDD body image obsessions and negative core beliefs can afflict people throughout their lives and impact individuals from different cultures, gender identities, sexual orientations, and ethnicities.[6] Though most people who posted to the forum were younger (twenty to thirty), one fifty-three-year-old man was suffering due to his appearance concerns and fear of getting older (gerascophobia). His BDD symptoms had started in his twenties, and he had "good face days and bad face days" due to his appearance changing in mirrors, photos, and with age:

Male-Initial Post: I don't quite remember when this started, but I'm sure it goes back to at least my late 20's, maybe even to my teens. It seemed to center around my neck, which is definitely less than aquiline. But I have also gone, and still go, back and forth, thinking I'm quite good looking and then see myself in a mirror or photo and think it was all a vain illusion, thousands of times. I have good face days and bad face days.

Exacerbating and intensifying this "BDD", maybe growing out of it, is my "gerascophobia". For years, I thought with the right diet, the right skin creams, the right supplements, the right youth elixirs and potions, I could keep ahead of the marring hand of father time and fool everybody I was 28 forever. The reality that this is a delusion terrifies me and gives me intense anxiety, that my battle is all but lost, that I'm doomed. Still, I cling to this delusion, if only "for one more summer".

A young Italian woman in her twenties was repulsed by her big nose and sticklike body. She constantly compared herself to other women with curves and felt so hideous that she was contemplating suicide:

Female-Initial Post: I am a petite Italian woman with a big disgusting nose and few curves. Basically, not attractive at all in society's eyes. I will go so far to even say hideous. For years, I always found myself comparing myself to other women who were taller, curvier, prettier. I can't tell you how many hours I've spent googling images of curvy women and comparing myself to them, or searching for others out there like me. I literally stare at these women for hours and cry, then stare at myself in the mirror and cry, wondering why I had to be born so awkward and hideous.

I hate who I've become as a person. Totally vain and self-absorbed, and constantly judging others by their appearance as well. I've started to have suicidal thoughts, and I don't know where to turn. I don't even know if I have BDD. I'm just sick of crying for hours, I'm sick of feeling hideous and ugly from the moment I wake up to the time I fall asleep. Honest truth? I really don't want to be around anymore. I just feel like it's a beautiful world, and I'm just an ugly girl who's forced to live in it and suffer through it.

A young Hispanic woman hated her body shape because she wanted a curvaceous body. She was an artist and lamented not having the pear-shaped body she desired:

> **Female-Initial Post:** I am an artist and I am constantly drawing bodies, different bodies, but most often female bodies that I would like to have, that look better than I do. I just don't get it. To me a beautiful female body is shaped like a pear, a beautiful pear, an hourglass with full hips and small upper bodies. The kind that fills jeans and looks like a coke bottle. It's so lovely. Like Beyonce or the Kardashians I suppose. (I am hispanic, by the way)... How can I love my shape if I think it is sooo ugly. I don't want to be bone thin, just shaped correctly! I draw beauty, and I just can never see myself as it, ever. I think about this too much... It ruins my outlook on myself...

Body image problems can be based on cultural norms and values.[7] Rather than wanting to be thinner, these two young women wanted to have more curves. I could empathize with the Hispanic woman because I used to draw nude models during college art classes. I preferred drawing women with more curves (both hips and breasts) because they were more interesting than thinner models. However, I disliked having the pear shape this young woman desired. My ideal was to look like a runway model with slender hips and long legs. I wanted that cultural ideal, despite knowing how models' body shapes have changed over time, from voluptuous Marilyn Monroe to skinny Twiggy.

NEGATIVE EMOTIONS: "I FEEL LIKE NOTHING"

Being obsessed with perceived appearance flaws can cause individuals to experience extreme self-hatred, shame, depression, and anxiety. Feelings of shame are prevalent in people with BDD symptoms.[8] Stigma and shame in individuals with body dysmorphic disorder can be caused by high levels of appearance-related rejection sensitivity, which is the fear others will negatively evaluate and reject a person based on one's appearance.[9] About two-thirds of people with BDD have delusions of reference, believing that other people are taking special notice of them in a negative way or mistreat them based on their appearance.[10]

Rejection sensitivity and delusions of reference were evident in many of the posts by BDD forum members. One man felt rejected by women due to his looks and described feeling hurt, scared, and distressed as a result:

> **Male-Initial Post:** I am simply self-conscious of my looks and my flaws because I am so hurt, scared and distressed by being seen as unattractive. Why am I so hurt, scared and distressed by being seen as unattractive? Because I just feel so worthless, inadequate, shameful, not good enough, a nobody, irrelevant, inferior to others, etc when seen as unattractive. I just am so hurt by it. That is how I have felt when put down for my looks, that is how I have felt when rejected and overlooked by women. I feel like nothing. I hate how I never seem to be good enough to be liked/wanted by women.

Another woman received compliments on her looks but was certain people were being sarcastic and mean by mocking her:

> **Female-Initial Post:** When people look at me I always feel like they're looking at me with disgust, thinking about how ugly I look. People always tell me they think I'm beautiful, customers at work and people at the grocery store, etc. and for the LONGEST time every time someone complimented me like that I would start crying because I felt like they were mocking me and making fun of me like they were being sarcastic and mean. I don't do that anymore, but I am struggling with

things. I still feel like when someone is looking at me they are disgusted.

Negative emotions such as guilt and remorse could be caused by regret over past cosmetic and dermatological procedures. These negative emotions were often turned inward, against the self. A young man felt extreme guilt because he had tried to fix moles on his face with a commercial product that left "4 large noticeable scars" instead. He recalled getting advice from a dermatologist to leave the moles alone but had persisted. The guilt and regret about his actions left him feeling suicidal and depressed more than two years later:

Male-Initial Post: Before I decided to do this, I had gone to a dermatologist to remove them. She told me not to do it, that it was not worth it, that the scars could look worse; her words have been echoing in my mind ever since. So, I put this cream on all 4 moles (all on the right side of my face, except 1 on the tip of my nose) because the dermatologist would not do it herself.

Needless to say, the cream left 4 large red craters on my face. After that, people just stared at my face (especially family) wondering what the hell happened. My mother even at one point told me I ruined a "beautiful" face. Since then, I have spent a couple thousand dollars at a plastic surgeon, trying to remove my mistakes. Not a day goes by when I'm not kicking myself for what I've done.

Other forum members believed their perceived ugliness was caused by fate and responded with anger. In the following example, a woman used all caps to emphasize the extreme frustration she felt about the "monster" staring back at her in the mirror:

Female-Initial Post: I am ugly, I am hideous, SO STOP LYING! If I wasn't men would at least give me a glance.

If I wasn't people wouldn't look at me with that horror look on their face.

If I wasn't I wouldn't see These DARK, DARK PURPLE RINGS AROUND MY EYES THAT MAKE ME APPEAR TO BE DEADLY OR SERIOUSLY ILL!

If I wasn't I would be desired by men. Or at least Lusted after. I would have friends. I wouldn't see what I see in the mirror. A monster staring back!

SO BEFORE YOU TRY TO MAKE ME FEEL BETTER BY TELLING ME I'M NOT UGLY...

spare me. Because I already Know I am.

The female poster did not ask for help, so forum members failed to reply, unable to ease her suffering. Some individuals with BDD are enraged by their perceived ugliness. Research has shown people with BDD have higher levels of anger/hostility than those with other psychiatric disorders.[11] They may be angry because of their perceived ugliness, because it isn't fair they are ugly, or because they can't fix their perceived appearance flaws.

People on the forum experienced a wide range of negative emotions, including shame, guilt, anger, and remorse. Some found living with their perceived ugliness such a hellish experience they wanted to end their lives. One woman hated the result of her eyelid procedure so much she wanted to commit suicide:

Female-Initial Post: Now i feel life is not worth living after all these years and what happened to my face made things worse I know lots of people who are going to say i am crazy but no. i am ruined.

i am giving myself max two months for my face and eyes to heal and my hair to heal i am using minoxidil. I am going to kill myself by hanging if it fails. 😢

Why do this to me? Why did god and luck let this happen? What am i to do?

The last time i was bullied i could take it. Sexual assault i could bear. But losing my eyes and face no. I want my looks backkkk... 😢

Some members tried to fix their perceived flaws with surgery. However, they were so unhappy with the results they wanted to end their lives. Members believed suicide was the only way to alleviate feelings of shame about their appearance. Shame is a painful emotion caused by the deep-rooted, inherent belief there is something so wrong with the person that the flaw must be concealed from others to avoid being negatively judged and humiliated.[12]

SUICIDALITY: "I FEEL TOO UGLY TO LIVE"

Disclaimer: Messages by forum members about suicidality could be triggering to readers with body dysmorphic disorder (BDD). If you are experiencing suicidal thoughts or behaviors, immediately contact your physician, call 911 or the emergency services in your area, and refer to the suicide prevention resources located in Appendix A2.

The desire to commit suicide was a recurring theme on the BDD forum. It was tragic and heartbreaking to read posts by young people who wanted to end their lives due to hating their appearance. I met the family of a young man at an International OCD Foundation conference who took his life because he suffered from BDD. Every day, his father, mother, and sister grieve his passing. Their lives have moved forward, but his is over, due to this debilitating disorder.

Having BDD is associated with many risk factors that predict attempted and completed suicide. These include poor social support, high rates of suicidal ideation, suicide attempts, psychiatric hospitalization, unemployment, disability, being single or divorced, and past abuse. Other risk factors include comorbidity with major depressive disorder, substance abuse disorders, eating disorders, anxiety, poor self-esteem, anger, and feelings of humiliation and shame.[13] Evidence indicates approximately 80 percent of individuals with BDD experience lifetime suicidal ideation, and 24 to 28 percent have attempted suicide.[14]

The BDD forum enabled people who lacked support from family members and friends to vent their negative emotions and get help. Feelings of shame and self-hatred can be fueled by guilt about being so focused on one's appearance. This is referred to as the "double whammy" of BDD.[15] People not only have distressing thoughts they cannot control, but they also berate themselves for having these thoughts. One female participant felt like an "idiot" for hating herself due to her appearance flaws but admitted she felt "too ugly to live":

> **Female-Initial Post:** I hate the way I look, and I am starting to hate myself for looking this way. I don't hide away all the time. Although sometimes I do. I will lie to my friends and say I'm not around when they want to meet up, because I can't handle what seeing them does to my self-esteem on a given day. Whenever I see them, however I might be feeling that day, my self-esteem will always shoot down 100% because I am reminded that they are beautiful, I am ugly, and that is how it will always be. I rue the day I joined Facebook, because now my stupid face and body are there for the world to see. I feel like an idiot for saying what I have just said, because I have studied psychology, philosophy, and education in quite a bit of detail, and I know that there is so much more to our existence than what we look like. I am going to die someday, so why am I wasting my life feeling like this? The problem is that I feel too ugly to live.

Another man was in therapy and on medication but still obsessed about his nose. He was suicidal despite being married to his "beautiful wife" with three children. It was only thinking about seeing his kids every day that kept him from committing suicide. His greatest fear was being right about his appearance. His self-loathing, hatred, and suicidal thoughts were interspersed with periods of acceptance. He ended his post by sharing his "love and support" for others who were also dealing with these issues:

> **Male-Initial Post:** I appreciate everybody sharing their story as it makes me feel less alone so I would like to share mine as well.

I am completely obsessed with my nose, have been my entire life after it grew very big in middle school and people started making fun of it, including my own mother.

I had rhinoplasty in my early 20s (twice because I didn't like the result the first time) and lived obsessed with but reasonably happy with my appearance for approx. 12 years.

5 years ago, I woke up, looked in the mirror and just come to a loathsome, disgusting hatred of myself and the way that I looked, mainly because of my nose. I had some troubles breathing so there was that component but I had a third nose job. I was happy with it for about 6 months and now I am in a completely loathsome place again where I cannot look at myself in the mirror without feeling like I am getting kicked in the gut. I am completely obsessed, and it never leaves my side ever.

I used to look in the mirror 100 times per day but now I try not to at all.

I have not made a new friend in 5 years and I try not to go out with the exception of work. It has damaged my career pretty seriously as I shrink into my office and have had opportunities for promotions but turned them down because I could not stand putting myself out there in front of people.

I have a beautiful wife (that I met during one of my relatively healthier times) and 3 great children and I have been seeing a therapist and take 40 mg of prozac (have been taking that for 10 years) and I don't know whether I need to mourn my appearance (take less prozac) or take more medication to help with the obsession.

I definitely have suicidal thoughts quite a bit. That is scary. Most of the time it is thinking about seeing my kids the next day that keeps me going.

I am lucky enough to live in a place with a lot of doctors and I am going to try to find a good psychiatrist (new) that maybe can help.

I oscillate between hatred/self-loathing/suicidal thoughts and getting by acceptance. Never better than that. Stress exacerbates the problem.

Of course, my fear is that yes, I am obsessed with my looks but I am also *right* about my appearance. you can be both you know and that is my greatest fear.

My love and support to anybody else dealing with these self image issues.

Many individuals on the forum who had plastic surgery were dismayed and suicidal due to the results. One man could not forgive himself for getting plastic surgery to trim his jawline. The outcome left him more distressed about his appearance. He wanted to get a second procedure to fix the first and planned to kill himself if that failed. He believed the surgery had left him uglier than before:

Male-Initial Post: I feel like I will never forgive myself.

I've been told I'm attractive my entire life. But I obsessed over certain features on my face that I hated. My nose, my flat cheeks, my jawline.

I impulsively decided to get a plastic surgery procedure to trim my jawline. Yes, I cut off my freaking bones. And I really regret it.

I used to have a strong, defined jawline. Now it's weak and uneven with a droopy chin. I look like I aged 10 years.

I don't know how I will ever forgive myself. I am going to try to get reconstructive surgery next month.

If I can't improve it, I have planned to kill myself in the next few years.

I will probably drive my car off a cliff and pretend it was an accident, and give all my assets to my mom.

I can't imagine living with this face anymore. This face I destroyed. I was born with it, I could accept it. But because I paid $$$$$ to alter it and ruined it, it now looks unnatural and weird and NOT ME. I don't think I can ever accept it. I wake up every day wanting to die. I look in the mirror and have panic attacks. The only way out is to end my life. I'd rather be dead than live with this ugly face I butchered.

A woman responded to his post and echoed his concerns about wanting to get a second procedure to fix the results from her first surgery. She was also suicidal and believed the plastic surgery had left her face unrecognizable. Both her mother and psychologist recommended she not get a second surgery, but she could not accept the results:

Female-Reply: oh my gosh me too I'm feeling the same way - I got a nose job and I hate it so much. It's not me anymore in the mirror. I can't deal with this change and I think about suicide every day. I did not know that I should not have done this but when I think back, I see all the signs for someone who should not have plastic surgery. I don't know how to deal with it and all the advice I get is to move on and accept it but when I look in the mirror I just can't. I don't feel like myself even when I'm not looking in the mirror because when people look at me now I'm wondering what they see. It's so strange and horrible. I can't get my life back on track. I want a revision so bad but my mom said I should not and my psychologist said that will not make me happy and they sound like they are right but I can't be happy with this.

A thirty-four-year-old woman believed she had "aged overnight" after taking ADHD medication (Adderall). She was socially isolated, unable to work, and suicidal: "I now have sunken eyes and facial wasting like a meth junky and I used to be so beautiful...I now have to take my life because I can't live this way. What would you guys do if this happened to you?? I am also in need of friends who are in a similar situation."

A male poster tried to help by providing advice and coping skills (Appendix B2): "It is important to tell someone in your offline life who can help you and can help you keep safe. Remember that thoughts about taking your life are just thoughts. They do not mean you have to act on them - no matter how overwhelming the thoughts are or how often you have them. They also don't mean that you will always have those thoughts."

On the BDD forum, the desire to commit suicide was fueled by a range of emotions, including shame, depression, guilt, and remorse. Members often regretted getting cosmetic surgery since they still hated their appearance. People with suicidal thoughts may feel hopeless, believing they will never achieve their inner, idealized representation of attractiveness.[16] Members disclosed negative appearance beliefs and suicidal thoughts along with their BDD-related behaviors. These behaviors included seeking cosmetic procedures, mirror checking or avoidance, camouflaging perceived flaws, taking selfies, seeking reassurance, and social comparison.

BDD-Related
Behaviors

Female-Initial Post: I had cosmetic surgery and now have two huge scars on my thighs and my butt looks distorted. Perhaps I had a form of BDD to even get this surgery... but now it has taken over my life. I am obsessed with hatred of my body. I feel horrific...like I am a freak. I feel like I want to die.

Male-Initial Post: I've thought extensively about plastic surgery, but to be honest, no surgery will be able to fix my face. It just won't - you can't play around with the skull to make the face look better, and in my case, the skull is the problem. Even if i do have cosmetic surgery, i'm scared that i'll still be ugly and the problems won't subside.

Seeking Cosmetic Procedures (Surgery)

Some members on the forum endorsed having cosmetic procedures as a way to feel better about their appearance. Pursuing cosmetic treatment (surgical, dermatological, and other types of cosmetic interventions) is common among adults with BDD. Research indicates 76 percent have contemplated cosmetic procedures to fix their perceived flaws, and 66 percent have received aesthetic treatments. However, even when individuals feel better about one part of their body after surgery, the image obsession often moves to one or more different body parts. [1]

The forum moderators and frequent posters usually reminded members that cosmetic surgery was not recommended to fix their appearance concerns, and having surgery could make their symptoms worse. This was the reason Roger refrained from having plastic surgery to fix his nose:

> **Roger-Reply:** i think about surgery often, but i've been regularly told that it won't achieve anything, one way or another i will scrutinise something else. It's the nature of the business and i had a think about it the other day, if i fixed my nose i would probably move onto my ears or something even though i have very little issue with them right now.

Other forum members wanted to find out if having surgery would help ease their BDD symptoms. In the following example, a male poster wanted to know if anyone on the forum had plastic surgery and liked the results. One man who had multiple procedures did not feel worse about his appearance. However, having the surgeries had not helped his BDD:

> **Male-Initial Post:** My question is: has anyone EVER had surgery with BDD and liked the results? Scratch that, has anyone ever had surgery with BDD and been unhappy with the results/preoccupied with something else but overall LESS upset with how they look?

> **Male-Reply 1:** I guess the best way to put it is that I have, for, 50 flaws that I feel make me god awful ugly. So I try to go down my list and correct each one. And yes, I have had extensive cosmetic surgery to correct many of my flaws with great success. Do I still have bdd after all the surgeries and procedures and alterations? Yes. Why? Because I may have only eliminated 20 or so defects off my list, so I still believe I am dog ugly, but not as severe as before my "transformation". I do not feel my surgeries have worsened my bdd.

Another woman who replied got surgery but was unhappy with the results. Her self-esteem had dropped, which was why she joined the forum. She realized in hindsight that plastic surgery could not make anyone more beautiful:

> **Female-Reply 2:** No, I got a rhinoplasty in November and its made my face worse. I'm disgusted with plastic surgery. In fact, the rhinoplasty has dropped my self-esteem 10-fold and that's why I'm on here. I remember being insecure, but the plastic surgery has made me so much more insecure. I was hoping to become more beautiful naturally, as I seemed to be doing in my late 20's but it seems to be going backwards again, i'm 32. Plastic surgery can't make anyone beautiful, I never saw that before, it just isn't possible.

Despite their attempts to fix their perceived flaws with plastic surgery, most participants ended up feeling worse after the procedures. A self-fulfilling prophecy BDD therapists often witness is a person getting a cosmetic procedure, being disappointed with the outcome, and then returning for a second, third, fourth, or even fifth procedure on the exact same body part.[2]

Cosmetic surgery was endorsed by some members to fix perceived appearance flaws. Getting cosmetic treatment (dermatological and surgery) is not viewed as deviant conduct and carries less social stigma than getting treatment for a mental health condition.[3] In a study of two hundred individuals with BDD, 64 percent had received cosmetic treatment (dermatological and surgery).[4] By comparison, only 30.5 percent of 401 people with symptoms consistent with moderately severe BDD had sought help from a psychiatrist.[5]

People with BDD symptoms may prefer cosmetic procedures over therapy because there are fewer barriers to finding and receiving treatment (Chapter 11). BDD specialists may be difficult to locate, expensive, and require patients to have health insurance. Cosmetic procedures, dermatologic treatments, fillers, and other noninvasive treatments are accessible to many people due to an abundance of practitioners, payment plans, and advances in medicine. These procedures are considered acts of beautification, altering the body to more closely resemble what is currently viewed as culturally attractive.[6]

In retrospect (and after recovery), I don't regret having the rhinoplasty since it made my nose thinner. However, I was consumed with guilt and shame after the procedure and unhappy with the results. Members seeking cosmetic surgery were often worried they would no longer recognize themselves or would look worse after the surgery. However, some individuals who had undergone surgery endorsed having cosmetic procedures. In the following example, one member desperately wanted a rhinoplasty procedure:

Undetermined-Initial Post: So, I'm very focused on a certain flaw; a bump in my nose. I told someone my worries about it and they said there's nothing there, and mentioned BDD. But the thing is, I have evidence proving it is there. I can feel it, and it seems as though I've inherited it, so how can I be imagining it if it's so obvious it's really there? I want a rhinoplasty and nobody is listening to me...

The first two members who replied endorsed getting surgery since the person's life was negatively impacted by fixating on the perceived flaw:

Female-Reply 1: I believe that if you indeed think your nose does not make the best of your face, you could have a rhinoplasty. Think long before you do one and choose the right type of surgery. I know people may disagree and say that we need to accept this fact, but I disagree. For us who have been good looking and lived years being treated in a certain NORMAL way, will be miserable after "the change of appearance".

Male-Reply 2: I personally think surgery is not necessary because I find nobody ugly and will always say no you really don't need that you look fine. But for people like us who fixate too much on them to a level that their lives are literally being destroyed—surgery can be a very effective cure, of course speaking from personal experience.

One of the forum moderators pointed out that even if the flaw did exist, focusing on the bump could be related to BDD. She cautioned against getting plastic surgery and recommended the person get advice from a therapist:

> **Anna (Moderator)-Reply 3:** Even if it is there, maybe you worrying about it and obsessing over it might be a sign of BDD or traits, though I couldn't tell you for sure and we're not professionals here. You could talk to a psych about this and see what they think and ask them to help you. Surgery is not how you treat BDD, the "obsession" just moves to another part of the body and it goes on forever with no therapy.

Forum leaders and moderators countered pro-surgical advice and reminded people surgery was not helpful in relieving symptoms. Members who had received effective clinical treatment also advised against getting plastic surgery. One such member quoted a respected BDD researcher and clinician (Dr. David Veale) to back up his advice that surgery was detrimental for individuals with BDD: "Even if patients are satisfied with cosmetic treatments, often the preoccupation moves to a different area of the body, so that the handicap of the disorder remains." In this way, the poor advice offered by some members was corrected by others.

Mirror Checking/Avoidance

Individuals on the forum often spent hours studying their reflection in mirrors and obsessing about their perceived defects. Even when people liked some aspects of their appearance, looking in mirrors made them feel ugly. The key reason was their belief the mirror doesn't lie. Unfortunately, for people with BDD, the image they see in the mirror is not accurate. They view a reflection that is distorted by their perceptions, where small flaws assume monumental proportions. Mirror checking or avoidance is a common BDD-related behavior; researchers have found 87 percent of people with BDD engage in mirror checking or avoidance behaviors.[7] Mirror checking by individuals with BDD is not related to being vain, though many people on the forum labeled themselves as vain for obsessing about their appearance.

One female poster asked if anyone had trouble knowing what they "really" looked like. She felt that she did not look human in photographs but could look pretty in mirrors:

> **Female-Initial Post:** Does anyone else on this forum also have trouble knowing what they really look like? There are days I can look in the mirror and look pretty, and then have my photo taken and see the photo and look grotesque... I want to cry every time I see a photo of myself next to a friend and I realize that I don't even look human. It is so confusing to me, like every day I look different, but the way I look is so fragile that if the weather is off or if I eat something heavy my appearance completely changes. And then there is the fact that I look completely different depending on the mirror I am looking into.

Another woman replied that she hated looking at her reflection in the mirror. Doing so caused her to spiral into a manic-depressive episode that would leave her sobbing all day about her body and life in general. She was caught between not wanting to be seen in public due to her appearance, yet she felt even worse if she stayed inside all day:

> **Female-Reply:** I also have phases of 'mirror obsession' and 'mirror avoidance.' I have periods where I deliberately don't look in mirrors or any reflective surface because I know I'll be sucked into that whole cycle of mirror checking, and I can't take it. But of course sometimes I'll catch sight of myself, be really shocked by how ugly my body is (or legs, in particular) and it'll send me spiraling into 'manic depressive' episodes where I'm just sobbing all day long about how I look, the pain of living in this body, and usually my life in general and how $#%^ it is, for instance being too afraid to leave the house, yet feeling even more depressed if I stay in all day.

The mirror became a trap that confirmed members' worst fears: their perceived flaws were visible to others. Like the previous female poster, some members avoided looking in mirrors due to becoming depressed and suicidal. The following poster succinctly describes typical avoidance behaviors:

> **Undetermined-Initial Post:** I avoid pictures being taken of me. I avoid mirrors or anything that can reflect light. I avoid videos being taken. I try not to look at myself in the mirror since I'll get a BDD attack.

Checking one's reflection occurred in shiny surfaces other than mirrors, such as cell phones and computer screens. One transgender male (Chapter 3) was dealing with obsessions about his hair, which he checked constantly using his phone:

> **Male-Initial Post:** I have dealt with anorexia for a few months, but I'm trying to recover right now. This morning, it rained and I was stuck outside without an umbrella, waiting for my school to open, and it completely ruined my hair. It didn't seem to bother other people and my friends were getting annoyed that I was constantly fixing my hair. I have my phone out literally all of the time during school. If I don't, it's only a few seconds before I use it again. I use it more for the reflection than I do for texting during school. I'm constantly looking at my face and hair because I can't see it without a reflection, of course.

Whereas many people can have good and bad hair days, for people with BDD, most days are bad. When people are convinced what they see in the mirror is real, they may try to hide their perceived defects with clothing, body position, or excessive use of makeup.[8] Fran (one of the forum leaders) used makeup to hide her perceived ugliness from everyone, including herself.

Hiding Flaws (Camouflaging)

Concealing (camouflaging) takes place when individuals use body posture, makeup, clothes, hands, hair, or hats to hide their perceived defects. This is considered the most common BDD behavior, with 91 percent of people using camouflaging to conceal their perceived flaws.[9]

One woman was convinced she had an ugly side and a good side to her face. As a result, she only wanted people to see her pretty side in pictures and in public:

Female-Initial Post: When i decide to actually go out, i am constantly planning how to position myself so that nobody is viewing my 'ugly' side. I hate photos, but when i do take them it's always of my good side. The other side looks like a different, uglier person. When people are on that 'ugly' side, i feel extremely self conscious and avoid looking at them. I hate it so much.

Hiding perceived facial flaws with makeup was a common BDD behavior by women on the forum. Fran admitted she wore makeup all the time, even when she slept at night. She dreaded having her boyfriend and other people see her face without her mask on:

Fran-Initial Post: This is very disabling, and inhibits greatly me from having a normal live like i want. People have commented on my make up, that i wear too much, wrong colour etc etc. I hate it and feel ashamed of that too, but if I could choose, I'd rather have them speaking bad about my makeup then about how ugly I am.

Another woman used fake tan and makeup to disguise her pale skin before leaving the house:

Female-Initial Post: But the thing i hate most right now is my pale skin. I'm not just a little bit pale i am literally the whitest color ever! people would say how white i was as well. So i've been wearing fake tan since i was about 14. And it made me feel a lot better wearing fake tan as well as make up. But now it's got to the point where i can't leave the house without fake tan on or a face full of make up. It takes me hours to get ready in the morning and if the slightest thing is wrong on my face i won't leave the house or go to school or out with my friends.

Having bad hair days caused forum members to avoid going out in public for fear of showing their perceived ugliness to others. One male poster described how debilitating it was when his hair looked bad:

Male-Initial Post: I am a real perfectionist with my hair, when my hair looks good I feel so much better about my appearance. When my hair looks crap I feel I look awful and I just want to hide. To be honest, everyone else's hair looks the same every day and I am sure my hair looks pretty similar every day. But today I had a bad hair day and I just felt like $#%^, I just didn't want to chat to people as I didn't want to be seen. Do others here feel totally distressed on bad hair days?

Many men on the BDD forum had bad hair days; they feared their hair was thinning or balding. Women used makeup and fake tan to hide their facial flaws. Seeing themselves in mirrors and other reflective surfaces was extremely distressing. However, even more difficult was comparing one's image in mirrors to how the person looked in photographs and videos. There was no way members could know what they really looked like, since their image kept changing based on the time of day, lighting, and how the image was taken.

TAKING SELFIES (PHOTOS AND VIDEOS)

Some forum members were tormented by the way their appearance changed during the day. The time of day, quality of light, and use of photographs, videos, and mirrors continually altered their appearance and self-perceptions. This instability led members to lament they didn't know what they "really" looked like to others. Were they hideous and ugly, or did they look normal? They struggled to solve this dilemma by creating elaborate rituals such as taking excessive selfies (using videos and cameras) before leaving the house. This was the only way some members could feel okay about being seen in public.

People with BDD may take hundreds of selfies a day with their cell phones, comparing one photo to another, while others videotape the disliked body areas from many different angles or under various types of lighting.[10] Two female forum members described in detail how they prepared themselves to leave the house. The first spent hours taking photographs and videos of herself. She wanted to practice making herself look pretty. Even so, she was still convinced others thought she was ugly:

> **Female-Initial Post:** I spend hours taking photos and videos of myself to try to see how I look to others. I analyse hundreds of photos to decide whether or not I look ok in them, and if I do, I try to work out what it is that makes me look ok, so I can practise doing it all the time. After analysing the photos I have made a list of things to do/not do in order to make myself look pretty, i.e. makeup styles, hairstyles, the way I move my mouth when I talk, etc.
>
> Before leaving the house, even just to buy milk, I spend ages in front of the mirror and will often change my outfit several times. If I meet new people my first thought is that they will think I'm ugly, and I worry constantly about what my friends think I look like.

This young woman was obsessed with the pictures her friends took with her. As a result, she spent hours checking photographs posted on Facebook to make sure they met with her approval. If not, she removed her name from them (untagged) so the images were unidentifiable.

> I still have nights out, and after hours of getting ready I can usually come to the conclusion that I look ok. But then the cameras come out, and there's that desperate need to see every photo taken of me. If I look ok, then fine, but if it's a bad photo I obsess over it for the rest of the night. The next day I will go on facebook and trawl through the photos taken, so that I can un-tag myself before anyone else has the chance to see.

Another young woman spent hours in front of a mirror, checking her body from every angle. She then took multiple videos and pictures using her computer's camera (webcam) before leaving the house. That way, she could remind herself later about one picture she liked:

Female-Initial Post: Now every time I go out on the weekends, I make at least three videos of myself just walking around my living room, and have to watch each several times. I also take tons of photos of my face to see if my make-up is okay/how my face looks. I'm talking like twenty pictures at least every time I go out. I'm very embarrassed of my actions sometimes when my fiancee notices. I know that I sound very shallow, but doing these things give me relief. If I finally get everything "just right" I can remind myself that I took a picture or a video earlier that night that I was happy with, and I can tell myself that's what I look like. It's the only thing that makes me not feel horribly self conscious when I go out.

People with BDD can feel that their appearance looks okay from one angle but not from another. One male poster liked the way his nose looked from the front but did not like his profile in pictures and videos. He wanted to know if others judged people's appearance based on their profile:

Male-Initial Post: Hey everyone. I have this weird paranoid addiction. I'm always checkin if my nose looks big. I'm always taking pictures...even video on my iphone to see if its big. I know its not huge. I've never been made fun of for it. But it looks so good from the front n then the side it sticks out and i feels it's a little long. Do you judge how good looking people are by the front of their face or the side (profile)???

Another man compared his image in mirrors to those in photographs and videos. He believed he looked ugly in mirrors, but fine in videos and pictures. As a result, he desperately wanted to overcome his perception problem:

Male-Initial Post: I've found recently with my "moderate" BDD that pictures are often different to what I see in the mirror (and I say this in a positive sense). For example, I can take a picture of myself on my phone, or a video clip, hold it up to the mirror and see it as DRASTICALLY different to my usual negatively perceived appearance. The funny thing is, my mum and friends say that the picture/videos are EXACTLY as they see me on a day to day basis, aside from minor things such as light exposure and so on, they tell me that the images ARE NOT distorted in any way.

I now need to know how I can overcome this clear perceptual problem, my desperation has led me to several near-miss suicide attempts and I'd really like to get my head sorted.

Fran replied to another man who wanted to know why his appearance changed using different cameras and lighting. She assured him this was normal and people with BDD wanted to control how they looked under different conditions:

Fran-Reply: Its definitely hard to get hot admiring looks in one place, and then in another avoidance of eye contact. I can relate to this. But I think for all people, different light brings out different aspects of their looks. Even the most beautiful person may look average/ugly in some lights. The difference with us is that we have this need of control, the need of knowing, to be able to accept and start progressing from there. We want the whole truth. We can make tables and statistics of how good looking on a scale we look in a white light, yellow light from right side, left side, with a hat, without hat...and we could go on and on! There is no point guys.

I think we can just accept the fact that we DO look different in certain angles and lights. It would be strange not to. Lighting is used for this reason in marketing, how many times did the jewelry, the watch look much better in the store than at home on you? In the modelling, or photo taking overall, photographers use all kinds of lights and umbrellas to play with the light on the face.

You and I have a disorder which makes us care way too much about these natural things that have a reasonable explanation.

I agree with Fran that lighting changes how people, objects, and images appear. Painting outdoors in nature (like the Impressionists) is a challenge; the lighting changes throughout the day. People with BDD are distressed there is no one "true" image of themselves. But as Fran pointed out, photographers use special lights to improve how people look during photo shoots. Without the presence of light, nothing is visible. With light, many details become visible. And in different lights and from different angles, faces and bodies change their appearance.

Seeking Reassurance: "I know she's lying"

Forum members frequently asked family members, friends, and significant others about their perceived appearance flaws. Loved ones wanted to help so responded they looked fine or provided compliments and positive feedback. Rather than being relieved, forum members responded with disbelief and anger. When I had BDD and received compliments from family and friends, they rolled off me like water off a duck's back. Only I knew what I REALLY looked like (so I told myself). Reassurance seeking occurs in about 54 percent of people with the disorder; people question others about their perceived flaws but providing assurance the person looks fine doesn't help.[11]

People with BDD experience cognitive dissonance[12] when their negative core beliefs about their appearance are contradicted by others' compliments. Individuals experience emotional and mental discomfort when their beliefs or behaviors are not consistent. They seek to reduce this discomfort by avoiding information that contradicts their beliefs or by aligning their beliefs or behaviors to be consistent. Unfortunately, there is no right answer to the question: "Do I look okay?" Reassuring people they look fine doesn't help, but agreeing with them only confirms their worst fears.[13]

One female member expressed disbelief and anger when her boyfriend and others complimented her because she was convinced she was ugly, fat, and revolting:

> **Female-Initial Post:** I believe that I am ugly, fat and revolting, and will never be anything more than that. People tell me I am pretty. My

boyfriend (god help him) tells me I am beautiful every day. He might as well be telling me the sky is red, not blue - it means absolutely nothing to me. Every time someone tells me I look nice, or I am pretty, I want to punch them, kick them, scream at them and call them liars, because I know it isn't true.

Another female poster was obsessed about the two sides of her face being asymmetrical. She was convinced one side of her face was pretty and the other side was ugly. Her mother was unable to observe any difference, so she believed her mother was lying to her. She wanted reassurance from others on the forum that her observations were accurate:

Female-Initial Post: Thing is, it's like I know I'm not imagining it because I've taken photos in secret to observe the differences between both sides and there still is a major difference and is exactly the same to what i see in the mirror. I don't want to tell anyone because i feel like they will notice it and see me as someone else... even though i know people can see it. It's really weird! I've told my mum about it, and she's observed both sides and doesn't see a difference but i know she's lying. She is my mother after all. If pictures prove it, then it must be there?

A male poster spent hours looking at his face in the mirror and researching cosmetic procedures on the internet. He told his parents he wanted plastic surgery to fix his flaws. They reassured him he was a "good-looking lad" who did not need surgery. He then booked a consultation with a plastic surgeon, who also assured him his face was symmetrical:

Male-Initial Post: I now spend most of my time either looking in the mirror, looking at pictures of myself and trying to pick out flaws or looking up surgical corrections on the internet. My parents have noticed this and I have told them about the way I feel but they just do not believe that I can feel this way and say things like "but your a good looking lad". I of course think that they are saying this just to make me feel better.

I felt so bad the other week that I booked a consultation with a plastic surgeon who's exact words were "I cannot find a problem and your face is actually more symmetrical than most peoples".

Get this though, I actually convinced myself that he was lying for a period of time. I CONVINCED myself that a professional whose main job is to identify and correct anomalies in the face was lying to me to make me feel better. Then I thought to myself, what would he have to gain from lying. He is a complete stranger to me who would obviously benefit from the identification of a facial problem or defect as I would pay him to correct it. But instead, he actually advised against surgery.

As shown by these examples, telling individuals with BDD they are good-looking, pretty, or beautiful does not alleviate their negative beliefs about perceived flaws. Even after his parents told him he was good-looking, the male poster wanted to get feedback from a plastic surgeon. However, neither the assurances from his parents nor the plastic surgeon had lasting results.

Another man was convinced he had a cone-shaped head, despite his friends and family members telling him otherwise:

Male-Initial Post: No matter how many times I fight with friends and family they insist that I do not have a deformed head. They insist my head is not a conehead and that it is normal. I cannot understand why they are lying to me. I don't want to live looking this way. Being bald is bad enough and people make jokes. But to be a conehead is pure torture. I don't know what I did to deserve this.

He was "1000% convinced" that his perception was not flawed and his family and friends were lying to him. As a result, his insight level could be considered delusional. A person's appearance beliefs are considered delusional if the person is convinced their perceived flaws are real.[14] Attempts by friends and family members to reassure him his head was normal resulted in fights and disagreements. Family members and friends should avoid trying to provide reassurance. Instead, calmly explain that reassurance seeking is a ritual, and you will not participate. Be consistent and kind in your resolve.[15] You can encourage the person to develop positive coping strategies to combat BDD rituals (Chapter 12).

Forum members also sought reassurance from each other about perceived flaws. One woman started a thread asking if other people found women with excessive body hair disgusting: "If you saw a woman and she had a really hairy face and arms and legs, would you think she was disgusting?" The first forum member who replied insisted she did not find excessive body hair disgusting but other people might be judgmental: "No, I definitely wouldn't. But some people out there are cruel and judgmental and if something is different to what THEY think is right then to them it's not socially acceptable."

Another person was similarly reassuring and provided an example of a female co-worker who had a "really hairy face" but was not perceived as disgusting: "I used to work with someone who had a really hairy face, it was blonde fine hair I'd never see someone quite like it before, but no I did not find it disgusting." The original poster responded to both members, thanking them for their positive perspective. She was obsessed with her hair and skin and was relieved to know neither person would be repulsed by her appearance: "Thank you for the positive perspective. You may already realize I'm obsessed with hair/skin. Hair removal is also an issue for me but I won't bore you with details. All I know is, medical and social standards are not matched. This is a real point of stress for me."

Members usually responded to these types of questions by assuring the person their defects were probably unnoticeable and advised them to get therapy. One woman explained to a male poster that seeking reassurance from family members was related to having BDD:

> **Female-Reply:** It is clear that this is an obsession of yours to find out "am I ugly, average/normal or good looking?" And the fact that your family does NOT see the flaw that you see points towards BDD. But your family is not lying. Nor can we EVER know what each individual of this planet thinks of our looks, since it is so different what people see as beautiful.

She noted even if he knew what he "really" looked like to women, he might still worry why all women did not find him attractive:

> And even IF you KNEW, you would probably still be preoccupied about WHY doesn't ALL of them think you look good, and how will I know who I got a chance with or not? And shall we all then wear labels that tells other people what we find attractive? And even if 90% of the population thinks you are beautiful/handsome, you will probably still take offense from those who don't, that gives you an uninterested or disgusted look. Do you see how this problem just can't get solved by thinking like this?

Questions about whether a person was ugly or had BDD were used both to seek reassurance and get information about diagnosis and treatment. Another female poster believed one side of her face looked better than the other side. She wanted to know if she had BDD or if she was an ugly girl who could not accept her ugliness: "I think only one side of my face looks good. The right side of my face looks smashed in and very ugly. I'm so confused. Do I have BDD? Or am I just a truly ugly girl who can't accept that she's ugly?"

The first person who responded reassured her she was not ugly and then provided a lengthy personal disclosure (about a thousand words) describing her own negative feelings and suicidal thoughts. She ended her message by advising the original poster to keep posting on the forum: "All I can tell you is to keep posting here and listening to the feedback that you get. I am sure that someone will come up with some ideas here sooner or later."

Another female poster asked members why she had recently developed an obsession about her skin complexion, despite getting reassurances from everyone that she looked fine: "I always ask everyone for reassurance and their answers are always the same...Your mind is playing tricks on you...seriously you look the same...etc. etc." Forum members and the moderator provided possible reasons for her recent appearance obsessions. Anna validated her mind was "playing tricks on her" based on the assurances she had received:

Anna (Moderator)-Reply: Assuming you trust these people to be honest, or you've asked several people separately, then I would say that yes, your mind is playing tricks. It's perhaps not that you're seeing something that isn't there, but your brain is interpreting what it sees differently to the other people. It's focusing on the exact shade of your skin and over-emphasising it to an unhealthy colour.

Seeking reassurance could backfire when members failed to provide positive feedback. A male poster wanted members to tell him if his "big head" was hidden by his hair; he was too embarrassed to ask family members. A female poster warned him she might look at his pictures and confirm his head really was big. She wanted to ask others about her nose but was afraid they would confirm it was huge: "I'd look at your pics, but what if your head really is big? would you be able to accept someone saying it is? I want people to look at my nose but i don't know if I can truly accept someone saying 'yes it definitely is huge.' Think about it!!"

Seeking assurances about one's appearance concerns occurred despite the visual anonymity offered by the forum. This behavior is considered harmful for those with BDD because it rarely makes the person feel better and often leads to more reassurance-seeking behavior.[16]

SOCIAL COMPARISON: "MY CLOSEST FRIEND IS BEAUTIFUL"

Forum members felt compelled to compare their appearance to models, actors, musicians, their friends, and people they saw in public. Their attention was drawn to others who looked more attractive or who possessed features they desired. About 88 percent of people with BDD compare their body parts to others or scrutinize others' appearance.[17] Upward social comparison[18] can be motivational for people with high self-esteem. Positive role models can help people improve their abilities, such as when people read recovery stories and are motivated to seek treatment.

Upward social comparison on dimensions like appearance may cause people with low self-esteem to feel worse about themselves. Most people with BDD have low self-esteem related to their perceived appearance flaws.[19] Two young women eloquently described the pain and suffering caused by comparing themselves to other "beautiful" girls:

Female-Initial Post: I feel like crying all the time. I see so many beautiful, beautiful girls around me everywhere I go, and I will never ever ever be as beautiful or thin as them. One of my closest friend is beautiful. She has perfect skin, perfect teeth, and a perfect body. She is everything I will never ever be. She is successful too, in her career. I feel it is her looks that have made her that way, because I am also well-qualified and experienced, yet I never seem to succeed, career-wise. I feel that the way I look is dragging every other part of my life down with it.

Female-Initial Post: I constantly compare my face to others, thinking 'why can't i have a normal nose/chin like her' or 'why can't I just have a normal face'. It's so unfair that these pretty girls are walking around having absolutely no idea what it's like having to deal with being ugly. When I walk down the street and see people laughing, I get a sinking feeling in my stomach because I'm convinced they're laughing at the way I look. Thoughts of my ugliness consume most of my day.

A male poster was suicidal due to comparing his appearance to other men and then hating all parts of his body. He wanted to achieve the same level of physical attractiveness he saw in male actors. His girlfriend did not understand why he avoided going to movies or the beach with her:

Male-Initial Post: I have suicidal thoughts if i see an attractive male actor. i could never achieve the level of physical attractiveness, i want to try to be over obsessed about my looks...then i think it's not worth it because i can never achieve this and proceed to eat a mass of food. I won't see any movie with my girlfriend with an attractive lead or male in general of any kind. I can't go to the beach or river because of other guys without their shirts off and my girl complains about not doing anything fun, i don't think she fully understands. I want plastic surgery really bad, but im afraid and its so expensive it would probably put me in debt. I don't want to live with these facts anymore, its not just one part of my body. It's ALL of it.

The BDD forum did not allow members to post personal images due to privacy concerns and the potentially harmful behaviors doing so could trigger in others. Despite moderators' attempts to dissuade them, members verbally compared their disliked features to those of other members. This behavior took place despite the visual anonymity offered by the text-based interactions on the forum.

Mia, one of the forum leaders, complained she had a bump on her nose and wanted to know if others had the same problem. She was seeking empathy and understanding: "Oh man...I've got a serious problem with my nose. Does anybody else? ...Even if it was a little bit smaller I'd be happy." In response, another member offered to swap noses with her, due to wanting a larger nose: "I'll swap you your nose for my nose. I have a small nose and frequently wish it was bigger." Despite not knowing what Mia's nose actually looked like, the other person was convinced it was better.

The drive for social comparison was so strong that one woman complained about her body when responding to a suicidal forum member. Rather than providing sympathy and concern, she expressed self-pity and dismay about her appearance. She insisted her body and face looked worse without having any physical basis for comparison:

Female-Initial Post: I feel like I am falling down a pit and screaming but no one can hear me. I hate my body so much.. I don't want to be in it anymore. I want this pain to end. I just want to die.

Female-Reply: my body looks worse than yours. ever since i was 10 i never wore anything that is not long sleeve or close to long sleeve and you don't know how it is like to be unable to wear any kind of cloth except super baggy ones, also even though my body looks terrible it's second problem, first problem is with my cursed face.

Negative social comparison is often exacerbated on social media sites, such as Instagram and Facebook, that are primarily image driven. These social media sites encourage individuals to engage in upward social comparison, which can result in increased levels of depression.[20] Some BDD forum members hated Facebook due to the social comparison that took place on the site:

Female-Initial Post: I hate Facebook. I'm sick of people's self taken pictures. I'm sick of people commenting on how gorgeous or hot they look. I hate that I get none of that... (maybe that's because I don't take pictures of myself but who knows)... I'm sick of hearing about whether or not someone I don't care about got a good night sleep. I don't care what disgusting garbage you ate for dinner and I most certainly do not want to look at it.

Male-Reply 1: I HATE facebook for the same reasons. That is why I permanently deleted my account. I decided to go on there and check my sisters account, I felt awful because she has lots of pictures of me, That even people who are not her friend can see. that made me angry and upset. I hate social networks.

Female-Reply 2: I feel the same way about facebook. There was this girl in hs who was absolutely horrible to me. I hate how I can see her fb and she is absolutely gorgeous, still and rich, and vacationing in Greece constantly, and graduated college on time, etc etc etc and I am here, years away from graduating, ugly, poor, and in a bad relationship. Ugh. Eff facebook.

Roger urged the young Italian woman (Chapter 7) to stop comparing herself to pictures posted on the internet because they were not real:

Roger-Reply: One thing i'd like to pick up on is comparing yourself to people on the internet. It's not going to give a true reflection. When you google them in your looking for something in particular, in your case curvy bodies and your going to end up with pictures of people who are perceived to have amazing curves. Now i'm guessing your from the States and one thing that we over in Britain get is the idea that all Americans have perfect teeth, are muscular, slim and incredibly witty but that's just the side that society shows you. Just like with curves it's not a perfect all round picture of what i call 'reality' where in fact none of us are perfect and there are very few people in the world who can even claim to have what we seek. In fact even the 'perfect' people that are in the movies, magazines etc have their apparent non perfect features hidden. That i tell you is a crying shame. It makes them not look human and does nothing to the 99.999% of the population that has to feel like they need to look like these people.

The Dove *Evolution of a Model* video demonstrates how lighting, makeup, and digital manipulation (Photoshop) can be used to transform a model's image from normal looking to unblemished and beautiful.[21] Forum members compared themselves to manipulated images of models, actors, and singers in the media. Their personal disclosures paint a vivid picture of the internal torment caused by having BDD. These negative appearance beliefs and BDD rituals crippled their career ambitions, family and personal relationships, and their performance at school and work.

Impact on Relationships and Career

Female-Initial Post: I have had BDD for almost a decade now, and I am currently in a serious relationship... I am supposed to move in with him in May, and he will see me without makeup when I shower at night. I am having serious anxiety issues dealing with this. I feel like he will break up with me when he sees what I really look like and not love me anymore.

Avoiding Social Gatherings

Imagine spending hours and hours every day obsessing about some aspect of your appearance you cannot change. Then imagine the added torture of believing others view the same deformity and are repulsed by what they see. What activities would you avoid? What family gatherings would become impossible to attend? My appearance concerns were constant when I had BDD, but they did not impact my social life, career, or educational goals. I was able to pursue my dream of managing an art gallery, I had multiple boyfriends and friends, and I attended family gatherings. However, many forum members were not as fortunate. Their symptoms led to social anxiety and isolation.

Forum members canceled plans with family members, friends, and significant others to avoid being seen in public. They refused to disclose their shame and embarrassment due to feeling misunderstood and alone in their suffering. One young man described how his BDD symptoms had negatively impacted his relationship with his family:

Male-Initial Post: Things just don't seem to be going my way at the moment. I missed a really important family event a couple days ago because i couldn't get myself to leave my house and pretty much everyone thinks badly of me cause of it. I don't know how to explain to them that I really, really wanted to come but I just couldn't.

Another man's best friend was confused and wanted to know why he avoided social gatherings. He didn't know how to tell his friends he "didn't look good enough to go out." Kathy empathized with his predicament and confessed her friends didn't know about her BDD:

Male-Initial Post: I have bdd, I am currently awaiting inpatient treatment for it. Fingers crossed..

But for now, I'm having a lot of problems with my friends. I sometimes make plans with them that I can't then make, because ... I don't know how better to say it than I don't look good enough to go out.

Some of my friends are like, 'oh 😢 I haven't seen you, try and come' My best friend however, I tell her I can't come out and she replies with something like, why??? Uh whateverrr

I know she has a right to be upset or angry, but how can i man up and deal with this? It really overwhelms me on top of the bdd, I'm not dealing well with it.

Kathy-Reply: I'm kind of in the same boat, my friends are like that too and it sucks. Do your friends know about BDD? Mine don't and I'm constantly making up new excuses but my friends are at their limit and they get really annoyed with me now I'm slowly losing them all, I have only one true friend and my boyfriend, they are the only people i like to be with, so I'm not complaining because for me that's enough but it's hard to try and make excuses and stuff to not socialise with other people.

DATING AND RELATIONSHIPS

One young man refused to date girls with ugly noses. He disliked his nose and did not want to inflict an ugly nose onto his children. This could be an example of BDD by proxy, which is when a person is fixated on another person's perceived appearance flaws:[1]

Male-Reply: I just think it's important I date a girl with a good nose so my kids don't get even worse noses. When I have an option to date a girl with a bad nose I just think it's wrong, it's like creating problems for my future children and I won't do it, I think this stems from my BDD and I think my sister felt the same way.

Female posters often worried about the impact BDD had on their lives and relationships. One twenty-six-year-old woman was unable to stay in school or attend work due to the severity of her BDD symptoms. She wanted to look "perfect" and spent hours putting on makeup, only to cancel plans at the last minute. Her boyfriend (bf) dismissed her concerns, so she turned to forum members for advice:

Female-Initial Post: Now at 26 yrs old I'm still struggling ...I cancel most things ...nights out ..dinners ..birthdays ...lunches ...anything really ..because it takes me hours to get ready and i end up crying and panicking and hating myself. One part of me knows I'm a good-looking girl and another part of me can't stop thinking about all my flaws. I feel the need to be perfect in every way and because i can't be ..i can't leave my house. I'm so depressed and sad and have nobody to talk to about it ..my bf just thinks I'm being a baby but he doesn't get how severe this is. job opportunities...school opportunities ...social opportunities..all ruined by this. Everyone sees this perfect person and thinks I'm so lucky for my life and my looks but nobody knows how much i hate everything inside and just am done with it all. i can't spend the rest of my life like this and i don't know what to do.

Some young women viewed getting married and having children as impossible due to how miserable they felt about their appearance. Being socially isolated and unable to go out in public made dating and relationships difficult. One female member believed her life would be better if she were good looking. She had no friends except her mother and believed her life was over at twenty-seven:

Female-Reply: I would love to be beautiful and stunning and hate that i've inherited ugly features and that i'm not perfect. Life would be so much better if I was good looking. I never get noticed or commented on my appearance. I hardly go out now as there are lots of people I compare myself to attractive people and feel inferior. I get very jealous of attractive people. I have 0 friends - my mum is my best friend. I've not been in a relationship since I was 21 and can't ever imagine anyone ever being interested in me. I've resigned myself to a life alone without marriage or a family. Just writing this makes me feel really pathetic that my life feels over at 27. Writing this down is weirdly therapeutic though. Sorry for being so long but I could go on forever.

Relationships were negatively impacted when participants became so depressed they wanted to end their lives. One woman posted to the forum while contemplating suicide. Her BDD symptoms were destroying her relationship because she hated herself so much:

Female-Initial Post: My BDD has been so bad lately, all I want to do is die. I have been contemplating suicide and how I would do it. In turn I am destroying my relationship with my boyfriend, I hurt him unintentionally because I am so hurt inside myself. I tell him he deserves better than me but he doesn't want to give up on me. I guess I am lucky in that sense.

I am too poor to afford visiting any sort of doctor or therapist. I don't know how to get better. I don't know what to do. It is so hard to get through every day.

Male forum members were primarily distressed about being unable to attract women for dating and sexual relationships. The following man liked everything about his body but felt trapped by his ugly face. He believed having an ugly face made him unattractive to women. He metaphorically compared his image with the portrait described in *The Picture of Dorian Gray* by Oscar Wilde, where the protagonist remains youthful and attractive while his portrait grows ever more hideous and grotesque with age:

Male-Initial Post: I love life. I really do. I love everything about myself except for one thing tho. My face. It is the one thing I can't change and feel trapped in. All my other imperfections I accept. I am 6'4" tall and muscular. I have sculpted my body into a Greek statue of fitness. I am smart, funny and passionate.

But my face is the one thing I can't change and can't seem to accept. And it's killing me. To get by, I have avoided looking at my face in pictures. When I have to look in the mirror, I take out my contacts or dim the lights. I have gotten by like this for years. It has enabled me to project confidence and function.

But one look at a picture or glance in a mirror, and it's like the story of Dorian Gray...my confidence shrivels and I realize I've been living a lie, I'm also a guy, which makes it hard. Men don't talk about this stuff.

Even having a body like a "Greek statue of fitness" and being "smart, funny and passionate" did not minimize the importance he placed on his face. Being handsome was more important to him than being wealthy or powerful. He felt helpless because he could not change his face, hide it, or work out and make it better:

> But all my life, I've been hyper aware of the importance of male handsomeness in today's society. And by that, I mean facial handsomeness. It doesn't seem to matter that I have a great body or am tall or am funny or smart. I've observed that initial female attraction seems to be heavily influenced by male facial attractiveness. This is not a swipe at women, I LOVE and respect women, and harbor zero blame on women. I think it's just nature.
>
> I think men and women are both visual when it comes to attraction. But from my observations, animal magnetism when it comes to female sexual selection on a purely visual basis seems to revolve around a man's face more than his body. Otherwise every guy pumping iron at the gym would be considered hot which obviously isn't true. Men however seem to look at a woman's body more. Meaning a woman with an average face will still be considered hot by a majority of men on a visual basis based on her body.
>
> Money or power might make average or even ugly men more attractive but that knowledge has never brought me any solace. No Matter how much money I had, I'd still know I was ugly. It really sucks. My face is like a prison I can't escape. I can't change it. I can't hide it. I can't work out and make it better. I am stuck with what I've got and it's the most helpless feeling in the world.

Unlike other men on the forum, he did not view plastic surgery as an option to fix his face. He believed his body was malleable and could be improved through a regimen of weightlifting, but his facial features were permanent and ugly. As he noted, most men don't talk about their appearance insecurities with other men. Posting a message to the forum enabled him to confess the reasons he felt inadequate without needing to reveal his identity.

Being too ugly to attract women was a common theme for men on the forum. Another male poster was devastated because he kept getting rejected by women and was convinced it was because he was ugly:

Male-Reply: Throughout my life I have been overlooked and rejected so many times because of how I look. I am just so hurt. I just can't handle being seen like that any more. Being looked down on as unattractive/ugly, not good enough to be liked/wanted romantically, I cannot even put into words how worthless, shameful, inadequate, inferior, not good enough, etc it has made me feel. It destroys me. I just hate being seen as someone who is unattractive/ugly and not good enough to be liked/wanted romantically.

We all are attracted to certain people and to feel like you're not good enough for people you're attracted to is soul destroying.

PARENTING WITH BDD

Parents with BDD were concerned their image-related obsessions, behaviors, and perceived flaws would either be passed on to their children or were interfering with their ability to be good caretakers. One father felt guilty because his symptoms were causing him to be a poor role model for his son. He described the shame, anger, and depression he felt about his perceived flaw, as well as the dichotomy between his outward appearance (a big strong tough guy) and his inner self (a weak pathetic excuse of a man). He was too ashamed about one of his "features" to name it even within the anonymity of the forum:

Male-Initial Post: Hi everyone don't want to say my name, I am 26 I have a lovely little son but I'm so wrapped up in my own fudged up world it's got to a point where i can't have fun with him or do what a normal dad should do for his son. I love him to bits but the majority of my Time Is spent looking in the mirror or feeling bitter and angry or depressed etc.....

He then went on to ask himself and others, rhetorically:

> What kind of a role model am i? I Rarely go out and when I do it's only because I have to. I am so deeply upset and hurt by my self image I don't want to do anything or go out or have fun because all I think about is what people think of me. I am very ashamed of one of my features that I don't want to share it.

> But I'm even more ashamed of the fact that I am no role model to my son. I am kind of a big strong tough guy on the outside but on the inside i am a weak pathetic excuse of a man, whether my obsession with my physical defect is imagined or real the point is I should be a Man and not let it bother me because it's not fair for my son.

A similar message was posted by a mother who was contemplating suicide due to her symptoms not improving after years of clinical treatment and multiple plastic surgery procedures. She was worried her depression and obsessions were having a negative impact on her daughter but knew committing suicide would leave her daughter without a mother:

> **Female-Initial Post:** I have had bdd for almost 17 years and I can't take it anymore. Had plastic surgery and wasted most of my life as I find no joy in anything as im so convinced I look ugly. I have an amazing daughter, but I can see that im starting to transfer my insecurities on to her...this kills me more than anything and honestly feel like she will be better off if im not around. I so badly cannot do this anymore....the depression is too much to handle....after trying cbt and ssris for years I can't see any way out. I'm planning my next surgery but I know it probably won't make me happy,.im losing hope and im terrified for my daughter...i believe that if im alive I will mentally scar her as im so troubled...or I will take my life and she will have no mummy at all.

The mother received a reply from another member, who tried to convince her she was valuable to her daughter, no matter how she felt about her appearance:

Female-Reply: Don't take your life, your daughter would be in much more pain for the rest of her life if she knows you left her like that... I'm sure your daughter will never judge you, reaffirm to her she is beautiful in every way as much as you can she will always be in need of your affection more so then a "perfect" looking mom. I like to think of nature and animals in a way, like how wild animals act off instinct and nature, there is no judgement or perception of looks, your a momma bear gotta protect ur cubs ^_^. If you were to look into her eyes now, and 10 years from now, you would still see the same unconditional love. As she gets older you will realize how lucky you are to have such a beautiful gift to give this world. We are all imperfect hun, society can be cruel and we can all have our flaws but your daughter is flawless is she not?! ☺ Hope your doing ok.

Although some forum members shared their struggles with family members, others wanted to project an outward appearance of being strong, capable, and normal. Revealing that one struggles with a mental health disorder can result in stigmatization. Forum members (like the parents just described) chose to disclose their shame and despair on the forum, where they could remain anonymous and keep their feelings hidden from their children and loved ones.

Changing Career Ambitions

Fran, Kathy, and other members had changed their career ambitions due to their BDD symptoms. Fran admitted her preoccupation with her appearance made becoming a surgeon unrealistic. She asked forum members how "feeling ugly" had impacted their career plans:

Fran-Initial Post: I was curious to see to what extent "feeling ugly" can impair us to reach our goals and ambitions in life. I see myself as a very ambitious person and have always been. I believe there is nothing

117

I cannot do. Unfortunately the last couple of years my condition of feeling ashamed of my looks has impaired me to live fully my capabilities, realized that it affects my daily life too much, so I had to cut down on some of those highest ambitions.

I am in my last year of medical school and always wanted to be a surgeon (im a woman), I think it was made for me. But lately I have come to a reality check that that kind of stressful life will not suit me anymore. I will not be able to dedicate myself to my job in that way, as I am still too occupied thinking about others perception of me. I am inhibited. So now I am considering other less time-consuming specialties.

Kathy replied to Fran since she no longer wanted to be a dancer due to her appearance concerns:

Kathy-Reply: Mine have changed! I wanted to be a dancer, I went to a dance school and I loved it! But it became to hard for me to perform in front of people, I got distracted from what I was doing because i was so concerned about how i looked! I cut down on my time spent in class because I felt so uncomfortable in front of all the other people there. So at 16 I quit and I don't really dance anymore. But I don't really mind to be honest, I think if it didn't work out then it wasn't meant to be.

One man's BDD symptoms had impacted his ability to advance in his career. He compared himself to his friend who was a consultant and millionaire. He asked members if they were able to fulfill their potential, despite having BDD:

Male-Initial Post: Is there anyone here who is able to fulfill their potential when it comes to jobs / career opportunities despite BDD/image concerns or does it prevent you from even working at all?

I ask because I read about an old friend from school who I was in the same classes as back in high school, he was quite a bit cleverer than me

I admit but he has his own consulting company now which has made him a millionaire. I however have had to just settle for a very basic office job doing admin work because I don't have the confidence due to my image issues to do things where attention is on me. I get so self conscious when eyes are on me, fearing being seen/judged as ugly/unattractive.

BDD poses significant challenges to those with the disorder. BDD symptoms can negatively impact one's personal relationships, social interactions, and career goals. Some people with body dysmorphic disorder are unable to work or go to college; 99 percent of people with BDD experience interference with social functioning (family, friends, or intimate relationships), 95 percent experience periods of avoidance of social interactions, and 90 percent experience interference with work or academic functioning.[2]

Forum members shared the devastating effects the disorder had on their relationships with family members and friends, and on their jobs and career ambitions. Friendships were negatively affected when people canceled plans due to their social anxiety. Relationships were impacted when individuals felt too ugly to be desired by others. Parents with BDD feared their symptoms made them poor role models and caretakers. However, not all personal experiences disclosed on the forum were negative. Members sought and shared information about overcoming BDD symptoms, getting diagnosed, and receiving treatment. Two members also served as positive role models by posting their recovery stories.

PART FOUR
OVERCOMING BDD

Getting Diagnosed

Janet-Reply: BDD can manifest itself in any part of the body from a number of different life experiences. I would suggest instead of trying to find if you fit the symptoms list of BDD, just get straight to a therapist who is specializing in the OCD spectrum. You will get a much better diagnosis this way. It's also easy to fall into the trap of diagnosing yourself via the Internet, which can get very upsetting pretty fast.

Diagnosis by Self, Friends, and Family

BDD forum members primarily diagnosed themselves with the disorder by searching for information on the internet and by comparing their symptoms to the General Information moderator post (copied from the Mayo Clinic website). The description of BDD read (in part):

Moderators-Initial Post: Body dysmorphic disorder is a type of chronic mental illness in which you can't stop thinking about a flaw with your appearance — a flaw either that is minor or that you imagine. But to you, your appearance seems so shameful and distressing that you don't want to be seen by anyone. Body dysmorphic disorder has sometimes been called "imagined ugliness."

When you have body dysmorphic disorder, you intensely obsess over your appearance and body image, often for many hours a day. You may seek out numerous cosmetic procedures to try to "fix" your perceived flaws but never are satisfied. Body dysmorphic disorder is also known as dysmorphophobia, or the fear of having a deformity.

I diagnosed myself with BDD by answering a series of ten self-diagnostic questions and reading about others' experiences in a *Shape* magazine article.[1] I recall thinking how familiar their experiences were, such as being depressed about perceived appearance flaws and staring in the mirror for hours at a time. The symptoms of BDD are distinctive, debilitating, and easy to recognize in oneself. Diagnosing myself with BDD enabled me to gain insight that I had a treatable mental health disorder. Self-diagnosis provided forum members with access to a supportive online community.

Doing internet research was the most common way individuals diagnosed themselves. One young woman from Canada posted to the forum after diagnosing herself with the disorder:

Female-Initial Post: I'm new to these forums. I hope to become a regular around here and meet some new people and make friends!

I'm a 26 year old female living in Canada. Returning to school in January and very nervous but also very excited about it!

I have never been diagnosed with BDD but after conducting a lot of research I do believe that I suffer from it and that I have for quite some time. I'm not going to go too far into detail in this post as it's a simple introduction post but I do have several insecurities that seem completely irrational to everybody else. I also suffer from severe anxiety including social anxiety, a sleep disorder, and occasional depression.

Getting diagnosed with BDD or self-diagnosing was important to forum members. Part of the appeal of having a mental health diagnosis lies in its ability to explain behaviors that would otherwise leave individuals open to blame and personal accountability.[2] The young woman I just described diagnosed herself with BDD and wanted to find others who shared her symptoms.

Some members expressed uncertainty as to whether they had BDD. As a result, they compared their symptoms to those found on the BDD forum or other websites, such as Wikipedia. The following male poster had many BDD symptoms listed in the General Information topic post but had not been clinically diagnosed. He was housebound and had become alienated from his family:

> **Male-Initial Post:** I'm unsure if I have body dysmorphic disorder or not. I have the majority, if not all of the symptoms posted in the General Information topic on here. I haven't been to the doctors to get myself diagnosed because well let's be honest, it's a little bit embarrassing. But I know this the time that I should say something because it's literally taken over my life, completely. I'm pretty much housebound now (Haven't left my house for 3 or so months now) My relationship with my family has deteriorated and is virtually nonexistent now.

Two of the most common reasons people don't seek treatment for their BDD symptoms are embarrassment about their problems or about needing help.[3] According to Dr. Phillips, there is no need to feel embarrassed or ashamed when speaking to your doctor or therapist. She recommends bringing an article or book about BDD to your appointment if you are worried about raising the topic.[4] A female poster used Google to find information related to her symptoms. She wanted to be "almost sure" she had BDD before seeking treatment to avoid wasting the doctor's time or embarrassing herself:

> **Female-Initial Post:** I Googled some of my symptoms (which I know you're not really supposed to do), and I found loads of stuff on BDD, but I'm reluctant to go to the doctor about it until I'm almost sure, as I don't want to embarrass myself or waste their time.

Some individuals diagnosed themselves after reading personal stories posted to the forum. One woman was too ashamed about her appearance obsessions to share them with her family but was relieved to know others felt the same way: "I have not been diagnosed with BDD, but reading about peoples' stories, I believe that it is the closest to what I am experiencing in my life, that I have yet encountered. And it feels somewhat of a relief knowing that it is not just me feeling like this."

Three forum members diagnosed themselves after being told by friends or family members they might have BDD. One woman had a friend with an eating disorder (ED) who diagnosed her with BDD after she confessed to feeling ugly:

> **Female-Initial Post:** I am new here but I thought I would introduce with a thread. I am 41 years old and I have NEVER thought about this disorder. I am very much into fitness and know a few people with ED but I never fell into that. I was talking to a friend of mine struggling with an ED and I told her, "well I'm having a harder time getting down to the weight I want and I can't look in the mirror. I think I look bulky and I just look ugly." She says "Oh right so just regular BDD". Like this is a normal thing? She is not a psychologist mind you but google is right? So I google BDD and low and behold my symptoms are all there mirror avoidance, hatred of photos of myself, panic disorder, low self-esteem, obsessive thoughts about my body. Everything I had gone through most of life was there!

Self-diagnosis was beneficial because members gained insight they had a treatable mental health disorder. Doing so could have increased their perceived self-efficacy,[5] which is the belief in one's ability to take action to produce desired outcomes. For example, I was relieved to self-diagnose myself with BDD since I could then get treatment for the disorder. Learning I had BDD was better than feeling helpless and unable to fix my appearance flaws.

How much time do you spend obsessing about your appearance and trying to fix perceived flaws? Do these activities take up more than one hour each day? Do they cause you significant emotional distress, pain, and torment? Do these feelings interfere with daily activities, such as going to school, work, or socializing with friends?[6] You will find more information about self-diagnosis in the BDD Resources (Appendix A4).

CLINICAL DIAGNOSIS: "AM I IN THE RIGHT PLACE?"

Psychiatrists and psychologists use the *Diagnostic and Statistical Manual of Mental Disorders* (DSM) published by the American Psychiatric Association (APA) to classify mental health disorders. BDD is classified in the DSM-5[7] as an obsessive-compulsive-related disorder. This alignment with OCD is based on multiple variables, including similar symptoms, comorbidity, genetic risk factors, and treatment options.[8] BDD is defined as a preoccupation with one or more perceived defects or flaws in physical appearance that are not observable or appear slight to others. The person also needs to have performed repetitive behaviors, such as social comparison and mirror checking (Chapter 8).

The perceived defects/flaws must cause clinically significant distress or impairment in social, occupational, or other important areas of functioning. Further, these appearance preoccupations are not restricted to concerns with body fat or weight as in an eating disorder. There is an additional indication for muscle dysmorphia, a form of BDD characterized by the belief one's body build is too small or insufficiently muscular.[9]

BDD is classified further according to a person's insight levels. People with good or fair insight recognize their BDD beliefs are definitely or probably not true. People with poor insight think their BDD beliefs are probably true. Those with delusional beliefs are completely convinced their BDD beliefs are true.[10] One forum member had BDD for ten years before revealing his symptoms during therapy. He was relieved to be diagnosed with BDD by his psychologist:

> **Male-Reply:** I had had BDD for 10 years before I finally decided I had to tell someone. I told them thinking I'd be laughed at. The Clinical Psychologist I "confessed" to, said (very casually) "Oh, you think like that because you have BDD."

One of the challenges when treating BDD is that individuals tend to delay seeking help for fifteen or more years after the onset of symptoms.[11] Some members who received a clinical diagnosis wanted to confirm their diagnosis on the forum. Asking peers about a diagnosis is common on mental health forums and can help reduce uncertainty about one's condition.[12] In the following example, a female poster wanted to confirm she was in the right place to get help after being diagnosed with BDD:

> **Female-Initial Post:** In late July 2012 I started seeing a councilor and it is only then that I was told I might have Body Dysmorphic Disorder. I'm not sure if I do or not but having read up on it now I certainly relate to a lot of it. The problem I now have is how to even begin to get through this? Do I sound like someone with BDD? Am I in the right place?

Questions from members about whether they had BDD were common, even after they received a clinical diagnosis. This was due to the conviction they were indeed ugly; receiving a clinical diagnosis did not alter this belief. Another member asked if she could have BDD if she was genuinely ugly. She had been given a tentative BDD diagnosis but disagreed with the therapist because she thought others were responding negatively to her "strange" facial features:

> **Female-Initial Post:** After years of therapy I've had BDD as a working diagnosis. They still don't know if it is BDD or not.
>
> I don't think its BDD. The things that fit are that I cover up my face, afraid of social interactions and generally depressed because of my appearance.
>
> However the things that don't fit are, I don't actually think I am ugly. Yet I keep getting negative reactions from people, I've had strangers comment on my 'strange' facial features. I am a girl yet have a heavy jawline, but I never thought it was a problem until I started getting all these comments. It never used to be a problem before. Also i am not

delusional, people actually say these things. And I think, if I am genuinely ugly then how can I have BDD?

Some people, like the following male poster, wanted to get a clinical diagnosis for BDD but didn't know how to do so. This lack of knowledge about getting diagnosed was prevalent on the forum:

> **Male-Initial Post:** i need to get diagnosed, if i definitely am suffering from it which only a doctor can tell me, really soon, because its having an impact on my studying and relationships and enjoyment of life. But i don't know how to get diagnosed? Do you walk into a doctor's surgery and tell them you think you have it, or tell them your symptoms and see what they say, or do you go to a doctor at all?

Kathy advised him to go to his doctor (GP) for a diagnosis. She suggested he write down his symptoms beforehand if he found it difficult to talk with his doctor:

> **Kathy-Reply:** You should make an appointment with your GP and discuss it with him/her. Tell them that you think you have BDD and why you think that. You could maybe write down how you feel and take it with you, that way if you find it hard to talk about it you can just hand it over to your doctor.

BDD was classified as a somatoform disorder in a previous version of the DSM (DSM-IV-TR).[13] Somatoform disorders are characterized by the presence of bodily symptoms that cause severe distress and impairment.[14] BDD was further classified in the DSM-IV-TR as a preoccupation with an imagined or slight defect in appearance, where the individual's concern about the defect is markedly excessive.[15] I disliked this BDD definition because the term "imagined" seemed to imply people with BDD were seeing things that did not exist. The issues I had with my nose and face were real to me even if they were minor or not apparent to other people. Thus, it was a relief when I learned the updated DSM-5[16] removed the term "imagined" from the classification.

Diagnosis on the Forum: "Do I have BDD?"

About 20 percent of the forum members had diagnosed themselves with BDD using internet searches or others' personal experiences posted on the forum. Some people received a clinical diagnosis but wanted members to provide a second opinion to supplement the professional diagnosis. A female poster copied symptoms from the BDD description in Wikipedia and wanted members to tell her if she had BDD: "Could you help me? Tell me if you think I have BDD or not. I copied over some symptoms of BDD from Wikipedia to help me out. These are all symptoms that I show. I took out all the symptoms that I don't show."

Most members who responded to these requests stated they were unable to provide a diagnosis and referred people to medical professionals. These referrals could have encouraged participants to seek help from clinicians familiar with treating BDD. On two occasions, members responded by providing reasons why they thought the person did or did not have the disorder. However, this was rare, and most individuals were referred to professionals, as shown in the following example:

> **Female-Reply:** I would say don't focus on whether you have BDD or OCD because it might cause you to stress more. Everybody experiences this differently and varying intensities. My advice would be, if you would like to live without worrying about being ugly or not, you should find a nice psychologist. Everybody experiences body worries but when it starts to take over and cause you distress it becomes a problem.

Roger declined to diagnose individuals with BDD when members asked if they had the disorder. Instead, he provided information about BDD based on reputable sources and referred them to doctors for diagnosis and treatment:

> **Roger-Reply:** My advice to you would be that if you really think that you have BDD then to discuss with a mental health professional if you have access to one and explain to them exactly like you have here about

how it pre-occupies you and they would certainly be in a better position than me to say whether or not you are.

I've noticed you saying you haven't read up on BDD, if you'd like i could write up a little synopsis of it and what it's about for you or i could point you to a good book called 'the broken mirror' if you have access to a library and like reading.

Rather than diagnose members, Roger queried them about their symptoms. One female poster had recovered from an eating disorder but was so obsessed with fat around her stomach that she couldn't be intimate with her boyfriend. Roger asked her about the extent of her obsession:

Roger-Reply 1: I don't want to get into the habit of diagnosing people so i can't directly answer your question but how much of your life does it affect you? Is it a constant pre-occupation for you? When your boyfriend compliments you do you find it makes you feel fine for a little while then wears off after a bit? BDD to me is more about the pre-occupations rather than the faults we find with ourselves because quite frankly everyone has faults! It's how we perceive and deal with them that is our biggest issue, do you find yourself looking in the mirror for really long periods of time and not being able to draw yourself away from it?

The woman acknowledged she stared at herself in the mirror for a good portion of the day:

Female-Reply 2 (OP): I guess yeah, it preoccupies my mind a lot of the time. All of the time if I'm not focused on something else. Even when I'm lying in bed trying to sleep or standing in the shower I'm conscious of how much I hate it. I stare at myself in the mirror for a good portion of the day looking for changes. If I'm walking past a mirror or a glass door, I hold in my stomach nearly all of the time, even if I'm wearing a big baggy coat or if no-one is around.

My boyfriend compliments me all the time but usually I brush it off or say 'that's not true'. When I think about it, that makes me a terrible person because I know he really does mean it, and I know it's really bitchy to not accept compliments, but I can't help it. I wish that I could not concentrate so much on my faults because it's getting in the way of everything in life.

Roger recommended she talk to a doctor about her symptoms and use CBT to challenge her core negative beliefs:

Roger-Reply 3: If you find it taking up a significant proportion of your life then my suggestion to you would be to see your local GP (or doctor if your not British), that's where i started out and they referred me to a counsellor who then referred me to a cognitive behavioural therapist. Now they are the best method for dealing with Body dysmorphia because they work on the behaviour of our mind and how we attribute negativity towards something.

Roger offered advice and opinions about getting a professional diagnosis and treatment for the disorder. He had read books about BDD by researchers and clinicians, such as *The Broken Mirror*.[17] He was on a mission to rid himself of his BDD symptoms using CBT and therapy. Thus, his knowledge about BDD diagnosis and treatment enabled him to offer advice in accordance with researchers and clinicians.

I had BDD symptoms for fifteen years before I gained insight about the disorder. There are varying levels of insight for people with BDD (good/fair, poor, and absent/delusional). The most severe level is absent/delusional, which means people are completely convinced their BDD beliefs are true.[18] I had the delusional form of BDD since I believed what I saw in the mirror was real. My insight level improved from delusional to good after seeking treatment. I was able to gain insight that the mirror *does* lie to people with BDD.

Treatment
Experiences

Undetermined-Initial Post: The things that have helped me get through my depression and anxiety have been seeing my therapist on a regular weekly basis and getting started on Prozac, which has put my brain exactly where it's supposed to be!

Roger-Reply: To my understanding BDD can be cured, the best way i've heard is through cognitive behavioural therapy which is basically a rewriting of your thought patterns. There are some that say CBT and use of Serotonin re-uptake inhibitors are the best combination although i've refrained from using any medication so far as a matter of personal principle.

Clinical Treatment

Seeking and sharing information about clinical treatment occurred frequently on the BDD forum. Clinical treatment included cognitive behavioral therapy (CBT) and medication using selective serotonin reuptake inhibitors (SSRIs). CBT involves exposing individuals to situations they would otherwise avoid in order to reduce or eliminate body checking behaviors.[1] SSRIs are antidepressant medications used to reduce or eliminate obsessive thoughts and compulsive behaviors so individuals feel less anxious and depressed.[2]

Four of the most frequent posters (Roger, Fran, Mia, and Janet) received clinical treatment for their BDD symptoms. Roger and Janet were using CBT, Fran had tried medication, and Mia sought help from a therapist. They were each receiving (or had received) effective clinical treatment for the disorder and shared their positive experiences on the forum.

Cognitive Behavioral Therapy (CBT)

Roger and Janet were both undergoing CBT treatment for BDD. They provided information about CBT and recommended the treatment to other members. CBT is considered the gold standard psychological treatment for BDD.[3] CBT involves modification of intrusive thoughts and beliefs about physical appearance (cognitions) and elimination of problematic body image behaviors. CBT consists of cognitive restructuring, exposure and behavioral exercises, ritual (response) prevention, perceptual retraining, and relapse prevention.[4]

Cognitive restructuring helps individuals identify and evaluate their negative beliefs and develop more accurate beliefs about their appearance. Exposure and behavioral exercises focus on facing, rather than avoiding, stressful situations caused by BDD. Doing so gradually reduces their intensity over time. Ritual prevention helps patients decrease and eventually stop doing compulsive behaviors, such as reassurance seeking. Through perceptual retraining, patients develop a healthy relationship with mirrors and view themselves less negatively. Finally, relapse prevention aims to keep symptoms from returning after treatment ends.[5]

Roger explained how CBT can be used to challenge core beliefs about one's appearance, such as believing other people are negatively judging a person's flaws:

Roger-Reply: Now challenging core beliefs are hard, because they are so deep rooted into our very consciousness and it is very difficult to change or delete them. It's not impossible however and it can be done. Along the way you probably will have picked up other core beliefs and one of them seems to be that "your appearance will be harshly judged by everyone else" or something along those lines.

In reality people generally don't care or give much notice to what people look like, mostly inside their heads are other bits of information like "did i remember to switch the oven on, or "where can i get that really good cat food" or even they themselves might be thinking similar things to you like "oh god i hope people aren't judging the clothes i'm wearing/what i look like etc."

Cognitive behavioural therapy is a good way to challenge these core beliefs that are rooted inside you and with it you can learn to challenge them and in time you may not even care what other people think of you. Have you tried CBT before by any chance?

Janet advised the fifty-three-year-old man with gerascophobia and BDD symptoms (Chapter 7) to get help from a therapist who specialized in treating OCD-spectrum disorders using CBT:

Male-Initial Post: I think my BDD and gerascophobia are closely related. But I have other issues as well, social anxiety being one of them. I don't want to seem disrespectful, but I don't think the answers clinical psychology offers for these conditions will quite work for me. I may use some of them, to some degree, like CBT, but I will have to fashion my own coping mechanisms. One thing I hope to start soon is journaling. I don't want to oversimplify or sugarcoat any of this. I also think BDD is a much more complicated issue than it's presented as. I feel I must confront and grapple with those complexities.

Janet-Reply: I would suggest instead of trying to find if you fit the symptoms list of BDD, just get straight to a therapist who is specializing in the OCD spectrum. You will get a much better diagnosis this way. It's also easy to fall into the trap of diagnosing yourself via the Internet, which can get very upsetting pretty fast. I think from your post you're very much on the right track back to health and happiness because you're actually acknowledging where you are in your life and the fact you want help, which is a big part of the whole process. You know you better than anyone else. You are also right with the fact you will have to fashion your own coping mechanisms eventually, despite using CBT/some kind of drug.

Janet knew BDD was classified as an OCD-spectrum disorder prior to the publication of the DSM-5.[6] This indicates she may have done research or been told by her therapist about the revised classification. The forum leaders were familiar with BDD treatment options, such as CBT, as a result of getting therapy or doing research on the disorder. They provided advice in alignment with recommendations by BDD treatment specialists.

One man who was worried about losing his hair feared going to the doctor for treatment. He asked others to share their experiences with CBT:

Male-Initial Post: So I am wondering about cognitive behavioral therapy. But I am deathly afraid to call to make an appointment. I'm afraid I am going to go and the doctor will say "but you are clearly going bald, why not just accept it?" or make me do things that will make me so uncomfortable that it will send me into a downward spiral that could last years. I guess it is a case of being more comfortable with the devil I know. Has anyone ever tried CBT for their body dysmorphic disorder and what was it like? Did it help? Are my fears unfounded (or more likely being caused by my disorder)?

Kathy replied and wanted to learn more about CBT and its effectiveness for treating BDD. In response, the original poster provided information about CBT and encouraged Kathy to call her doctor (GP) and make an appointment. He and Kathy exchanged forty messages from November 2011 to January 2012. After just two months in treatment, he was making progress toward recovery. In January, he told Kathy how much better he felt and regretted not getting treatment sooner:

> **Male-Reply (OP):** I am getting to the point where each day is better than the last. I am seeing improvements on a daily basis now. All of the defects that I once saw are disappearing. I just can't find anything wrong with my appearance anymore.
>
> Each morning I wake up and run to the bathroom to take my medication and every Monday, I race to my therapist's office, ready to talk about something that I kept hidden from everyone for so long. Instead of just living from day to day, trying to maintain my sanity, I find that I am actually enjoying myself, I am actually looking forward to the future, and I am glad to be with people instead of fearing social situations. After just two months, this experience has been amazing. I still have a lot of issues to work through and this is going to take more time but I finally feel like I am getting my life back. The best thing you can do for yourself, if you have BDD, is get into treatment. It absolutely works. Waiting so long to do this was the biggest mistake of my life.
>
> It is so surreal when you start taking the medication how much your view of everything changes. It is like waking up from a bad dream. Why was I so afraid of getting treatment?

MEDICATION (SSRIs)

Prescription medication is another effective treatment for people with BDD. People may be prescribed SSRIs along with CBT treatment, especially if they have delusional insight or are suicidal.[7] Medication is used to treat BDD symptoms because it normalizes chemical imbalances in the brain (neurotransmitters). The SSRIs increase the amount of serotonin available between nerve cells and improve brain functioning.

SSRIs can reduce or eliminate cognitive distortions, depression, anxiety, negative beliefs, and compulsive behaviors. They can also increase levels of insight and improve daily functioning.[8]

SSRIs are prescribed by psychiatrists, physicians, and in some states, nurses.[9] There are seven SSRIs commonly used to treat BDD. They are Lexapro (escitalopram), Prozac (fluoxetine), Luvox (fluvoxamine), Zoloft (sertraline), Paxil (paroxetine), Anafranil (clomipramine), and Celexa (citalopram). SSRIs may take from three weeks to three months or more (twelve to sixteen weeks) to become effective. Treatment with SSRIs usually requires higher dosages for BDD, similar to OCD. All SSRIs have side effects, but these are usually minor. Psychiatrists recommend staying on an effective SSRI for at least a year or two, even after symptoms improve.[10]

A female member who was suffering from BDD and depression used sertraline (Zoloft) to control her symptoms:

> **Female-Reply:** For me BDD died down in my early 20's but has now come back with a vengeance. I'm 27 and have had BDD since I was 17. I also suffer from depression and body focussed repetitive behaviours. I find stress does make it worse as well. I'm going through a particularly tough point in my life and it's really worsened my BDD. I'm currently on 100mg of sertraline and have had counselling. I'm now starting CBT which I hope will help a bit. I'm resigned to the fact I can't be cured but that the illness can be managed. Since I've gone on a high dosage of SSRI's it has helped my obsessive thoughts which is good as I can now function day to day whereas before I got to the point where I wasn't functioning or thinking clearly and rationally.

Another member who was prescribed sertraline (Zoloft) by a nurse sought advice about whether he should continue taking the medication. A female poster told him to see a "real doctor" and to get a referral to a BDD specialist:

> **Female-Reply:** Next time you are in the hospital, demand to see a real doctor, I am surprised a nurse was allowed to do the consultation and decide your treatment. And I hope that you received a proper plan

from her on how to take the sertraline, which dose and how to increase them with time..? Insist next time to get a proper consultation, and try to underline the importance of your BDD symptoms, because in these cases doctors shall refer you further to psychotherapy, CBT etc. Medication alone will never cure us BDDers.

One woman wanted to know how to get a prescription since she believed medication could help alleviate her symptoms. She also wanted to know about others' experiences with medication:

Female-Initial Post: I have finally decided to get help. I have anxiety and OCD problems along with my BDD. I think medication would be the best thing for me. How do I go about getting it? Can I just go to a therapist, explain my problems and why I feel medication would be best for me, and they would diagnose me and I can get the medication from there? I doubt it is that simple.

What are your experiences with medication? Do you feel medicine would be the best thing for someone like me? I feel like I have way too many problems that would take more than therapy to fix.

Fran advised her to seek professional help and follow the treatment regimen outlined by the doctor. She had stopped taking medication two years earlier but decided to ask her psychiatrist for "another round." This example demonstrates how one member's desire to use medication could motivate another person to act:

Fran-Reply 1: Listen to your psychiatrist about how long you should use the medicine and stay by those indications and the dosages, do not make the mistake I did and stop when you feel better. I stopped after 6 months and got worse. Haven't had meds now for approx. 2 years, but I think any day I will go and ask the lady for another round.

Roger urged the original poster to discuss her concerns with her therapist since "everyone is different" and some people need CBT, medication, or a combination of both. The original poster found both responses helpful and looked forward to getting help:

> **Roger-Reply 2:** Many people say that the best form of treatment for BDD is a combination of cognitive behavioural therapy and serotonin re-uptake inhibitors and then once treatment with CBT has finished you may not need the meds after it. Everybody is different though and some people can tackle it with just CBT or psychotherapy and others may require medication or both, there's no right or wrong way but it would definitely be adviseable to make it a discussion point with your therapist because with their 1-to-1 interaction with you they will be in a much better position to offer you concrete advice.

> **Female-Reply 3 (OP):** Your responses really helped a lot and make me look forward to finally getting help. Luckily I have seen the therapist before so I will be comfortable talking with her.

BARRIERS TO TREATMENT

Forum members disclosed a variety of barriers to getting clinical treatment, including shame, stigma, embarrassment, fear of being called ugly, cost, using drugs and alcohol to self-medicate, and being unable to find therapists knowledgeable about BDD. In an internet survey of 175 people who had self-diagnosed themselves with BDD, less than 20 percent were receiving clinical treatment or taking medication for their symptoms.[11] Other barriers to treatment for people with BDD symptoms include logistical and financial constraints, discrimination, low treatment satisfaction, misperceptions about treatment, lack of insight, and low knowledge of BDD, even among mental health professionals.[12]

FEAR, SHAME, AND LACK OF KNOWLEDGE

Some forum members were being treated for depression and anxiety but felt too ashamed to tell physicians about their appearance concerns. The most common reasons people do not disclose BDD symptoms to doctors are fear of feeling embarrassed or negatively judged, the belief that clinicians will not understand their appearance concerns, and lack of awareness that effective mental health treatments are available.[13] It takes an enormous leap of faith and courage to request a professional BDD assessment.[14] Some members felt relieved and empowered after receiving a clinical diagnosis, while others were too embarrassed or scared to seek treatment.

One woman received a tentative diagnosis from her counselor but had not received an "official diagnosis" or treatment for BDD. She wasn't sure where to go for help and feared her doctor (GP) would dismiss her concerns:

> **Female-Reply:** I'm not sure I have a diagnosis. I don't know how you'd get an official diagnosis.
>
> Up until now I've been in denial and/or prodding about in the dark trying to find the right person to help me. Hypnotherapy wasn't the answer. I'm unsure about counciling.
>
> I'd briefly thought of asking my GP, but never did as I felt like I was wasting an appointment that a genuinely sick person could have used, and that I'd be dismissed as being silly.

A female college student could get free counseling sessions from her campus therapist, but she was terrified the clinician would either dismiss her concerns or tell her she was ugly:

> **Female-Initial Post:** So, I found out my campus gives students 10 free therapy sessions a year and after that it is all sliding scale (which, based on my income, would make my copays very, very cheap.) I am planning to go but I am truly SCARED. I was diagnosed, sure, but I am scared that this person will laugh at me if I tell her my diagnosis as if he or she would assume I am fishing for complements, or that they would tell me I am simply unattractive and trying to obtain something I will never have. I know this is crazy but I am absolutely terrified.

Roger replied and encouraged her to get treatment from her campus therapist. However, a father cautioned her against using the campus therapist based on his daughter's experiences. His daughter went to a campus counselor for help with her OCD symptoms, which resulted in her being committed to a psychiatric ward and expelled from school. He suggested she seek treatment off campus and offered to provide her with more information:

> **Male-Reply 2:** Not to be a naysayer, but I have a lot of experience with a campus mental health center and would advise you to be very cautious about seeking assistance at yours. We encouraged our daughter who was struggling with OCD to seek counseling at her campus mental center. . . In our case, my daughter was unnecessarily and involuntarily committed to a psych ward and then subsequently denied enrollment and housing. Ultimately, her enrollment was reinstated, but she declined to return.

> There's a lot about this issue on the internet. I'll try to find some links that may be helpful. I understand how it may be appealing to utilize the campus resource, but it can be problematic. What about getting some insurance coverage through the college? Do you think it's a possibility?

There are a variety of barriers college students face when seeking help from college counselors. The top three barriers are embarrassment, denial, and stigma about being labeled as "crazy." About 50 percent of college students listed "fear of counselors" as a barrier to treatment.[15] The father's experiences could have reinforced the student's fears about getting help from her campus therapist.

The man who believed he had a "conehead" (Chapter 8) feared treatment would make him delusional by forcing him to accept his flaws:

> **Male-Initial Post:** I had 2 assessments with a BDD expert and she is taking me on as a patient next week. I am 1000% convinced that my perception is not flawed and that I see things accurately. What is the

point of doing this treatment? Is it to make me feel okay and accept myself this way? Is it to make me delusional? If that is the case then they should just stop lying and tell me to accept myself from the start. I'm sorry for sounding frustrated I just needed a place to vent and get some advice.

Kathy expressed sympathy for his plight and advised him to get therapy: "I'm sorry your having a hard time at the moment. I think you should stick with the therapy, try it out and see how it goes. You are very welcome to come here and vent and we will try to give you advice if we can." In response, the original poster repeated his fears about treatment: "What's the point of treatment if it's the truth? To make me feel less bothered by it? If that's the case I would rather not be made delusional. You know?"

Kathy asked him to consider the possibility his beliefs about his appearance were not true, and as a result, therapy could help him. She confessed she would "give anything" to become more accepting of her flaws and live a normal, happy life:

> **Kathy-Reply 3:** But what if it's not the truth? I'm not saying you are wrong at all, but what if you are? And if that's the case this could really help you. And don't you want to be happy? If this makes you happy and less concerned about it, wouldn't that be worth it? To be able to a live a normal happy life and not have to bother about it. I would give anything to have that!! I understand that you don't want to be made delusional, but what if it's not about being made delusional but about becoming accepting of it?

Lack of knowledge about where and how to get professional treatment was another barrier for people with BDD. One poster asked members where to find BDD treatment centers in Canada: "Are there any treatment centres in Canada? I live in Ottawa Ontario Canada and cannot find anyone in Canada that is specialised in BDD." There were no responses to this person's inquiry. One possible reason is that knowledge about where to find help for BDD is low among individuals with the disorder.[16]

Kathy replied to a female member in the UK who did not know how to get clinical treatment. She advised the woman to visit her GP and get a referral to a specialist:

> **Female-Reply:** I am not seeking any treatment at the moment, because I am not even sure about what it is that is wrong with me. Are you? And if you don't mind me asking, how does a person go about this? Does a GP make a diagnosis and refer you to someone? Are GPs even knowledgeable about this kind of thing? I have no idea, so please excuse my ignorance.

> **Kathy-Reply:** yeah you just go and speak to your GP and they will refer you. I actually just went to see my GP today. She was very helpful and very knowledgeable about it, i'm getting referred to someone else but she said it could take a while as therapy etc isn't very good on the NHS.

If you are unsure where and how to get help for yourself or a loved one, refer to the treatment resources and therapists listed in Appendix A. Additional resources and clinicians are provided on the International OCD Foundation and BDD Foundation websites.

INEFFECTIVE DIAGNOSIS AND TREATMENT

The fear, shame, and stigma felt by those with BDD were reinforced when clinicians lacked knowledge about how to diagnose and treat the disorder. A male poster shared the negative experience he had with a doctor who did not know about BDD and referred him to a specialist:

> **Male-Reply:** Well the doctor was a moron. Wasn't even aware of the condition! He was clueless, he told me he had never heard of it and just made me feel like a bit of an idiot.

It took a lot of courage to go in there and just talk face to face about it to someone. I told him how hard it is for the sufferer and how much emotional anxiety and constant negative thoughts weigh on the mind.

He has referred me to a specialist. Hopefully this person will have some knowledge and isn't a complete demoralizing moron. I am not done fighting.

Finding therapists who knew how to diagnose and treat BDD was difficult. Clinicians either misdiagnosed people with depression or anxiety (which can be comorbid with BDD) or tried to assure them they looked fine and dismissed their concerns. Two female posters were told they looked "pretty" or "attractive" by therapists. A young woman was seeing a university counselor for depression but had never been diagnosed with BDD: "I was seeing a counsellor at my university for 3 years and she suspected I had BDD. I never got diagnosed by a doctor mostly because anytime I'd say I was sad they'd say well you must not be sad about how you look and then go on to list physical traits of mine and say I'm good looking. so yes, I'd say I have BDD."

Another therapist dismissed a member's appearance concerns and the negative comments she received about her looks:

Female-Initial Post: What does your therapist say when you explain your issues? All I get is "you're attractive, there's nothing to worry about" or when I try to explain what people have said to me or done to me they say "why do you care about looks so much?" or "maybe that person is having a bad day" or something. It NEVER helps me. Does it help you?"

A male poster expressed sympathy for the woman's plight and provided a letter from the BDD Foundation meant to be shared with clinicians: "I am sorry to hear you had a poor experience with a therapist. Many therapists (unfortunately) are not very aware of BDD and how to screen for it. Here is something you may want to print off and take to your therapist or a new therapist..." The letter/card for doctors is meant to help people in the United Kingdom explain their symptoms when seeking referrals to a BDD specialist.[17]

Therapy could also be ineffective due to the stigma involved with disclosing one's appearance concerns. According to one man who recovered from BDD (Appendix B7): "In the early days when i was hospitalized and put into a BDD group, pretty much the whole group used to analyze me and put me down physically!" Another patient believed her therapist was judging her, so she was afraid to share her insecurities: "I also wanna say that I go to therapy but I normally don't tell her much about myself while in it . . . I know that it's a little strange to say, but I'm quite scared that she's judging me for some reason."

One woman had dermatillomania (skin picking disorder) and bulimia for years but had never been diagnosed with BDD. She found the BDD forum after one therapist advised her to blog about her feelings:

> **Female-Initial Post:** I've had (undiagnosed) severe dermatillomania since age ten and have been an on again off again bulimic since age 15. I'm 43 now and just learned BOTH are related to BDD. I don't know what to do...I have broached the subject of my conditions with two different counselors but neither recognized the root problem. Both diagnosed me with depression/anxiety. Consequently, I have never received true help. I started a blog to "journal" my feelings (on the recommendation of my most recent therapist) and found this group as a result. To be honest, my life (on the inside) is pure hell and I do want to get help but don't know how to get it. If my therapists can't see it, can I walk in and say, "I have BDD. Find me some help!"

COST AND LACK OF INSURANCE

The high cost of therapy, along with lack of health insurance, presented more barriers to getting clinical treatment. A young Asian woman was saving money for laser hair removal because therapy was too expensive:

Female-Initial Post: ...normally, asians don't have lots of body hair but i think i'm a freak of nature & somehow born with so much hair...even both my mom and dad don't have much body hair....worse of all, my parents don't understand the pains i go through... i've had guy friends who commented about my body hair and it was so embarrassing... & they don't even wanna pay for waxing and laser... i have to save up for my own $$$$ to get it done. plus i'm still schooling so it's impossible for me to work full time to save up enough $$, school starts next month and i've only earned $500 so far which i've spent on nicer clothes and hair...

a therapist is kinda out of the question, went to one before and it was so expensive!!!! $100 for one session, just to talk to the therapist and draw about how i feel?!?!? THATS CRAZY.

Lack of health insurance was a barrier for some members who lived in the United States. One woman recommended getting CBT therapy, even though she could not afford clinical treatment herself: "Have you considered seeing anybody about your symptoms? A doctor or a therapist? I have never had CBT or any real therapy since I live in the states and lack health insurance...but I have heard from some that CBT works wonders."

I lived with depression for fifteen years before diagnosing myself and seeking treatment. After diagnosing myself with BDD, I got help from a psychiatrist and psychologist. I am grateful their treatment methods worked and were covered by health insurance. My psychiatrist diagnosed me with depression and put me on 20mg of Prozac (fluoxetine). The psychologist used talk therapy to help me overcome my negative thoughts and behaviors. Both were effective in treating my BDD symptoms. There are resources available to overcome treatment barriers, so don't lose hope, and keep trying!

Self-Medicating with Drugs and Alcohol

While SSRIs can be effective in alleviating BDD symptoms, using drugs and alcohol to self-medicate can make BDD symptoms worse.[18] Some forum members used drugs and alcohol to cope with stress and social anxiety. The young woman who was afraid of seeing her campus therapist used marijuana (pot) to deal with stress. Unfortunately, smoking pot made her symptoms worse:

> **Female-Initial Post:** I admit I have turned to smoking pot to deal with some of the stress. Not a lot...but maybe once every 10 days. Funny enough, my BDD symptoms have been getting worse from it, so I have cut back. I would immediately start panicking and crying because I would just suddenly think of the visual image I have of myself and just feel disgusted and ashamed.

Mia could relate to people who used drugs or alcohol to self-medicate. She responded to a male poster who was nineteen years old and felt he had a big head. He had other appearance concerns including puffy eyes, pimples, and lack of facial hair. His appearance obsessions kept him from socializing and meeting girls since he could not make eye contact with them.

When he went to parties with friends and had some beers or marijuana, he felt better about his appearance. He wanted to know if the drugs alleviated or even eliminated his BDD symptoms. Both Mia and Fran advised him to get clinical treatment for his BDD symptoms. Mia warned him not to become addicted to drugs or alcohol:

> **Mia-Reply 1:** I'm not a psychiatrist or anything but a lot of young people are self-conscience about how they look, however, if you're finding that these thoughts are consuming you then speaking to someone about it may help. Besides, if it really is BDD then getting help for it early will be way better than waiting.
>
> As for the drinking and smoking, it may just be how your body reacts to it, but please don't become dependent on those substances to make

you feel better because then you'll just acquire another problem---substance abuse! as for me, when i drink i either get really sad about how i look or sad in general or just too drunk to care...so i don't drink. as for smoking well that's something i thoroughly enjoy, but just be careful!!!

Fran echoed Mia's advice about getting professional help for BDD. She was a medical student and had undergone BDD treatment, so her advice was based on her educational and personal experiences:

Fran-Reply 2: Just to add, if you are dealing with BDD, then you are doing the right thing to go and seek up a psychiatrist asap, do not drag it out because it may become worse. There is treatment and management but works best the earlier you start. As it sounds to me you are still able to go to parties, and to your work, so you are doing well compared to many BDD sufferers who may not be able to leave their homes. Don't let it get that far. Take care of it now.

BDD treatment specialists caution individuals to avoid self-medicating since doing so can lead to substance abuse. Seventy percent of people with BDD and a substance abuse disorder said BDD contributed to their problem. Substance abuse disorders may cause symptoms to worsen and can increase the risk of suicide attempts in people with BDD.[19]

TREATMENT RESOURCES AND INFORMATION

Forum members often provided resources and information about effective treatment in their replies. One woman became "obsessed" with finding information about BDD after her diagnosis. She wanted members to direct her to additional reading, including books and websites, so she could learn more about BDD:

Female-Initial Post: So I just now found this site and so far have found some interesting information. I was diagnosed with BDD a little over a month ago. I have Googled BDD only God knows how many times and I still feel like I am not fully informed. Every site I see says basically the same thing! I know the symptoms and everything, but I feel like I am still not getting all the info I can. (I have kinda been obsessed with researching it ever since my diagnosis, lol.) I just feel like there HAS to be more to this. Something so severe and debilitating cannot be that simple! Can anyone refer me to some good reading, on the web or books? Maybe link me to some good forums?

A female member recommended she talk to a therapist and referred her to books about BDD, including *The Broken Mirror*[20] and *Body Dysmorphic Disorder. The Broken Mirror* is considered a seminal work on BDD. The second reference could be the updated edition titled *Understanding Body Dysmorphic Disorder:*[21]

> **Female-Reply 1:** I always suggest talking to a therapist first, but if you can't do that, read as much as you can online about BDD. Check your local library or bookstore for books on BDD (two I always recommend are "The Broken Mirror" and "Body Dysmorphic Disorder"). If you have a couple dollars to buy them I recommend doing that because I find it really helpful to be able to go back and reference those books whenever I need to, I prefer to have them on hand. I'm no professional, that's just what has helped me over the years.

Dr. Phillips provides practical suggestions and advice for getting help in *Understanding Body Dysmorphic Disorder: An Essential Guide.*[22] Her advice includes how to overcome barriers to treatment, how to cope with medication costs and lack of insurance, and how to approach treatment professionals for help.[23] For example, ask a local medical school or mental health center if they charge less for uninsured patients. Consult your doctor or psychiatrist about patient assistance programs to lower medication costs.

Another member recommended a self-help guide for overcoming body image problems, including BDD:[24]

Undetermined-Reply 2: I'm new here was hoping to join the bdd central but it appears to have gone off line but anyway, I am currently receiving CBT for my BDD and I was recommended a book by my therapist which I bought straightaway and it's so far very useful, it is from a series called Over Coming. So overcoming body image problems including bdd, self help guide with CBT techniques by David Veale, Rob Willson and Alex Clarke, not sure If you can get it on a kindle though...

Two of the forum leaders (Roger and Fran) recommended *The Broken Mirror* to members. Fran planned to share the book with her family since they did not know about her BDD diagnosis. Roger agreed the book was helpful for educating people about the disorder:

Fran-Initial Post: I have just ordered home the book "The Broken Mirror", for the highest purpose being info resource for my thesis, but can also benefit myself.

It is supposed to be a very useful book for sufferers, but also for the family and friends.

Because it's hard to understand Body Dysmorphic Disorder from an outsider point of view, don't be afraid of giving this book to your family to read.

A lot of the recovery lays in the support we are getting, no matter what mental disorder we are talking about

Roger-Reply: Yeh that book is definitely advisable for anyone suffering from BDD or wanting to learn more about BDD in order to help another. Full of lots of useful statistics and surveys as well.

There are additional books, websites, clinics, and information about BDD in Appendix A. Please use these resources to get the help you need to overcome your BDD symptoms. They can also be shared with family members, friends, and clinicians to educate them about the disorder. Forum members who were battling BDD provided strategies for coping with their symptoms. These included self-acceptance, finding hobbies they enjoyed, exercising, getting outdoors in nature, posting to the forum, and recasting their problems in a more positive light.

Coping with BDD Symptoms

Undetermined-Initial Post: I was thinking it would be good to share tips/strategies/ideas about how to lessen the symptoms of BDD. For me, constantly telling myself, "No one thinks I am as ugly as I think I am" helps me put things in perspective sometimes. We are our own worst enemy. When I start obsessing, I try to exercise because it kills two birds with one stone -- takes my mind off obsessing and makes me feel like I am doing something to change my despicable appearance. Does anyone else have coping mechanisms they could share? May tomorrow be a better day...

Self-Acceptance/Accepting Flaws

Many individuals on the forum wanted to know how to cope with and effectively manage their BDD symptoms. Coping strategies shared by members included self-acceptance, fun hobbies, listening to music, exercise, being outdoors in nature, posting to the forum, and focusing on positive aspects of having BDD (positive reappraisal). Self-acceptance was the first choice among many for coping with BDD symptoms. One man viewed self-acceptance as a transformative process. He shared advice from an American Buddhist nun (Pema Chödrön) about accepting one's imperfections with compassion, kindness, and patience:

> **Male-Reply:** Although self-improvement can have temporary results, lasting change occurs only when we honor ourselves by approaching our imperfections with kindness, compassion, and patience. It is only when we begin to relax with ourselves, instead of relaxing our body, that acceptance becomes a transformative process (Chodron, 2001). Accepting ourselves is changing ourselves.

Another male poster reflected on the pros and cons of self-acceptance for people with body image disorders:

> **Male-Initial Post:** Yes, there have been a few times in the last 6 months where I have felt 100 % full self acceptance. The periods lasted very short, maybe just a few hours max. But they felt great. I am not saying I looked like Brad Pitt during these periods of self-acceptance, but I didn't need to. I was just happy with myself and therefore felt very attractive.

> You may say "Woah this is great that you have experienced this lately, it proves you are on the road to happiness and nearly there". Yes I suppose you are right in one sense. However... it does make you question it all.

> There is something very degrading about self-acceptance. It is almost as if you have just decided that there is no way you are going to achieve what you want, and that you are going to settle for the non ideal version of you. Now I know nothing is ideal, and nothing is perfect. Especially in the looks department.... I read before that there is no such thing as a perfectly symmetrical face. But surely you can relate to what I mean. I want to look a certain way but I can't due to natural genetics. Plastic surgery is an option but it is a dangerous and costly route... therefore self-acceptance is the only option.

I spent the last 8 years of my life dreaming of the day I would look a certain way, dreaming of the day I would have a beautiful face in the mirror. I am reaching a stage now where I am about to let go of all that self pride and accept that I just look the way I do, which is average-below average. My true beauty could well shine through then and I could love what I see in the mirror, as well as attracting girls who I find beautiful in both a physical and spiritual/personality sense. When I accept myself fully I will be able to carry myself extremely well and will look really attractive. There is a good chance I will get loads of girls and naturally attract people.

So yeah, self-acceptance seems great. But it also seems like a bit of a lie in a way.... and I just don't know what to think. Letting go of all your dreams, hopes, self pride and accepting something you don't like... it just seems irrational, even if it makes you happy.

Using exposure exercises helped another man accept his appearance flaws. Exposure and response prevention (ERP) involves exposing oneself to thoughts, images, and situations that trigger anxiety. Response prevention refers to not engaging in compulsive behaviors (rituals) after one's anxiety has been triggered. Over time, a person's anxiety and rituals will diminish.[1] The male poster forced himself to look at his reflection in the mirror (something he usually avoided). He also went out in public without caring how he looked. At first, this triggered feelings of depression and hopelessness. However, after a short time, he was able to accept his appearance:

Male-Initial Post: My way to cope with this is to make me get used to the feeling of being ugly. The actions include not caring about how you look, not dressing up properly, not making your hair properly while still going out as usual, trying to look at the mirror as much as possible of course. With all of these in place, you would feel very hopeless, probably like the most serious depression state you could get. It may last for a week or so. After that, you would not be depressed anymore because you have already reached the final stage- the true acceptance. For those who have tried this method, please let me know if it works for you.

No one responded to his post, perhaps because exposure exercises can be difficult and are usually guided by a therapist. One type of exposure common in my virtual BDD support groups is turning on one's video camera during meetings. Some people hate seeing their face on a video camera. That is why I let members join with just their audio, if desired. However, I enjoy watching people's facial expressions when cameras are on, since faces convey emotions better than voices alone.

HOBBIES/MUSIC/EXERCISE/NATURE

Anna (one of the moderators) advised a forum member to find a hobby unrelated to one's appearance. Anna had the BDD forum, which gave her a feeling of belonging and being good at something, especially when she first started posting:

> **Anna (Moderator)-Reply:** People here say that it helps to have something you're passionate about that has nothing to do with the way you look. Do you have anything like that? It could help with your self esteem a lot. I have this forum, and it gave me a feeling of belonging and of being good at something especially when I first started posting here. It could be any kind of hobby that's not related to looks, really.

Another woman reminded herself that BDD-related attacks were not real. She distracted herself by doing something fun:

> **Female-Reply:** Basically, whenever I feel an avalanche of negative emotions building up, I pause and remember that I know it's only my perception tricking me, and it isn't how things truly are. So now instead of having a really miserable day, crying for hours and contemplating killing myself, I literally just decide to do something fun to distract myself while my mood gets back in balance. It may sound weird, but "training" myself that way really worked for me. I

learned that "BDD attacks" or whatever you want to call them, aren't real. They're not how I truly perceive things.

Fran shared seven of her coping strategies for managing a bad day (Appendix B5). These included physical activity (running/jogging), connecting with friends via email, talking to her boyfriend, making future plans, cuddling her cat, and creating a soothing space at home. Fran used music to ease her social anxiety while exercising outdoors:

Fran-Reply: I place the headphones deep into the ears, I put on loud sound, I put on my sunglasses (without works ok also) and I walk on the streets looking only at the beauty around me. I don't look at any person, or car. I live into the music and i sing along (not too loud). You will never meet somebody's look or hear a laughter or feel strangely perceived, because you just walk there and you just don't care. I feel so good in those moments, because I got no clue whatsoever what happens around me. Just check out for cars when you cross the road and so on.

I am not encouraging these methods of avoidance as a cure, but as management, so that you don't feel scared of going out taking a jog or walk which feels so good.

Mia also liked to spend time outdoors in nature. Doing so made her feel more at peace with herself and her appearance. She replied to a young woman who was suicidal by expressing empathy and disclosed that counseling had saved her life. Her counselor helped her to develop coping skills, including spending time in nature:

Mia-Reply: Please don't kill yourself <3, I've been there and it's not a good place to be and often people giving you help doesn't help. A few years back I was extremely depressed and it's around that time that I met my counsellor and I swear she saved my life. She helped me determine coping skills and the major one for me is to go outside and be with nature and love nature because nature loves you no matter if you think you're ugly or not.

157

Like Mia and Fran, I enjoy spending time outdoors in nature. I took long walks in the woods while living in New England and currently enjoy hiking in the Rocky Mountains. My other outdoor activities include gardening, biking, swimming, meditating, and jogging/running on trails. Even taking a short walk with my cat makes me feel better. Plus, walking a cat is a great way to meet the neighbors and become more social. Walking a dog is also an excellent way to get exercise outdoors.

POSTING TO THE FORUM

Writing about one's experiences can provide a sense of relief by exposing one's inner feelings, which can lead to emotional catharsis.[2] The female poster who was suicidal and felt "too ugly to live" (Chapter 7) admitted she felt better after sharing her story on the forum (Appendix B8):

> **Female-Initial Post**: I don't know what to do. I am frightened, sad and I feel very alone about this problem. I know that society has bred insecurity in girls, but this is something much much worse. I want to get help but I am 1) embarrassed and 2) unsure as to what help I could even get.

> Thank you if you happened to read this. I feel better for even having typed it out. But I can't ever, ever say that to anyone.

Writing about difficult experiences has been found to decrease negative emotions and increase positive ones.[3, 4] Sharing mental health struggles can normalize difficult emotions and lessen stigma and shame. For example, one member reassured another that her appearance obsessions were common on the forum: "Everyone here has the obsessions. It isn't normal but you certainly aren't alone and you certainly aren't a freak."

Many members and the forum leaders praised the BDD forum as a place where they could meet others who shared their struggles and feel less alone (Chapter 15). In the following example, a female runner with a "happy heart and soul" was afraid to tell her friends and family about her recent BDD diagnosis. She came to the forum looking for coping strategies:

Female-Initial Post: I was recently diagnosed with body dysmorphic disorder. I've had it for almost two years now, and I have no idea how to cope with it. No one knows, and I'm too afraid to tell anyone besides my doctor. I just need a friend and some strategies to suppress my anxiety.

I'm a runner, I have a happy heart and soul, but a depressed mind. I'm creative and funny.. But I'm just hideous. Does anyone have an iPhone where we can group chat? Or is anyone willing just to help me..?

Both Roger and Janet replied, along with other forum members, and welcomed her to the forum. Roger suggested she might be able to help other members, along with getting help from them:

Roger-Reply 1: Welcome to the forum. You have come to a good place to talk to other people who are in the same boat as you regarding BDD, there are a few regulars on here who are excellent contributors to this forum and we get a lot of people who come on every now and then too.

Maybe you should post on here for a little bit you might strike some common ground with some people on here, and also you could be able to help people yourself.

Janet-Reply 2: 😊 thanks for posting! I love how you said you have a happy heart and soul! That is already a step in the right direction. It's ok if you haven't told anyone else yet, you can post on here, there are some really nice people on this forum to talk to. There are lots of strategies to help with your anxiety, lots of information that you can work with.

I've had BDD for many many years and only started treatment this year, so it's never too late. I don't have an iPhone but please feel free to message me on here, i will do anything to help.

POSITIVE REAPPRAISAL

Kathy's way of coping was self-harm (SH), which was not helpful for dealing with her BDD symptoms: "My coping strategies are not very good! I SH, it helps in the short term but causing more damage in the long run!!" However, Kathy used positive reappraisal when she stated that having BDD had made her more compassionate and understanding: "I am 99 percent sure that BDD has shaped my personality in a positive way."

Roger was grateful for the people he met due to having BDD: "BDD may have wrecked my life as i know it but it also allowed me to find some of the most amazing people i will ever have the privilege to know, you are all stars and you will have your chance to shine!!" Another young woman viewed her perceived ugliness as a blessing rather than a curse. Instead of lashing out in anger and frustration at her fate, she wore her ugliness as a badge of honor from God:

> **Female-Reply:** well i am trying to learn to wear my ugliness as a badge of honor, which is extremely hard to do, but i definitely think God made me ugly because he wanted to bless my **soul**. not my outer body which will rot someday, but my soul. i wish that all "ugly people" would be able to "wear their ugliness as a badge of honor".

She was deeply religious and compared herself to Jesus, who was also one of the "ugly people" and a social outcast:

> God thought i was special enough to be ugly like Jesus was, and to learn the life lessons that many beautiful people will never figure out (like how to treat other people regardless of how they look, like how badly it hurts to be judged on something you can't control, like how it feels to be a social outcast). ooooooh yes i think that God loves ugly people, God loves an underdog.

Acceptance of one's fate as a "blessing in disguise" is an emotional coping strategy used by people suffering from stigmatizing physical or mental health conditions.[5] My positive reappraisal of BDD is recognizing how much recovery has increased my self-esteem and confidence. I now have loving relationships and close friendships, and I can accept my appearance flaws.

RECOVERY STORIES

Male-Initial Post: So, what do i think of the treatment i received? It worked. I still take medication everyday but i haven't been to my therapist in over a month, and for a long time, i was going less and less, because i didn't need to. Still some minor, lingering symptoms but i don't feel like i have BDD anymore. I am happy and calm and this is the best my life has been for years. It isn't easy but even if it had taken 10 years, it would have been worth it.

FROM RECOVERY TO ADVOCACY

Two men posted their recovery stories on the forum to provide hope, advice, and information about BDD treatment. They became positive role models for other members and exemplified that BDD could be beaten. Recovery from a mental health disorder is defined as a process of change through which individuals improve their health and wellness, live a self-directed life, and strive to reach their full potential.[1]

A Wikipedia entry about BDD led one male college student down the road to recovery. Discovering he was not alone caused a "piano sized weight" to come off his back. He planned to use a portion of the proceeds from his memoir to start a counseling center for BDD. His goal was to have support groups for BDD on every college campus throughout the country:

Male-Initial Post: I sought counseling at school in Miami and subsequently wrote a book about living with BDD. I plan to use a portion of the proceeds to start a counseling center for people with BDD. My ultimate goal is to have support groups on every college campus and in other settings like 12 step programs have throughout the country. I still have only told a few people, but with the publication of my book I am ready to come out with my story. I want to help fellow BDD sufferers and know that all of my pain and suffering can serve some greater purpose. I want to start an awareness campaign to help people not only realize they may have BDD, but to seek treatment when they do. I never knew I had BDD, but was typing in the symptoms of my obsessive thoughts a few years back and came across the Wikipedia page on BDD. I felt a piano sized weight come off my back when I found out I wasn't the only one suffering with these symptoms. Learning that I had an actual disorder that affects millions of Americans made me feel much less alone.

He hoped posting an excerpt from his book would inspire other people to enter counseling: "I hope you read my story and feel less alone. Maybe it will inspire you to enter counseling and no longer be ashamed of your thoughts. Maybe it will inspire you to help others who may be suffering." He then provided an excerpt detailing his mirror obsession and how he overcame the disorder using clinical treatment (Appendix B6).

BEATING BDD STORY

Another man also shared his story about recovery and beating BDD. He ended his post by urging others to believe recovery was possible and described the feeling of completeness "post" BDD:

Male-Initial Post: The reason i wrote here was to create a perception for you all on what it's like "post" BDD. I know alot of you won't believe it's possible to reach this level, but i urge you to keep pushing and pushing... I want you to know it's possible. I've done stupid things, lost friends family and partners cus of my BDD fuelled behaviour. I know what it's like, but i urge you to keep going, you will get there, and when you do you'll feel complete. That feeling of completeness is so much more than anything you might be looking for.

Kathy and a male poster were encouraged to know BDD could be beaten. The male poster asked for specific steps he could use to manage his symptoms:

Kathy-Reply 1: Thanks for your post 😄 it's really inspiring and motivating.

It's great to hear from someone who is beating BDD! I often wonder if it is truly beatable, but you prove that it is 😄

Male-Reply 2: I thank you also for this great post. What you've put here is very encouraging. I think you've hit the nail on the head focusing on management rather than cure. I've come to realize the same in regards to my own Bdd - questing for complete freedom from it I've found to be futile at best, counterproductive and damaging at worst.

I'm at the stage where I'm thinking this stuff, similar to what you've outlined in your post, but not yet applying it. I can't seem to move beyond the theory into actual real life practice. Can you give me some specifics as to how you did it, as in the actual application of your new outlook/thought processes? All the best with continued recovery.

In response, the original poster provided five strategies he had used to beat BDD (Appendix B7): 1) attention training every morning, 2) regular exposure and response, 3) spot your avoidances and target them immediately, 4) positive data logging with a therapist to find your core beliefs that cause your BDD, and 5) trauma work. He encouraged the male poster to do exposures, such as going to a sports club, even if he was feeling insecure about his appearance:

Male-Reply 3 (OP): you said you can't seem to put the theory into real life and practise. This is a very very interesting statement for both of us! For example i know im avoiding going to a sports club to try and find friends at the moment because im overweight due to my medication. I want to go but the fear of being overweight is stopping me literally putting the theory of exposure into practise. The answer is simple for both of us: We must put the theory into practise. we owe it to ourselves and deserve better than what BDD tells us. We deserve happiness and we will get this if we put the theory into practise and expose ourselves to places and situations that our BDD makes us anxious in.

These five strategies were developed with the help of his therapist during counseling, including the exposure and response prevention exercise he described. He urged Kathy and the other male poster to get therapy to heal their childhood trauma:

Most people with BDD believe it or not have had a history of social anxiety and trauma (myself included). addressing these traumas with your therapist using specific techniques they give you can help massively. At the root of BDD is trauma, and if the trauma is not resolved by the brain it will always resurface in one way or another. Most of us think we're ugly because we've been traumatized into thinking so. So, by treating BDD like a post trauma occurence, we can resolve it and dampen it loads by emotionally resolving and coming to terms with what happened in our childhood/early life.

The two men who shared their recovery stories served as positive role models since they encouraged others to get treatment. Interactive media (like the BDD forum) connect individuals to social networks and community settings where they can find role models for behavioral change.[2] These role models can increase people's outcome expectations and motivate them to take positive actions. The BDD forum enabled participants to connect with each other, disclose their struggles and coping strategies, and learn about diagnosis and treatment options.

Most members wanted to find people who could empathize with and understand their struggles. They provided positive support to each other, such as compliments, gratitude, encouragement, and validation. The forum leaders were committed to keeping the BDD forum a supportive online community. Roger and Kathy, in particular, defended the forum against flaming and trolling and supported each other when disagreements arose between members.

PART FIVE
SUPPORTIVE ONLINE COMMUNITY

Emotional Support

Roger-Initial Post: Everybody starts from the beginning, you cannot expect to be a pro when you first start something. You will fail, you will hit the wall on occasion but you will get better and you will progress. Every pro started off exactly where you did. When you take up that new hobby or new coping technique just remember you will not master it immediately. Perseverance will get you there in the end.

Forum Leaders

The five forum leaders responded to individuals struggling with feelings of ugliness, loneliness, and suicidality by expressing sympathy, compassion, empathy, and encouragement. Roger provided emotional support to other members without asking for support in return. Kathy indirectly asked for support when she expressed insecurity and doubt in replies to other members. Mia and Fran both sought and provided support in their messages, whereas Janet only provided emotional support to others.

ROGER: "I'M SORRY YOU ARE STRUGGLING"

Roger was fully focused on providing emotional support to other members. He advised a woman who had tried to commit suicide to see a doctor (GP) and offered to support her as well:

> **Roger-Reply:** if you go to your GP and tell them your symptoms and how it affects you they can put you onto CBT and they can help work with you to change your mindset.
>
> A big part of BDD is perceptions, if you believe yourself to be 'ugly' in some way have you not thought that it could be BDD causing a lot of it? Please don't be so quick to try and throw your life away, it's not a lost cause.
>
> You have obviously come on here for a reason. Please keep in touch with us on here, we will help however we can, i swear it!

Some members asked for support at night when they were alone and there was no one else to confide in. For example, one female poster was having a panic attack and desperately wanted to talk to someone:

> **Female-Initial Post:** Is anyone up or can someone talk to me? I'm laying in bed, but I can't sleep and I am having a panic attack...
>
> I ate some stuff today that will probably make me gain a lot of weight and my mind is racing about everything...I feel so disgusting and worthless I don't want to be here anymore. Someone please help me. I don't know what to do anymore. I just want everything to disappear..

Roger replied the next day and wanted to know if she was okay: "Sorry i wasn't around when you typed this, are you alright?" The original poster was grateful for his reply: "I completely appreciate you replying, regardless of the time." Roger expressed sympathy for another woman who was struggling with BDD symptoms: "I'm sorry you are struggling, and I'm glad you've already found the forum helpful."

Roger started a thread to celebrate the "little victories" he and other members achieved on their road to recovery:

> **Roger-Initial Post:** The road to freeing yourself from the clutches of Body Dysmorphia can be a long and arduous path, in it we sometimes forget the little victories we achieve on the way.
>
> I want this to be a thread about the victories we do have, no matter how little no matter how big, i want it to reach 1,000 and be here to remind us what we are truly capable of. 😎 I'll set us off down the path with numero uno; 1) Today i have looked in the mirror for half as much time as i normally do, and have been able to leave it promptly without being compelled to keep looking.

Janet was the first to reply to Roger's thread, and she shared two recent accomplishments:

> **Janet-Reply:** Hey Roger. Good thread. I had a great day today so I'm happy to contribute 😃
>
> 1) I was surprised by a friend coming to my house this morning. Seconds prior I was practicing a mindfulness technique. It allowed me to speak without fear and we went for a really long drive.
>
> 2) I am writing down my thoughts and "editing" them to the way I would like them. Getting it down on paper is a good reference point for me.

Roger posted a picture of a Christmas tree on Christmas Eve (US time) and wished everyone on the forum Merry Christmas and a happy new year. Fran replied and returned the greeting. Another BDD forum member replied to both and shared holiday greetings with the "BDD family" on the forum: "Merry Christmas Roger, Fran, and the rest of the BDD family. 😃"

FEMALE FORUM LEADERS: "NEVER GIVE UP ON YOU"

Kathy, Janet, Mia, and Fran often responded to members who felt rejected, depressed, suicidal, and socially isolated. Kathy provided encouragement, empathy, and sympathy to the female poster who felt "too ugly to live" (Chapter 7).

> **Kathy-Reply:** Hi, welcome to the forum 😄 I'm so sorry that you are going through all of this! Thanks for sharing your story, I can relate with some of the things you have said and it's awful.
>
> Are you receiving any treatment for this? I hope you like the forum, feel free to join any discussions or message me if you ever need to talk about anything.

She expressed sympathy for another woman who was lonely and encouraged her to try meeting people:

> **Kathy-Reply:** I'm sorry you feel lonely. It's so hard to trust people, especially with our hearts but maybe if you give a little then the reward will be so much greater than the potential hurt. It's a risk that sometimes we have to take, I'm saying this and I know I'm not able to do it but maybe you could give it a go! Take the plunge, go out and meet people. Everyone deserves to be happy and it's so sad that this illness is holding you back.

Mia offered compassion and encouragement to a woman who attributed childhood abuse to the onset of her eating disorder and BDD symptoms:

> **Mia-Reply:** Stop being so hard on yourself!! You've made it through such hard times and you deserve to be nice to yourself and to love yourself. I've been through a hard childhood too and I think that my problems with how I look stems from it because whenever I'm sad or whenever anything goes wrong I think it's because I'm ugly.

But we're survivors, we're strong, resilient and that's what makes us beautiful.

Fran empathized with another poster who was experiencing suicidal thoughts. She also had suicidal thoughts despite having friends and a boyfriend. Fran expressed her frustration with the forum because she wanted to provide physical comfort by giving her a hug:

Fran-Reply: I'm just so sad to read this. It's absolutely devastating. I have also felt the same way, despite the fact that I have a few friends and a boyfriend to back me up.

But I know those feelings so well... they come often, and you feel you are better off gone.

In moments like these I wish that we lived close by so that we could meet and talk to each other, show that we are real people who understand and care and won't judge! And because I really feel the urge of going and hugging you now!

I want to make you have hope, but I don't know what to say, I have the same damn curse.

There is hope there is hope, there must be sweety. Hugs to you, hugs for all the dumb people who missed the privilege to give you one.

Janet comforted a woman who was socially isolated and suicidal due to fears about people seeing the fat around her stomach (Chapter 10). She had recovered from anorexia but was trapped in her house and felt "alone in a black hole." The longer she was alone, the less real the world seemed, and the more she contemplated suicide. Janet congratulated her on being a survivor, urged her to keep going, and promised her the days would become brighter:

Janet-Reply: My gosh. Do you know how amazing it is that you actually survived through all of that? You must have a strength you do not realize yet, because I read your story and it's clear you are a survivor. Congratulate yourself on making it this far in life despite it all. And thanks for posting your story so others like myself can also relate to you. I've not experienced anorexia but lots of the other things you said I can very much relate to (I'm in therapy for BDD with my skin).

It's ok to acknowledge all this pain, sometimes we just need to be alone and acknowledge that yes, this is not where we want to be, but it's undeniably where we are, and that's ok. It's a part of the beginning process of healing. I recommend keeping on posting here because trust me it does get better and feels like you actually get some kind of help from it. 😄 In the meantime just remember there is a light at the end of the tunnel, a way out, which we are all heading for. Never give up on you, you are a human being and just doing the best with the knowledge you have, keep going, the days become brighter I promise you.

MEMBERS AND MODERATORS

Most members came to the BDD forum seeking empathy from others who could understand their struggles. Expressions of empathy often overlapped with and extended members' painful BDD experiences. In addition, forum members provided compassion, gratitude, sympathy, compliments, encouragement, and validation. These supportive responses helped fulfill the forum's function as an online peer support group.

EXPRESSING EMPATHY: "I FEEL THE SAME"

Members sought empathy by asking if others felt the same way or had similar experiences. For example, a young man was obsessed with "stretch marks" on his body and wanted to know if others on the forum could relate to his experiences:

Male-Initial Post: I was diagnosed with BDD a couple months ago. At first I didn't think I had it but now I'm certain I do. I am a 23 year old guy and for some reason I developed a ton of stretch marks. I hate my body because of them and whenever I see them I get angry. I get told I'm handsome and get looked at all the time, but all that goes through my head is "if only they knew what was under these clothes." I've never dated because of them even though I want to. I'm just sick and tired of these things ruining my life when they shouldn't be. I just thought it would be nice to hear others experiences and if there's anyone that can relate to me.

Another man without BDD empathized with him due to having third-degree burns on his body. He encouraged the male poster not to focus on his flaws and assured him he was not alone:

Male-Reply: Well, I can relate to the whole "what's under the clothes" thing and I'm 25 never dated or anything as well. I don't have BDD btw, but I have similar compulsive worries due to 3rd degree burns and dentures at 25 lol, so yeah I can't offer much experience advice considering I never really overcame anything yet so I'm in your boat but, keep your head up bud. I know your opinion on your body matters a lot more to you then someone else's opinion that implies you look fine, I try not to focus on my flaws a lot but it's very hard to do, so don't feel alone!

Another man hated his ugly face and worried he would always be unattractive to women. A woman empathized with his pain because she was "tired of being ugly too." She assured him they both had as much value as the most beautiful people in the world:

Female-Reply: hi i am sooooo tired of being ugly too. so very tired of it. and it's hard a lot of times, when i have to look in a mirror or see a picture of myself and i just really don't want to look at it anymore. i feel like my soul belongs in a different body, a pretty one. please remember you and i, we have every bit as much value as the most beautiful people in the world. they did nothing special or good to deserve being born with beauty and i did nothing "bad" to deserve being born without beauty.

Individuals on the forum who had plastic surgery and were unhappy with the results often sought empathy from others. A female poster hated the results of her rhinoplasty and asked if anyone could understand. She felt the surgery had made her face unrecognizable: "What a nightmare this year has been for me. I had low self-esteem before I got the rhinoplasty so I thought maybe it could make me feel better. HUGE mistake, I am so lost right now. I don't feel like the self i used to feel anymore. I am not strong anymore, I cry every day. When i look in the mirror i don't recognize myself. Does anyone understand this?" Another person responded and empathized with her plight: "I got rhinoplasty 5 days ago. And I feel the same. I have got drastic change on my face. Is it beautiful? surely not. It is the ugliest thing in the world."

Forum members were relieved to find others who shared their appearance concerns. One man had "exactly" the same feelings as another about the devasting effects of his weak jawline. They both believed having a weak jawline rendered them sexually unattractive to women:

Male-Initial Post: Anyway, I've thought about all this stuff for years. Why do I do this? What is the real core belief driving my BDD? I don't hate my jawline because of my jawline. I hate it because of what it symbolizes: that I am not sexually attractive to women. That I am not one of those men that women look at and feel sexually attracted to. I have no idea why that is such a huge deal to me but it is. And that's really the core of my BDD: a feeling that my ugly, dorky face makes me a valueless pariah in the sexual marketplace. Those are the truly painful emotions underneath it all.

Male-Reply: For a second I thought I wrote this. You and I have EXACTLY the same story. I have a problem with my jawline as well. This thread blew me away, because it captured the feelings I feel everyday as a man with a weak jawline and how hard it is to cope with being unattractive to women and society because of it. There is TREMENDOUS pressure on men to be HOT and attractive too.

A female member was astonished to be "reading about herself" when replying to another woman's post. Both were the same age and shared similar body image concerns and BDD behaviors:

Female-Reply: Wow, reading this I literally felt like I was reading about myself. I'm 22 too and I'm extremely pale, i have a huge nose, i have small weird eyes, my face is weird, wrinkles and I'm too short. I know how you feel, don't you wish you could just go to a bar like other people our age and feel normal?!?!?!? And the picture part, I hate it, I always make sure I'm facing the camera straight forward and I'll go on facebook so much the next few days just to check pictures that were tagged of me.

Concern, Gratitude, Compliments, Encouragement, and Validation

Forum members frequently responded to others' posts by expressing concern, gratitude, compliments, encouragement, and validation. They cared about other members who were suicidal; one man responded by offering to help a young woman with anything she needed: "I really really wish you the best as you sound like a nice person and you don't deserve what you're going through. I really hope I've covered everything, but please if there is anything you'd like me to help with please ask." Another member expressed concern and offered to pray for her: "How are you? I hope you're doing okay. I'll keep you in my prayers."

Expressions of gratitude were shared in initial message posts and in replies. In initial posts, members offered thanks in anticipation of receiving help and advice ("Thanks in advance for your help") and thanked others for taking time to read the message: "Thanks for reading this!" One female poster had been lurking on the forum for a few weeks and was grateful for the advice given to others:

Female-Initial Post: I've been reading the posts on here for a few weeks trying to sort myself out and you guys really seem to know what you're talking about, I just want to say thanks for the advice I've picked up from the replies off the other posts.

Sharing stories about one's suffering could be, in itself, emotionally beneficial. A woman asked for help with her reassurance-seeking behavior and expressed gratitude for any replies she received:

Female-Initial Post: i feel ugly and disgusting even though from what i hear i'm def. not. i just can't believe it. i've been accused of fishing for complements when i can't get my hair right, or i think jeans don't fit me perfectly right and i look decent otherwise. i'm just running out of options. i really wish i didn't have these feelings about myself, i'm the only one who should pass judgement on myself and instead i'm relying on others and instead not believing a word they say. i really need some help and would be thankful for anyone that replies to this. wow. it feels good to get that all out. thank you all so much.

One man who posted his recovery story received replies from Kathy and another member expressing gratitude for his great post (Chapter 13). They found it inspiring, motivating, and were glad to know beating BDD was possible. The original poster thanked them for their positive responses and assured them they could also beat BDD (Appendix B7):

Male-Reply 3 (OP): Thank you for your replies, it's great to meet people who are going through the same battle as me, sometimes you can feel so alone but it's great to know there are people out there that share the same problems as me, and have felt the same as me.

Another poster used a "forgetting box" to put away her negative feelings and thoughts caused by her BDD symptoms. A male poster complimented her on this coping technique: "If your point is what i think it is then it's a good one. Yeh it is a lot easier to remember the bad things that happen in your life rather than the easier ones, it's a psychological way of making sure it doesn't happen to you again by keeping it in the mind. Your 'forgetting box' is a good idea, if it works for you then that's fantastic."

The young woman who was trying to accept her ugliness as a blessing from God (Chapter 12) received praise from another member. He copied parts of her message into his reply and complimented her after each excerpt:

> **Male-Reply:** That's a beautiful thing you write. Why does it have to be ugly? Why aren't you just unique in who you are? . . . The way you see yourself, in leaps and bounds. That's awesome in your ability to do that. If only more people thought like this, I think the world would be filled with a lot less depression, self-persecution, and otherwise. . . You're a positive role-model for diversity of character and being... That's just grand.

Members were encouraged to keep posting after expressing negative feelings: "The good news is you are talking about it! It can be the hardest thing just to post on here. Just know there are so many options for you. So many things out there you can benefit from, loads of people that can and will love and support you, so don't lose hope, you can overcome this. keep posting if you want. I'm here pretty often." Another member responded to a female poster who was contemplating suicide. She empathized with her struggles, encouraged her to continue fighting, and praised her strength:

> **Female-Reply:** And I know how it is to hate something that is yourself so much that you want to die. It comes in waves and we need to survive those days hun, we can, we are so many fighting here with the same thing, a self-disgust! Stay with us and fight. Shared pain is half pain! Give me some right now. Hang in there, don't give up, you are very strong! <3

Forum members also validated each other's ideas and advice about coping with BDD. One man agreed he needed to distract himself from obsessing about his jawline: "You are right - I have to focus on other things besides my jawline. I'm actually a lot better about this than I used to be but I still have problems with it, obviously. I wrote the OP when I was feeling particularly bad. It's a struggle each day." In another post, a woman announced she was finally starting CBT treatment after years of "muddling" through various medications and therapists. Rose agreed with her reservations about CBT treatment:

> **Rose (Moderator)-Reply:** I definitely agree with the wait and see, though. I did a brief course of CBT for stress and anxiety and it was very helpful. But not a magic wand. I'd hope it'll help you in places, but I think you're right to have a few reservations and not to go in expecting a miracle.

Rose encouraged members to express gratitude to people who had supported them. Her request received three replies thanking other members, and one man thanked his family:

> **Female-Reply 1:** I would like to thank you all for all the encouragement you give each other.

> **Female-Reply 2:** I'm new to this forum and having people to talk to. Everyone on here is so nice. You guys offer me so much to think about and you give me a place to talk.

> **Female-Reply 3:** I would love to say a huge thank you to Janet. She pm me and has kept a steady convo with me, giving me the most encouraging thoughts I could ask for. You're the best, and its nice to have you to vent to a little each day. SO MUCH APPRECIATED.😀

> **Male-Reply 4:** I'd like to thank my family, if it wasn't for their support I'm positive I wouldn't be alive right now.

Members provided empathy, concern, compliments, encouragement, gratitude, and validation to others. Online forums are valuable for individuals with mental health conditions due to finding others who can empathize with their feelings. Active members are empowered by helping others, and by doing so, feel less alone in coping with their health conditions.[1] BDD forum members appreciated meeting similar others who understood their struggles. Four of the forum leaders (Roger, Kathy, Mia, and Janet) also formed strong bonds that extended their social network beyond the constraints of the BDD forum.

Network Support

Female-Initial Post: The most difficult part of this is dealing with it in the high school setting. I compare myself to everyone. The few friends I have are all very confident and outspoken, and it often feels like no one understands how real and serious this is to me-- which is why I found this forum. I really hope I can meet someone to correspond with and provide mutual support to. I need to talk about this with someone who understands. Nothing is working or helping.

Forum Leaders: "We are always here"

Members appreciated the BDD forum because it was filled with people who understood what they were going through. Connecting with similar others (companions) made them feel less alone, isolated, and stigmatized. Some members were unable to leave their homes due to their social anxiety about perceived appearance flaws. Many new members had decided to join the forum after reading others' posts and the supportive replies. Roger and Kathy greeted new members and encouraged them to become active participants so the forum could continue to thrive.

Roger provided most of the network support on the forum. He welcomed new members and praised the forum as a place where they could meet others who understood their situation:

Roger-Reply: Congratulations on posting by the way, it can be hard for people to discuss these kind of things and you've come to the right place the people on this forum are fantastic.

Nobody is here to judge, this is a great neutral environment for you to vent out anything you feel you need to and for people like me who understand your situation to read and help where we can.

Honestly there is nothing wrong with talking to people about any of this, even if it's just on the forum for now, and then eventually a doctor maybe if you feel you need to. We are always here though if you feel you need to vent anything out, that's what this forum is for.

Roger reached out to members who were displaced by the loss of BDD Central. He started a thread in September 2012, on the same day BDD Central went offline, wanting to know the status of the defunct site. He specifically targeted his post to other BDD Central members: "Where has BDD Central gone?" Members from BDD Central answered and provided support to him and each other:

Roger-Initial Post: Went to go on this morning and it's just disappeared, replaced by those webpages that link you to all sorts of rubbish.

Don't know if there's any BDD Central users on here that can shed any light on the matter?

Male-Reply 1: I know, I was like what the hell? I have no idea... I hope they haven't shut it down. I'm like so sad 😢

Roger-Reply 2: It's good to see you chief!! 😄 You getting the same thing then? No warning or nuthin!

After facing the loss of BDD Central, Roger realized he shared a common bond with other BDD forum members. He viewed them as his extended family. As a result, he no longer felt alone in his fight against the disorder:

Roger-Initial Post: We all share something here. We all have a common ground. We all know what's it like to be like we are and that is something i don't even share with my friends, or people of my blood.

And because of that, and with the loss of BDD Central to ram this point home in my mind, i have realised one thing. This one thing that makes us unique, makes us a family. As far as i'm concerned you are all my brothers, you are all my sisters. You are not alone, you never will be alone. I don't care if you're a regular on here, a lost connection from BDD Central or a passerby who has joined because they have discovered who they are, you are **all** family to me.

BDD may have wrecked my life as i know it but it also allowed me to find some of the most amazing people i will ever have the privilege to know, you are all stars and you will have your chance to shine!!

May we take the future on together, and unlock the potential within all of us. The potential to be free from our mind. Hell i'll drink to that. You are all legends! 😎

Roger was an advocate for the BDD forum since he missed BDD Central. He replied to a high school student who wanted to connect with other members and assured her she was not alone: "... this forum is a great place to get info on BDD or just chat to other people who go through the same things that you do. You are not alone chief, welcome. 😎"

Kathy also welcomed new members and praised the forum as a place where people could find others who understood the disorder:

Kathy-Reply: The forum is great, I love it! You should post some things in the BDD forum just for fun, it's a great way to get to know people. At first I found it a bit daunting and I thought people wouldn't want me to post there but everyone here is so nice, it's a great little community. There are so many people going through the same or a similar thing so it's great to chat to people here as they understand.

Roger, Kathy, and Mia often replied to member posts and reinforced each other's advice and support. Roger welcomed a new member who was unsure if she was ugly or had BDD. He advised her to get therapy (CBT) and invited her to communicate with him and other regulars: "Please feel free to stay on the forum for the meantime there are a few regulars on, myself included and speaking to people in the same boat as yourself is a really good start. Keep us updated." Kathy and Mia validated Roger's recommendation that she find a qualified therapist and offered to talk to her at any time:

Kathy-Reply 2: I'm sorry your going through this! The advice I would give you is the same as what Roger said, the best thing you can do is go and speak to your doctor. It's a hard thing to do but it's also the best thing to do. And the forum is a great place, it's helped me out significantly over the past year. Like Roger said there are a few regulars who would be more than happy to help you however they can. If you need anyone to chat to I'm always here,

Mia-Reply 3: Like the other two said, go see your doctor...but if I were you, I'd only tell them if you really trust them because they might just shut you down if they're not a good doctor and it could make you feel worse. But ya please get help before it gets worse. you can talk to me and the others on here anytime!!

Roger responded to the loss of BDD Central by recreating the popular "Off Topic" thread. The thread enabled members to share anecdotes unrelated to having BDD. Kathy was the first one to respond, and she and Roger were clearly pleased to connect there:

Roger-Initial Post: Almost feels a bit disrespectful to BDD Central making this but seen as though it was such a popular thread on there, and entertaining at times (seagull talk 😄) hopefully it will make things seem a bit familarish in the meantime. Well it's here anyway.

Kathy-Reply 1: Good thread!!! 😄

Roger-Reply 2: I thought you would be first on!! 😄😹

Kathy-Reply 3: Haha of course!!!

The "Off Topic" thread had more than 1,500 replies during 2012 (more than any other topic). The first hundred messages were exchanges between Roger and Kathy containing jokes, teasing, and topics about everyday events in their lives. The second hundred posts in the thread contained exchanges between Roger, Kathy, Mia, and Janet, primarily about experiences unrelated to having BDD.

The forum leaders increased their affinity for one another by sharing their favorite movies, songs, and hobbies (Chapter 5). Similar instances of chatting, teasing, and off-topic posts have been found in other health-related online support groups.[1, 2] These off-topic conversations can fulfill members' entertainment needs by diverting attention away from their problems. Exchanging friendly banter and humor in online groups can foster supportive communication between members.[3]

Fran wanted to create a live chat on the forum so she and other members could speak and form friendships. However, she was dissuaded from doing so by Anna, due to issues around privacy and anonymity:

Anna (Moderator)-Reply: I can see how they could be good in some ways, Fran. It was before my time here. But I think the BDD forum did have one or more linked chatrooms for a while. And there were some major problems, I think over privacy and anonymity. So that's why the Rules now explicitly mention "no chatrooms" in unsolicited PMs, posts or sigs.

Mia started a thread in October, letting members know why she had not posted in months. She was feeling better due to taking time away from the BDD forum and Facebook. Mia missed interacting with Roger, Kathy, and Janet. She assured them she had not deleted them off Facebook. Instead, she had deleted her Facebook account altogether. Both Roger and Kathy were pleased to know she was doing well.

Mia-Initial Post: I just wanted to say that, especially to Kathy and Roger and Janet (i didn't delete you guys off facebook, i deleted it all together lol) but I wanted to say that everyone on here is beautiful, please stop obsessing about your flaws, everyone has flaws but the world is beautiful, everyday you're here is a blessing and maybe you see this but you still can't stop thinking about how you look.

Roger-Reply 1: Wheeey Captain Canada!! 😄 Good to see you again chief, me and Kathy were talking about you the other day. We were wondering if you were ok and it's good to hear that your well!!! 😎

Kathy-Reply 2: Hi 😄 it's good to hear from you! I'm glad things are better for you!

Roger epitomized the motto he espoused about the BDD family; he greeted new forum members to make them feel welcome, recommended helpful BDD resources, and offered advice and encouragement about professional diagnosis and treatment. As a result, he was appointed a forum moderator in 2014.

MODERATORS AND MEMBERS: "WELCOME TO THE FORUM"

Less frequent posters and the two moderators (Anna and Rose) also welcomed members and praised the forum as a supportive place for people with BDD. Anna responded to new members and encouraged them to post to the forum. One young woman from Canada was looking to make new friends. Anna greeted her and invited her to post in other members' threads: "Welcome to the forum. I hope you find what you're looking for here. There are many personal experiences in this part of the forum, and some other areas may be relevant too. And don't be shy about posting in other people's threads 😉." Anna welcomed a woman who was seeking a BDD diagnosis and acknowledged she had much in common with other members: "No-one here can confirm a diagnosis, but it does seem like you have much in common with others here. So I hope you find the forum helpful and supportive. 😄 I'm glad you've found us."

Rose encouraged a young man whose symptoms were putting a "terrific strain" on his family to participate in the forum. He couldn't leave his house, had dropped out of school, and could not hold down a job. He concluded by expressing gratitude to other members: "Thank you for reading. It can get extremely lonely at times so it's nice to know there are others out there who feel the same, and that you're not completely alone." Rose suggested he read through the messages and post to the forum: "You could read through this forum a bit if you like, see if it helps, and post here too."

Another member offered praise and assistance to a new poster: "I think it's great that you posted this and are talking through it, it's hard to write about our experiences. Feel free to keep posting about your thoughts, feelings, and experiences. We'll do our best to listen and support you." A female college student invited members to visit her school's Beat BDD Facebook page filled with "positive energy." The page was created to raise awareness about the disorder:

> **Female-Initial Post:** I just wanted to share our Beat BDD Facebook page with all of you. It started as a small project dedicated to my

friend's uncle who struggled with BDD, but turned into a campus-wide campaign. We worked hard trying to spread the word about this highly unnoticed illness.

Below is an event we did to spread awareness and an animation I made to help others develop a greater understanding of BDD. I know that sometimes it can seem lonely, and so we created a Facebook page filled with positive energy and a place for others to connect with another. Our group has disbanded after graduating college, but we hope to keep up this site in hopes of further spreading BDD awareness.

Forum members appreciated finding similar others who understood their struggles. One woman had tried to explain her symptoms to friends, but they could not understand her negative thoughts about her appearance:

Female-Reply: More importantly, everyone here understands your struggles. That isn't the case with people who don't have BDD symptoms. I've attempted to explain my situation to close friends in the past, and they just don't understand. Which isn't to say they aren't caring and supportive, but they can't understand why I'm having those thoughts in the first place. There's nothing rational about BDD, and I think you need to feel those symptoms in order to truly understand how terrifying it can be.

A former BDD Central member agreed that talking to other people with BDD was important. She advised a male poster to get a professional diagnosis and encouraged him to share his feelings on the forum: "I think that one of the key things that every BDDer needs is someone to talk to, someone to understand them. Hence the forum. Feel free to share anything. At the previous forum I was at it really helped me....being able to share very private matters with other people who understood me."

Actively participating in support groups can reduce feelings of loneliness and social isolation. By providing support to others, individuals learn new coping skills and gain new perspectives, leading to a reduction in emotional distress.[4] Unfortunately, conflicts and disagreements between members also occurred. One person, in particular, started trolling the forum by posting nasty messages. The forum flamer insisted people were ugly and needed surgery to fix their flaws. He urged members to be skeptical about BDD and believed being ugly was a valid reason to commit suicide. Thankfully, the forum leaders took action to combat these hurtful and potentially harmful messages.

Conflicts between Members

Flamer-Reply: *Ugly people typically have very few opportunities for deep friendships or relationships because, well, no one wants to be around ugly people. The result of this is that most ugly people go through life being very lonely and unloved.*

I'm skeptical of counseling because it won't change your face. I've been doing it for a year and have nothing to show for it. My only hope is surgery, and I'm scheduled to undergo several major procedures next year.

Kathy-Reply: *Seriously?? What part of this is a support forum do you not get? I understand your not happy with the way you look but this isn't a place to tell people whether they need surgery or not. You are making people feel bad, does this give you a kick or something?*

Not everyone is so looks obsessed like you! It wouldn't bother me if a man had a "weak" jaw line! There are far more Important things!

THE FORUM FLAMER

Roger and Kathy clearly wanted the BDD forum to be a supportive online community. They welcomed new members and encouraged them to keep posting. Roger and Kathy both disapproved of posts by a male forum member who consistently portrayed himself and others as ugly and in need of plastic surgery. I labeled him the forum flamer (Flamer) due to his critical and offensive comments directed at other members. The forum flamer could be considered the *aggressor* in the group. The aggressor expresses disapproval of the values, acts, or feelings of others by attacking the group or the problem the group is addressing.[1]

BDD forum members openly shared their painful feelings while remaining anonymous. Online anonymity enabled the forum flamer to attack other members with impunity. Individuals who troll do so for amusement; to vent their hurt, anger, and frustration; and to get attention. However, trolling and flaming are subjective since people have the option to ignore the comments rather than engage with the trolls.[2]

The forum flamer was in therapy but still hated his appearance. He was convinced he was ugly and wanted multiple plastic surgery procedures. He seemed to have little knowledge about BDD symptoms, diagnosis, or treatment options. The Flamer expressed dismay that physicians insisted on diagnosing ugly people with BDD rather than suggesting they get surgery to fix their flaws: "Diagnosing ugly people with BDD is cruel." His post was extremely disturbing since he suggested being ugly is a legitimate reason to commit suicide:

Flamer-Initial Post: I'm so sick of psychiatrists failing to distinguish between legitimate ugliness and imagined ugliness. By failing to make this distinction, they incorrectly diagnose thousands of people with BDD and end up making their lives worse.

The fact of the matter is that beauty is overwhelmingly objective: It comes down to the symmetry of your facial halves and the proportions of your facial landmarks. That's it -- there's hardly any subjectivity involved in interpreting beauty.

I should also add that attractiveness plays an enormous role in determining the quality of one's life (duh!). Therefore, people who are legitimately ugly have every reason to be distraught over their appearance. They have every reason to be depressed and -- depending on the severity of their ugliness -- suicidal.

What legitimately ugly people need is not counseling but surgery. Cosmetic surgery doesn't perform miracles, but it can provide significant and objective improvements to one's facial appearance. Someone with a wide, humped, crooked nose would probably benefit much more from a quality rhinoplasty than therapy. Unlike therapy, surgery treats the *problem* (unattractive facial features), not the *symptoms* (depression and anxiety over appearance).

So if you are readings this, I implore you: Be skeptical of BDD. If you are legitimately ugly, then your best option is to correct what is making you unattractive. If after correcting these problems you still believe you are ugly, then perhaps you should seek a counselor. But do NOT be lured by the comforting diagnosis of BDD, which seems to suggest that no one is ugly. That's a fairy tale.

Kathy responded by pointing out his post might be upsetting to other members. She asked him to clarify his intentions and offered to support him:

Kathy-Reply 1: I don't mean to be rude but I think your post is very insensitive. I'm not sure what your aim was in posting it, maybe you could clarify this? If you are looking for support then we are more than happy to help you out, but please remember there are people here who are dealing with some hard things and your post may be upsetting to some people.

Roger, unlike Kathy, clearly expressed disapproval toward the forum flamer's post and insisted that beauty is subjective rather than objective:

Roger-Reply 2: Hahaahaha I'm going to have some fun with you.

First of all, this ugliness thing, it's subjective not objective. You see the world has this wonderful way of making certain things attractive to different people. Some people like blonde hair others prefer dark, ginger etc. Some people prefer men with a bit of body hair others prefer their men clean shaven.

THERE IS NOBODY IN THIS WORLD THAT EVERYBODY THINKS IS BEAUTIFUL,

SIMILARLY, THERE WILL BE NOBODY IN THIS WORLD THAT EVERYBODY IS NOT ATTRACTED TO.

Now i'm not sure where your going with your post, personally i think your out to get a few people upset, make them feel hopeless, but i'm going to wager that most people that read your post just like i have done will see what you have put as the type of crap some self-obsessed jock would put up to troll people into replying and guess what? All your post is going to do is make people more determined to prove the likes of you wrong cos that's most definitely what it's done to me! So i thank you very much kind sir, your post is actually quite ENLIGHTENING.

Roger voiced strong opposition to the forum flamer's opinion about people needing plastic surgery to fix their perceived ugliness. Individuals who witness trolling can choose to ignore the nasty comments or to engage with and expose the troll by mocking, critiquing, or reciprocating.[3] Roger clearly was repulsed by the forum flamer's offensive comments telling members they needed surgery rather than therapy. He chose to expose the forum flamer using sarcasm and by labeling his comments as trolling.

Further down in the thread, Mia let Roger know the forum flamer was born with a condition called hemifacial microsomia: "... i guess it's like half your face is caved in and you can be deaf from it and stuff. so...i dunno..could you diagnose someone like that with BDD??????" Roger replied that he did not know, and that he was also confused: "Oh right, i didn't know that he had that, and again i don't know if you could describe it as BDD either."

The condition Mia mentioned is often corrected with surgery during childhood. The forum flamer posted a picture of his face (against the forum rules), and his features were not noticeably disfigured. I do not know if he had surgery to correct his birth defects or if Mia was incorrect in her assessment. Either way, the forum flamer believed it was insulting to dissuade ugly people from getting plastic surgery: "Telling ugly people to just accept their terrible fate is incredibly insulting. It's basically saying they should be content with a lower quality of life."

TROLLING ON THE FORUM

The forum flamer believed he and others were as ugly as they felt. He did make an exception for one female poster whom he referred to as "pretty" when she sent him her picture. However, when another woman did the same, she was met with the opposite response. The forum flamer told her she was "extremely ugly" and suggested she commit suicide. She posted a message asking if others on the forum had experienced the same outcome:

> **Female-Initial Post:** Well, he said I am SO EXTREMELY UGLY that even surgery wouldn't help me so I'm doomed to stay ugly forever. Flamer even said that I was spoiled for thinking I had the right to be pretty. It has really made me feel like crap. Even the tiniest bit of self-confidence I had left is gone now. All the random strangers that used to call me ugly were right. I am not going to commit suicide like he suggested, but I sure hate my life right now. And most of all the harsh society that values looks over personality, most of the time.

Fran was shocked and angry at the Flamer and sympathetic to the woman's plight: "That's one crazy mothafacka that Flamer and his genuine help. I am sorry that you had to read those arse words of his."

In another post, a female member asked if she was ugly or had BDD. The forum flamer responded by affirming the woman's perceived ugliness. However, she did not seem upset by his reply and instead wanted to know if she could still have BDD:

Female-Reply 2 (OP): So I am ugly. Fact. But does that eliminate the possibility of BDD?

Flamer-Reply 3: I would say so. I mean, you probably have the symptoms of BDD, but if these symptoms are due to *real* flaws, then I don't see how you could call it BDD. Being ugly is extremely painful, and it's natural to be upset over it and want to get surgery to fix it.

Like beauty, it seems that "bullying is in the eye of the beholder."[4] Whereas you and I might take offense at being called ugly, the female poster did not. The Flamer was confirming her negative core beliefs about her appearance. Denying her perceived ugliness could have elicited an angry response, but confirming her ugliness was met with acceptance.

The Flamer's answer that having "*real*" appearance flaws means a person does not have BDD is misleading. BDD is classified as a preoccupation with flaws that appear minor or are not observable to others.[5] If a person has visible physical flaws, such as burn scars or birth defects, then the person is diagnosed as having a BDD-like disorder with actual flaws. The exception is when people have visible scars caused by skin picking meant to improve their appearance.[6] Feeling ugly while looking objectively normal or attractive is characteristic of the disorder.

Roger, Kathy, and Fran were not the only members who responded negatively to the forum flamer's posts. In another thread, a male poster complained that women were constantly rejecting him due to his looks. The Flamer and another man (Male 2) were the first to respond; Male 2 urged him to take steroids and the Flamer advised him to get plastic surgery. A personal trainer vehemently disagreed with the advice about taking steroids and getting surgery:

Male-Reply 3: first of all Flamer and Male 2 have zero understanding of what BDD is and what keeps the obsession going. I'd say they were deliberately acting stupid to troll the site if I didn't know better. The advice to take steroids is plain retarded on so many levels. Firstly, you can get a very impressive physique with just training and diet, I work as a personal trainer and the vast majority of women are repulsed by bodybuilder physiques and the poser personality that tends to go with it. Secondly it would be counterproductive to encourage obsessive behaviour like bodybuilding and steroids certainly are. Thirdly, they are illegal in most countries so you won't be able to get a doctor's advice about them.

Flamer, your comments are consistently mindless, every clinician in the world knows that surgery doesn't work for BDD, it will never take away the obsession, if the surgery is perfect the obsession will shift to another feature. Very often the surgery doesn't even satisfy the patient and repeated revisions are sought. On a practical level, it's impossible to correct many facial imperfections with surgery and perfection is totally impossible.

The forum leaders did their best to make the forum a supportive online community. Their contributions were vital to the successful functioning of the BDD forum. The forum flamer's negative comments were a tiny percentage (less than 1 percent) of the primarily supportive messages posted to the forum. However, the question of whether beauty is in the eye of the beholder became another topic for disagreement and debate.

BEAUTY OR THE BEAST?

Debates about labeling people as beautiful or ugly occurred primarily between the Flamer and BDD forum leaders. Other members also chimed in and provided their opinions. Mia believed beauty is subjective, thus everyone had the potential to be beautiful:

Mia-Initial Post: I was just thinking that I find the thing that really bothers me about beauty is the subjectiveness. I think that's what gets me ... Maybe I don't have a strong enough positive opinion on my looks which allows other people's OPINIONS (NOT FACTS) to determine how I feel. I should probably tell myself every single day that I am beautiful.

Kathy and Roger agreed with Mia's opinion about beauty, but other members did not. One woman pointed out that Angelina Jolie (an American actress) is considered beautiful by many people. She believed those who disagreed were jealous of the "hype" around her beauty:

Female-Reply: I think there is SOME objectiveness in beauty. I see you mentioned Angelina Jolie in your other post, I think she is beautiful too and I don't believe people that say she is not. I think most people that say she is not are either jealous or just tired of the hype about her beauty. I think this is beautiful and I think most people would agree about her face being beautiful, and if they say no I think it's her style or something else that they hate.

Another male poster also believed that beauty is objective. He claimed: "Beauty is very objective. It's all about symmetry, good skin, golden ratios. 'Beauty is in the eye of beholder' or 'beauty is subjective' is what ugly people tell themselves and each other to feel better." The forum flamer also believed there was one objective standard of beauty:

Flamer-Reply: Beauty and ugliness are pretty objective. They basically come down to a few factors: 1. Symmetry 2. Proportion 3. Sexual Dimorphism 4. Coloring (e.g, smooth, even skin or healthy red lips) 5. Low body fat. If you have all of these, you're seen as beautiful. The fewer you have, the uglier you are.

Some forum members felt they did not measure up to societal standards for physical beauty. They believed only two standards existed: beauty or ugliness. This type of black-or-white thinking is typical of individuals with BDD.[7] The moderators did not dissuade participants from debating topics or stop members from flaming. Perhaps it was difficult for them to distinguish between disagreements and arguments. As a result, the forum moderators let members regulate each other's comments. Most times, the forum leaders took on the role of *arbiter*[8] when they judged whether content posted to the forum was appropriate. Roger took on the arbiter role when he disapproved of Fran's decision to raise awareness about BDD on Facebook.

FRAN AND ROGER COLLIDE

Fran liked to share her personal triumphs and struggles with forum members. She was proud of herself for posting information about BDD on her Facebook page:

> **Fran-Initial Post:** I just did a massive difficult thing!!!!!!! I shared a page on my facebook about BDD, and also wrote some short information of how common and under-diagnosed it is, but very disabling. Linked to a couple of pages to find more info, to be able to understand and support a family member/friend. I'm excited and scared, but mostly proud that I took this decision and went through with it.

Roger did not approve of her actions; he believed posting on Facebook did little to increase public awareness about the disorder:

> **Roger Reply 1:** I don't agree though that force feeding information about BDD to other people on facebook is the right way to go about it though. People, in general, aren't interested in things that don't affect them or people in their circle and although your family, partner, friends etc might be interested most people will probably scoff at it. The main thing is that BDD is better known than it was 10 years ago, which is better than it was 10 years before it and that's the way to look at it I think.

Roger and Fran each had firm convictions about how to help individuals with BDD. Roger advocated for the BDD forum and provided support to his extended "BDD family." Fran wanted to raise awareness among her friends and family members using social media. She accused Roger of giving up and being selfish in terms of not teaching others about the disorder. She added that the post had received a positive response:

Fran-Reply 2 (OP): No offense, but it sounds a bit as giving up. And not seeing further than to your own self and that YOU don't need to explain YOURSELF.

Just like any foundation wants to spread their knowledge about Breast cancer, Prostate cancer, Stroke or whatever it might be, I am doing my part on a subject which I am passionate about. You are entitled to your own opinion, but a "force feeding" of information to open people's eyes, I think some years ago when you weren't this laid back about your BDD, you might have appreciated it. (Just to add that the post had a positive response.)

Kathy came to Roger's defense by asking Fran why she was criticizing Roger and expressed admiration for his opinions:

Kathy-Reply 3: How does what Roger say sound like he is giving up? All he is saying is that for him it doesn't matter what people think, if they know they know it doesn't embarrass him or make him feel ashamed, and I think that's great! I hope to be like that one day, because the only person in my life that actually really knows me and about bdd is my boyfriend, I can't bear the thought of anyone knowing about it.

Roger, Kathy, Mia, and Janet formed connections that extended beyond the BDD forum. Their friendship supplemented the support offered by family members and significant others. Healthy support groups consist of members who are emotionally tied to one another and who are viewed as important or influential in one another's lives.[9] The friendships they formed may have made their bonds stronger, while excluding members like Fran, who did not belong in their primary group.

ROGER TARGETS THE FORUM FLAMER

Roger was appointed forum moderator in 2014 and posted two additional rules for members (Appendix B10). BDD members could no longer ask for or send photographs to other members without moderator approval. In addition, members could no longer recommend plastic surgery procedures as an effective treatment for BDD symptoms:

> **Roger (Moderator)-Initial Post:** In keeping with the principles of the forum rules and the purpose of the forum as a support forum, we wish to clarify what is acceptable with regards to mentioning cosmetic surgery on the forum. Cosmetic surgery is universally regarded as a bad treatment plan for people suffering with Body Dysmorphic Disorder. Medical professionals/psychologists etc strictly advise against cosmetic surgery as a method of combating the symptoms of BDD. Offering treatment advice that is contrary to professional opinion is strictly against the rules.

Roger concluded by summarizing his vision for the forum—to help members cope with BDD symptoms and to provide a safe and pleasant experience for members:

> We want this forum to be a pleasant experience for all, where members can discuss their experience with BDD without the more unpleasant aspect of malicious intent from anyone who may have an agenda which does not involve the betterment of yourself and people around you. If you see anything unpleasant, anything you feel is not beneficial to the treatment of others or anything that breaks these rules then please feel free to use the report function in the top right hand corner of a post or contact a moderator. Thanks for your co-operation and understanding.

These rules seemed to target the Flamer's desire to have members send him their pictures to determine if they were pretty or ugly. The forum flamer also urged members to get plastic surgery to fix their perceived flaws. Roger and the other leaders wanted to keep members safe from people with "malicious intent," like the forum flamer. Active members in online forums often act as quality control by correcting misinformation and by providing empathy, encouragement, advice, and information to other members.[10]

I found it reassuring that Roger was able to regain control of the BDD forum by becoming a moderator. His passion and dedication to the forum were admirable, especially considering that the active members and moderators were volunteers. Many peer support groups are facilitated by volunteers who truly care about helping those affected by mental health disorders like BDD. Please take the opportunity to participate in an online or local peer support group. Your participation will enable you to connect with and support others with BDD.

PART SIX
CONCLUSION

Support Group Pros
and Cons

Roger-Reply: Honestly there is nothing wrong with talking to people about any of this, even if it's just on the forum for now, and then eventually a doctor maybe if you feel you need to. We are always here though if you feel you need to vent anything out, that's what this forum is for.

Mia-Initial Post: I'm getting to a point where I'm so sick of the ups and downs and I feel like talking about it almost makes it worse. I've been extremely depressed before and talking helped me but I feel like talking about BDD just makes me think about it more. So I feel lonely and lost, like no matter how many people said I'm pretty it wouldn't matter because I'll never think I am.

Benefits

There are multiple benefits to participating in a supportive online community. For BDD forum members, these benefits included finding other people who understood their experiences; having easy access to peer support; learning more about BDD symptoms, diagnosis, and treatment; and developing supportive relationships. In particular,

Roger, Kathy, Mia, and Janet formed personal connections and friendships that extended beyond the BDD forum.

People Who Understand: "We all understand"

BDD forum members were able to connect with others who understood the disorder. A young woman felt out of place in a therapy group for general anxiety disorder. She was more comfortable on the BDD forum since members could understand what she was going through:

> **Female-Initial Post:** I didn't go to group last week and I honestly don't plan on going back. I attended a couple of group therapies before and made a lot of progress. One was for general unhappiness with life and the other was for helping with assertiveness. I just feel out of place at the one I'm at now. I want to let people know about my issues, but I feel like things are moving too fast. I posted on here because I feel like at least people on this board will understand what I'm going through. I fear that people at group will tell me I have nothing to worry about. I'm not strong enough to face that possibility.

Another member valued the support she had received on BDD Central. She assured a new member the BDD forum could help since everyone understood the disorder:

> **Female-Reply:** the forum I was previously on worked wonders for me. This forum may help you quite a bit. Just knowing that others go through the SAME stuff as you makes it easier to endure. It kind of helps you put a perspective on things and helps you realize that other people have been where you have been...some are almost recovered, some are getting by...some are only just getting better, but we all understand.

There are benefits to being part of a supportive community consisting of people who share the same condition. Similar others have an in-depth understanding that primary group members may lack. Also, it may not be easy to ask for or get support from loved ones. Family members and friends may withdraw due to the person's excessive reassurance-seeking and social anxiety. Individuals with BDD often avoid social situations due to fears about being rejected for their perceived appearance flaws.[1] I did not reveal my BDD symptoms to family members until after I recovered. My fear was they would either criticize me for having a mental health disorder or agree that my perceived appearance flaws were real.

Easy Access to Support: "You can talk to me"

Online support groups (like the BDD forum) enable individuals to disclose their problems, vent negative emotions, and get help. People can retain their cloak of anonymity and still receive information, advice, and support anytime, at no cost. In contrast, there are significant barriers to seeking professional help, including fear and shame, uncertainty about how to get help, ineffective diagnosis and treatment, and the cost of therapy (Chapter 11). Peer support groups encourage individuals to take responsibility for their own care and seek support when needed.

One woman was alone without her boyfriend and was obsessing about her appearance flaws. She was taking multiple videos of herself, crying, and felt like throwing up. She had to be at work in less than two hours, so she posted to the forum: "I'm so depressed I'm just laying around crying and staring at every angle of my face in the mirror completely obsessing over it figuring out how to fix things but I can't. HELP. 😞😞 " Mia was one of the first members to respond. She empathized and offered to talk with her: "you can talk to me if you want. I'm 22 too and I understand. I hope you made it through your shift alright, it's hard to work customer service when the last thing you want people to do is look at you. i hope you're feeling better..."

Research has shown that self-help and mutual-help groups are among the most effective vehicles for fostering empowerment in participants, especially in the context of mental health-related conditions. This is because support groups are directly associated with the three main attributes of individual empowerment. First is reliance on self and peers, rather than on authoritative professionals, which contributes to a sense of personal competence. Next is voluntary participation and free choice, which contribute to feelings of self-determination. Finally, peoples' perceptions of social engagement are enhanced by helping others and socially identifying with others.[2]

KNOWLEDGE IS POWER: "YOUR RESPONSES REALLY HELPED"

Online support groups can foster individual empowerment through the exchange of information perceived to be relevant, credible, and reliable. It is not only access to information that empowers people; it is the ability to share information with others. Both the receiver and provider are empowered, with the latter taking the role of guide, instructor, or helper.[3]

Two men who posted recovery stories (Chapter 13) could have served as positive role models for other members. Kathy wanted to learn more about CBT after reading one man's recovery story. She was also encouraged to know BDD could be beaten: "Thanks for your post. 😊 it's really inspiring and motivating. It's great to hear from someone who is beating BDD!" A female member was looking forward to getting treatment based on advice from Roger and Fran: "Your responses really helped a lot and make me look forward to finally getting help. Luckily I have seen the therapist before so I will be comfortable talking with her."

Some of the empowering outcomes for participants in online support groups are increased help-seeking behavior[4] and motivation to seek therapeutic treatment.[5] Empowerment in online groups comes from exchanging information, encountering emotional support, finding recognition, sharing experiences, and helping others.[6, 7] Outcomes of participation in health-related support groups are reduced stress, increased positive coping, increased quality of life, reduced depression, and increased self-efficacy in managing one's health problems.[8]

Building Relationships: "This is a great thread"

Online communities like the BDD forum that lack vibrant graphics, in-depth member profiles, self-starting videos, and personal photographs, seem to be almost an anachronism in today's era of social networking sites. However, posting to the forum was preferable since members could form connections without comparing their appearance to their "friends" on Facebook. Part of projecting a positive self-image on Facebook is choosing to upload flattering photographs of oneself[9] and not disclosing health-related problems.[10]

BDD forum members were not allowed to share personal images on the site. Text-based messages (using emojis) enabled them to connect with others without revealing their physical appearance. They built relationships by seeking and sharing personal experiences, information, advice, and social support. Connecting to other people with similar experiences can become the reason for joining an online group, remaining a member, and providing support to others.[11]

The development of interpersonal relationships was evident when Roger, Kathy, Mia, and Janet greeted one another by name, validated each other's comments, and chatted in the "Off Topic" thread Roger started. The four forum leaders used the Off Topic thread to create their own forum—a quasi-public place to deepen their relationships. A former BDD Central member started a creativity thread to replace one from the defunct site. Several members replied, including Kathy and Fran:

> **Male-Initial Post:** We used to have a drawing thread in BDD Central, so we could institute a similar one here too 😀
>
> You can post your creative artwork for others to see. I am making some ancient city miniature sets, ancient Greek and Babylonian
>
> **Fran-Reply 1:** Such cute little things. How did you make them?
>
> **Male-Reply 2 (OP):** Thanks 😀 These were made as 3d models using the free modelling program Blender.

Kathy-Reply 3: This is a great thread 😄 I'm not very creative so I'm not sure I'll have anything to offer, but I will enjoy seeing what everyone else has to offer.

Building personal relationships in support groups can be beneficial for people with BDD. Doing so can alter a person's dysfunctional (and often abusive) relationship with one's appearance. The primary relationship most people with BDD have is with their distorted body image. BDD support groups enable participants to develop genuine, authentic, and healthy relationships with other human beings.[12] Participants are able to connect with other people and increase their social well-being.[13]

DRAWBACKS

There were potential downsides to joining the BDD forum, despite the benefits offered by participating in a supportive online community. These included feeling worse rather than better, getting poor advice from other members, reading nasty comments, and having the group disappear (like BDD Central). I often felt worse after reading the many disturbing messages by forum members. I was further dismayed by the forum flamer trying to convince members they were ugly, and I was disappointed by Fran's desire to leave the forum.

FEELING WORSE: "I REALLY WANTED TO HELP"

Reading and posting messages to the BDD forum could increase members' negative thoughts and feelings. For example, Mia found sharing her experiences made her feel less alone but more obsessed with her appearance flaws: "this forum helped me a lot and made me feel like I wasn't alone, but it started consuming me and the more I came on here the more I thought about how ugly I am." Expressing negative feelings can bring about a cathartic experience and emotional relief for individuals with mental health conditions.[14] However, sharing negative emotions and experiences can be maladaptive when people continue to ruminate on them. Continued rumination makes negative feelings more salient, intensifying feelings of stress, anxiety, and shame.[15]

Fran wanted to make friends, get help, and provide support to other people, especially those who were suicidal. However, she felt her efforts and positive comments were not appreciated nor reciprocated. Thus, one month after joining the forum, she wanted to leave and asked the moderators to delete her posts and blog content.

Fran believed people with BDD were too self-focused to provide proper support to others: "But it is not a strange thing, we are so very preoccupied with our selves, so how can we dedicate proper support to a stranger?" Fran replied to her post about wanting to leave the forum by explaining her reasons to the moderators and other members (Appendix B9). She rhetorically asked whether participating in the forum had made her feel better and if she had been able to help others. Fran responded negatively to both questions:

> **Fran-Reply 1 (OP):** In this forum though I have found it hard to relate to others, except in the beginning when I saw there were more with BDD. That's as far as it reached.
>
> In the end we have two questions to ask:
> Is my contribution here making others feel better?
> Is my membership here making ME feel better?
>
> I think in my case both answers are NO. Therefore I have to go where I can do more use.
>
> I hope that this forum will continue to be a very useful page for those who seek support, comfort and answers. It was just not right for me, it kind of hurt me more than it helped. I was seeking a normality within this chaos. Just some understanding.
>
> I hope that anyone at all has had any kind of use in whatever I have written, I have always good intentions, I really wanted to help.

Two forum members replied to her post. One woman advised Fran to keep her posts on the forum to help sort out her feelings:

Female-Reply 2: What i would like to say is just hang on, don't be quick to delete your posts as now you are still facing problems. Just keep your posts as references to help you sort out your feelings.

Another member provided reasons why Fran's positivity was not appreciated on the forum: people with BDD preferred to focus on their problems rather than on finding concrete solutions:

Undetermined-Reply 3: Your reasons for leaving are exactly the reasons I had for leaving BDD central forums: positivity doesn't seem to be welcome. I think that's just how forums for people with certain mental issues work. They serve as an outlet for people to be like "omg, I'm in the same sucky situation, I feel less alone now", but they don't focus enough on finding concrete solutions to get out of that paralyzing mindset. People who are enthusiastic and try to bring some positivity quickly get dragged down by everyone else's negativity.

Fran was encouraged by the responses to her post. Rather than leaving the forum, she stayed and continued providing support to other members.

Fran-Reply 4 (OP): Firstly, thank you both for your understanding and great replies. I was honestly expecting an attack from various places, I am really grateful that somebody can relate to this.

As Fran's comments indicate, online groups can both enhance and impede participants' ability to cope with symptoms. She posted on good days when she felt confident and happy, though these were rare. However, she rarely received positive responses, and sometimes her posts were criticized by others. Fran spent a lot of time on a drawing she posted to the creativity thread but only received two responses: "Posted a wonderful drawing which I am very proud of, but it seems like it was too much, and nobody wanted to give complements...why?? I cannot have BDD and be talented and successful and smart? I am, but I am also often in suicidal thoughts, I am fighting with them on a daily basis."

Fran was trying to make friends on the forum and get positive feedback for her accomplishments. She wanted to be able to connect with other members, hug them, and provide ongoing support. Being unable to connect physically with others is one of the disempowering processes of online support forums. Other downsides include inappropriate behavior (being verbally attacked), declining real-life relationships, and information overload and misinformation.[16] BDD forum members also received poor advice, along with inappropriate responses to messages, and were targeted by the forum flamer's nasty comments.

INAPPROPRIATE ADVICE: "THAT IS AWFUL ADVICE"

Information and advice provided on the BDD forum were anecdotal and could contain inaccurate or potentially harmful information, such as when forum members recommended cosmetic surgery or taking steroids to improve one's appearance. For example, one male poster lamented that he was being rejected by women. The first poster who responded recommended taking steroids as a solution. Another member replied to both by discouraging the use of steroids: "That is awful advice to give somebody. If a woman says she does not like a guy who takes steroids then she means it. Taking steroids will NOT make you appear more manly and it won't boost your confidence."

Fortunately, when posters gave poor advice to others, the forum leaders, moderators, or other members offered advice that was more in line with professional clinicians and therapists. In the previous example, another person suggested the original poster get clinical treatment to help his symptoms: "Go to a doctor, tell them you have BDD. It's not easy to do but you will never regret it once you finally take that step." The forum primarily contained supportive replies to others' posts, and inappropriate advice was usually corrected by the moderators and other members.

Some members, like the forum flamer, seemed to lack empathy or compassion for others' suffering. The young woman who felt too ugly to live (Chapter 7) had recovered from anorexia and then gained weight. As a result, she felt fat and disgusting. Her boyfriend told her she was attractive, but she believed he was lying. The forum flamer and another man were the first to provide advice and reassurance about her appearance:

Male-Reply 1: If you are fat, you shouldn't have BDD about it, since it is easily fixable with the right diet and exercise.

Flamer-Reply 2: If you have a boyfriend who wants to marry you, then you probably aren't ugly. Also if people compliment your looks often, that's another sign.

If you were truly ugly, you wouldn't have friends, much less a boyfriend, and you wouldn't receive compliments on your looks.

Offering reassurance and advice about fixing one's appearance does not help people with BDD.[17] Fortunately, Kathy responded with sympathy, empathy, and an offer to help her:

Kathy-Reply 3: Hi, welcome to the forum 😃 I'm so sorry that you are going through all of this! Thanks for sharing your story, I can relate with some of the things you have said and it's awful.

Are you receiving any treatment for this? I hope you like the forum, feel free to join any discussions or message me if you ever need to talk about anything.

The young woman thanked them all for their replies and attempts to help her. She subsequently congratulated Kathy for seeking help from her GP (Appendix B8):

Female-Reply 6 (OP): Congratulations, that must have taken a lot for you to go and seek help. 😃 I'm sure it will be a very positive experience for you once you are able to talk to someone professional about this. I think I might try and do the same. I live in Ireland and have health insurance but for some reason, it doesn't cover me for therapy, I don't think. Crazy world. 😮

Nasty Comments: "Be skeptical of BDD"

Most members and the forum leaders responded with empathy, compassion, and helpful advice to those who needed support. However, the forum flamer provided inappropriate advice and nasty comments in his messages. He urged members to be skeptical about BDD and instead get surgery to fix their flaws (Chapter 16):

> **Flamer-Initial Post:** If you are legitimately ugly, then your best option is to correct what is making you unattractive. If after correcting these problems you still believe you are ugly, then perhaps you should seek a counselor. But do NOT be lured by the comforting diagnosis of BDD, which seems to suggest that no one is ugly. That's a fairy tale.

Kathy vented her anger and frustration over his nasty comments because she had felt comfortable expressing herself on the forum before they were posted:

> **Kathy-Initial Post:** I just wanted to say that in all the time I've been here I've never seen this place so negative and with so many blunt and in my opinion nasty comments! This is supposed to be a place where we can come for support, to talk to others like our selves or even to meet new people and have a little fun! It's not a place to point out people's flaws or to put them down!
>
> In the last couple weeks I've never felt so down because of this forum! I normally can't wait to come here, to let my self be myself! No one knows about my problems and here is the only place I can freely talk about it.

To be honest I don't understand why the moderators haven't done anything about this!

If you want to be horrible to someone then quite frankly piss off and do it somewhere else because I've had enough of this! How dare people come and behave like this, I hope you realise your posts could be the fine line between someone severely hurting themselves or not! Because I know you've put me in a bad place! I've been working so hard to feel better and to not SH but coming here is making me feel worse now! Not better like it was before. Grow up!!!!!!!!

Kathy wanted the moderators to block the nasty comments, but they were unable to delete the forum flamer's messages. The forum regulations did not allow them to delete posts: "Please understand that for technical reasons and in accordance with the rules of the forum we will be unable to accommodate requests to delete." As a result, the Flamer's thread urging people to be skeptical about BDD remained on the forum and became the most viewed post from 2012 to 2021.

THE GROUP IS GONE: "NO WARNING OR NUTHIN!"

Peer support groups are valuable stepping stones on one's journey to recovery. However, they may be removed, cease to exist, or stop being active. For ten years, the BDD Central website was a thriving hub of support for millions of members. Then without warning, it ceased to exist. Think about returning home after a trip to find your house gone. Not burned down, not in ruins, but nonexistent. That is the loss BDD Central members faced on September 28, 2012. The BDD forum is also no longer active. The most recent messages were posted in September 2021.

The post Roger started by asking "Where has BDD Central gone?" (Chapter 15) had more than two hundred replies between September 2012 and March 2014. One member posted a notice from Britney (the founder), explaining what had happened to the site. She lost control of the domain and was unable to get it back: "the domain is no longer pointing to the host, so nobody can even access the site or forums. What complicates things, is I got a new computer, and have limited information on what I did over a decade ago...trying to remember passwords and contact information is proving to be very challenging! Hopefully we can get this remedied. And thanks for the heads up that people are aware and standing by....please let them know, I'm looking into it :)"

Fortunately, there are multiple online support groups, podcasts, forums, and treatment resources available on the International OCD Foundation and BDD Foundation websites. Peer support groups work best when combined with therapy and other sources of support. Remember, even in your darkest hour, you are not alone. There are suicide prevention resources, books, and clinics that offer inpatient and outpatient treatment (Appendix A). Find people to support you, care about you, and help you overcome your BDD symptoms. You CAN win the battle with your BDD bully. Create a strong network of support to help you succeed.

Moving Beyond BDD

Male-Reply: Regardless of whatever ways we may put ourselves down, we exist on this planet and we are all trying to be happy in this life, and i really really hope that one day we can all come out of this fully recovered and look back on it as a thing of the past.

This book fulfills my goal from fifteen years ago to share people's personal experiences with BDD and to increase awareness about the disorder. My lengthy dissertation has become a useful tool for people with BDD, along with their friends and loved ones. I knew when I started my dissertation research that my story was one of many. The hundreds of messages I read confirmed that. Every person who posted had a different perspective on the topic of BDD. Although our symptoms are similar, we are all different.

Twenty-five years ago, I diagnosed myself with BDD. I started the Recovery from BDD online support group in 2021 for those suffering from BDD symptoms. I was inspired by Roger, who was committed to supporting BDD forum members since he considered them part of his extended BDD family. I have come to realize that everyone I met during my recovery journey is part of my BDD family. BDD has had a significant impact on my life for almost forty years. My symptoms began when I was sixteen, my treatment and recovery took place from 2000 to 2002, I completed my dissertation in 2016, and I started two peer support groups during the pandemic.

I am thankful I sought medical treatment for the disorder. However, for many people, there are considerable barriers to getting professional help. Seeking peer support may also seem difficult. But what is the alternative? To keep struggling for years with feelings of self-hatred, anger, shame, guilt, anxiety, and depression?

For fifteen years, I was convinced being beautiful would lead to happiness and success. As a result, I felt miserable when comparing my life to others who seemed to have everything I desired. It breaks my heart to read posts from young men and women so consumed with delusional beliefs about their appearance they want to commit suicide. I understand these feelings of self-hatred; I had them myself. But there is so much more value to a human being than what appears on the outside, and there are so many ways to cope with and overcome BDD symptoms.

Some forum members echoed my feelings about beauty when I had the disorder. The best example was the conversation about beauty being objective versus subjective: "Beauty is very objective. It's all about symmetry, good skin, golden ratios. 'Beauty is in the eye of beholder' or 'beauty is subjective' is what ugly people tell themselves and each other to feel better." I know this thinking is reinforced by modern society, where seeking outer perfection seems like an attainable goal—a goal that is reinforced by the many social media influencers who peddle the illusion that beauty is a commodity to be bought and sold. This is the reason so many people with BDD (including myself) get cosmetic surgery; it's a socially acceptable answer to the perceived problem of being ugly or unattractive.

Maybe for other people, plastic surgery provides good outcomes. Maybe other people are satisfied and pleased by the results. People with BDD are more often angry and upset and may become suicidal. This does not always happen, and some people on the forum were pleased with the results of one (or more) procedures. However, they were still not happy with their appearance and often hated how they looked. This is because the disorder cannot be fixed with surgery, only with therapy.

Work with a skilled psychiatrist and/or psychologist to begin your road to recovery. However, know that recovery can be difficult and may take years. Reach out to your peers on online forums and in support groups, and find a therapist you like and trust. These are the first steps to take, and the ones that will help you move beyond BDD.

I still have "good face days and bad face days," to quote one of the older forum posters. There are days when I am pleased with my appearance and other days when I wish I looked younger, thinner, etc. But the wish is not an obsession, and I don't lament getting older, since doing so is the cost of living. Everyone faces struggles, hardships, and problems, no matter how wonderful their lives look from an outsider's perspective. I hope that by reading other peoples' stories and BDD experiences, you have learned more about the disorder and how to get help. I wish you much success on your recovery journey. Do not lose hope; no matter where you are on the road to recovery, keep moving forward, and you will reach your goal.

APPENDIX A: BDD
RESOURCES

The resources provided in Appendix A are for reference only and are not personally endorsed by the author. The author has made every effort to confirm the reliability and accuracy of the resources provided. The author is not liable for any errors or omissions in the resources or for any use you or others may make of the resources.

A1: ORGANIZATIONS AND WEBSITES

BDD Foundation
45b Stanford Road
London, London N11 3HY
United Kingdom
https://bddfoundation.org/

International OCD Foundation
P.O. Box 961029
Boston, MA 02196
https://bdd.iocdf.org/

Mental Health America
500 Montgomery Street, Suite 820
Alexandria, VA 22314
https://www.mhanational.org/

National Alliance on Mental Illness (NAMI)
4301 Wilson Blvd., Suite 300
Arlington, VA 22203
https://www.nami.org/

A2: SUICIDE PREVENTION RESOURCES

Suicide Prevention Resources USA

- Mental Health Hotline: **988**
- National Suicide Prevention Lifeline: **1-800-273-TALK (8255); En Español 1-888-628-9454**
- Use the online Lifeline Crisis Chat
- For more information, visit the National Suicide Prevention Lifeline
- Connect 24/7 to a crisis counselor by texting the Crisis Text Line: Text **HOME** to **741741**
- National Institute on Mental Health (NIMH): https://www.nimh.nih.gov/health/topics/suicide-prevention

Suicide Prevention Resources UK

- Samaritans – **Call 116 123** (open 24 hours, 365 days a year) or email jo@samaritans.org for a reply within 24 hours
- HOPELineUK (for young people up to the age of 35) – **Call 0800 068 41 41** (open weekdays 10 a.m.–10 p.m., weekends 2 p.m.–10 p.m.), text **07786 209697** or email pat@papyrus-uk.org

- Shout Crisis Text Line – **Text "SHOUT" to 85258** to start a conversation with a trained Shout Volunteer, or text "YM" if you're under 19.
- Saneline: **Call 08457 67 80 00** (open every day, 6 p.m.–11 p.m.)

Suicide Prevention Resources Canada

- Talk Suicide Canada: **1-833-456-4566;** Quebec: **1-866-277-3553**
- **Text 45645** (4pm-midnight ET)

A3: BDD CLINICS AND THERAPISTS

Bio Behavioral Institute
Fugen Neziroglu, PhD
935 Northern Blvd
Great Neck, NY 11021
516-487-7116
www.biobehavioralinstitute.com
info@biobehavioralinstitute.com

Center for OCD and Related Disorders
Sabine Wilhelm, PhD
Massachusetts General Hospital
185 Cambridge Street, Suite 2000
Boston, MA 02114
www.mghocd.org
617-726-6766
cordclinic@mgh.harvard.edu

Harvard Medical School
Roberto Olivardia, PhD
57 Bedford Street
Suite 230
Lexington, MA 02420
781-999-3000
roberto_olivardia@hms.harvard.edu

Instituto Bio – Behavioral
Tania Borda
Teléfono: 4812 5904
Celular: +54 9 11 3358-5496
Sede CABA: Av. del Libertador 930 piso 4° 2do cuerpo
Sede Zona Norte: Gral. Las Heras 2145, Florida
info@institutobiobehavioral.com

Los Angeles BDD & Body Image Clinic
Arie Winograd, MA, LMFT
310-741-2000
http://www.BDDclinic.com

Obsessive-Compulsive Disorders Institute
McLean Hospital
115 Mill St.
Belmont, MA 02478
617-855-2776
ocdiadmissions@partners.org
https://www.mcleanhospital.org/treatment/ocd-institute

OCD NYC
Steven Poskar, MD
308 East 38th St., Suite 201
New York, NY 10016
646-415-7268
https://www.ocdnyc.com/

Spectrum Neuroscience and Treatment Institute
Eric Hollander, MD
901 Fifth Avenue
New York, NY 10021
646-351-0220
https://spectrumneuroscience.com/

The BDD and OCD Centre of Greater New York
Robyn Leigh Stern, LCSW, PC
Teletherapy (New York, California, New Jersey, Florida)
917-232-7788
www.rlsterntherapy.com
bddresources@gmail.com

The Gateway Institute
Chris Trondsen, MS, AMFT, APCC
940 S. Coast Dr. #235
Costa Mesa, CA 92626
christrondsen@gatewayocd.com
714-549-1030
https://www.gatewayocd.com/

The OCD-BDD Clinic of Northern California
Scott M. Granet, LCSW
501 Seaport Court, Suite 106
Redwood City, CA 94063
650-599-3325
sgranet@ocd-bddclinic.com
www.ocd-bddclinic.com

Weill Cornell Psychiatry Specialty Center
Katharine Phillips, MD
315 East 62nd Street
New York, NY 10065
646-962-2820
https://weillcornell.org/katharine-phillips-md
www.katharinephillipsmd.com

A4: SELF-DIAGNOSIS INFORMATION

BDD Foundation: https://bddfoundation.org/information/do-i-have-bdd-test/

International OCD Foundation: https://bdd.iocdf.org/about-bdd/do-i-have-bdd/

A5: BOOKS ABOUT BDD

- Baughan, R. (2008). *The butterfly girl.* William Clowes.
- Claiborn, J., & Pedrick, C. (2002). *The BDD workbook: Overcome body dysmorphic disorder and end body image obsessions.* New Harbinger Publications.
- Cuban, B. (2013). *Shattered image: My triumph over body dysmorphic disorder.* Net Minds Corporation.
- Fugen, N. (2012). *Overcoming body dysmorphic disorder: A cognitive behavioral approach to reclaiming your life.* New Harbinger Publications.
- Granet, S. (2020). *Body dysmorphic disorder, mine and yours: A personal and clinical perspective.* Toplight.
- Phillips, K. A. (2005). *The broken mirror: Understanding and treating body dysmorphic disorder.* Oxford University Press.
- Phillips, K. A. (2009). *Understanding body dysmorphic disorder: An essential guide.* Oxford University Press.

- Phillips, K. A. (Ed.) (2017). *Body dysmorphic disorder: Advances in research and clinical practice.* Oxford University Press.
- Schnackenberg, N., & Petro, S. (Eds.) (2016). *Reflections on body dysmorphic disorder.* Body Dysmorphic Disorder Foundation.
- Veale, D., Willson, R., & Clarke, A. (2009). *Overcoming body image problems including body dysmorphic disorder (overcoming books).* Constable & Robinson, LTD.
- Westwood, S. (2012). *Body dysmorphic disorder-memoir.* Chipmunka Publishing.
- Wilhelm, S. (2006). *Feeling good about the way you look: A program for overcoming body image problems.* The Guilford Press.
- Winograd, A. M. (2017). *Face to face with body dysmorphic disorder.* Taylor & Francis Group.
- Wolf, J. (2003). *Mirror mirror off the wall: A personal experience of intertwined obsessive/compulsive spectrum disorders: Body dysmorphic disorder and trichotillomania.* Writers Club Press.

APPENDIX B:
MESSAGES (FULL TEXT)

Certain online forum quotes originally authored by third parties are published in the book for education and informational purposes only and qualify as a fair use under federal law. The uses and integrations of quotations from online forums are made for fair use purposes, such as criticism, comment, education, research, teaching, and scholarship. If you wish to use any copyrighted materials for purposes that go beyond "fair use," you must obtain permission from the copyright owner.

B1: FRAN'S STORY/INTRODUCTION POST

Fran-Initial Post: Body dysmorphic disorder is a disorder of how we perceive ourselves. Thats why I dont think this is what I got, but I may exaggerate my feeling of ugliness? I dont think so, but one thing is for sure, and that is that it is interfering with my life, and I have reached a point of absolute totally exhaustion and hopelessness.

My story:

I am 28. I have a very demanding life which had made me come to the very top of all my frustrations. I am a medical student in my last year. I have managed until now in a way i dont understand how it was possible.

I think I am ugly, since I can remember. Not in the way that i have a big nose or ears or so, but i think its the mix of them all, my fathers eyes, the eyebrows that are long gone (little left), and all the little small things...that together just created a nasty reflection in the mirror. I wear makeup ALL THE TIME. Also when I sleep. I wake up, first thing i do is check the mirror to know what the day will have in store for me. It is almost always a big dissapointment, sometimes a smaller dissapointment which may be corrected if lucky. Every morning, looking with fear and some hope into that mirror, as if i wait for my face to have changed all of the sudden over the night.

I try to hide being ugly from any person by wearing make up. But it doesnt always work to spend 5 hours per day, washing off putting on washing off putting on, sometimes i just remain ugly and there is exhaustion, facial, mental. I dont know what to do, i have reached the end, there is no way out of this. If i was to make surgeries to my face, it will take ages to afford, what am i to do until then? Will surgery even help, I dont even know where i would start? Eye shape? Make my allready normal nose perfect? Since I can look somewhat normal with the right way of make up, I think that some kind of eye re-shaping would benefit me.If the eyes are crap, it doesnt matter the rest.

Make up used to work for me, at least enough times so that i could be showing myself in public, live for kind of life, even though i try to hide as much as i can. Now it just doesnt cut it, rarely rarely do the makeup sessions create something relatively normal. When they do, i can go out, by food, and go to classes, just to accidentally look into a mirror somewhere which just turns my world around and makes me depressed and want to run home as soon as possible.

This is very disabling, and inhibits greatly me from having a normal live like i want. People have commented on my make up, that i wear too much, wrong colour etc etc. I hate it and feel ashamed of that too, but if I could choose, Id rather have them speaking bad about my makeup then about how ugly I am.

When I was little, I didnt have thoughts about beauty or ugly, life just happens. And as years pass I realize that i do not look good. I experimented with hair and clothes to make me look better, this was a young age still. I recall a day when I was wearing my makeup for one of the first times... what a difference in peoples approach to me. I looked much better, and guys told me i was pretty for the first time. Since then, I understand how different beautiful people are treated on a normal basis. When I manage to make myself look ok, I notice how people act differently, they act normal. I feel then almost normal, but at the same time sad that it has to be like this. This word is not made for me.

I have had a relatively normal life despite all this, because of the many many hours spent doing makeup. I have had my wild party years, the many boyfriends and the normal life, but always this shaddow was above me, in my secrecy, doing makeup to survive the next day.

The "bad mirrors", is a common thing for me. I can be relatively ok with how i look in one mirror, but looking into another may show a very ugly person. And when i am in the stores, shopping, looking in my reflection, I hope that what i see will be ok, but it rarely is, and i start to look only down at the ground, wishing i could be home faster.

Psychologists may want to related this ugly-feeling to a deeper personal insecurity, but I really must disagree, at least in my case. I am a very talented woman, on my "good days" i am the most social and fun person, and there is nothing I cannot do, I am VERY good at most sports, smart and intelligent in my studies, inventive, handy, loving and caring of humans and animals, and I think I am really a great person that can accomplish anything. I just wish my face would match all this. I just wish to be looking ok, to be able to fullfill my life. And my lovely boyfriends life.

How shall we go from here? I have seen there are many like me, and even though surgery (in best case) may help, until I can afford that there are many days that i need to get through. Many frustrated exhausted moments, which will make me wish I was dead. Because that what I do wish when everything is bad, I just dont want to do this anymore. I love the outline of my life, the medical degree that is just a year away, my fantastic one in a million boyfriend and the wonderful future we can have. But my face doesnt match this...

Why do we have to accept that we look ugly? And even if other people saw me without makeup, and thought i wasnt ugly (which i really doubt), that wouldnt make a difference to me. I am so unsatisfied with the way I was created to look. This look, one look, to live though this one life. It is just not fair.

And why do I feel ashamed of feeling ugly? I dont know, maybe because the world and the human mind is created to love beauty and hate ugly. Push the ugly away.

I know this is not a delusion by me, because I notice in every way the day I manage to look ok, normal, pretty, rarely beautiful, the difference in how the world greets me. It is right here, infront of me, the proof.

I think my biggest fear is to loose my fantastic boyfriend because of my problems, or that he will agree with me that i do look ugly without makeup. Or that people will go around saying how can that handsome guy be together with that ugly girl. My boyfriend has during these 4,5 years together never seen me completely without makeup, allthough I have reveled an eye or eyebrow for him once in a while. Not even him saying he prefers me to have less make up, or that he will love me no matter how I look, is it changing the way I feel. I simple will not accept being ugly. And I cannot continue trying to put on makeup for hours, getting exhausted, get migraines daily, give up hope in life and wish I was gone. I just want to live my life.

B2: Coping with Suicidal Thoughts

Male-Reply: Do you have any strategies that you use for suicide prevention, i.e. what do you do or could you do to stop yourself?

Do you really want to die or is it that you want the pain to stop and you know no other way?

Try to remember that thoughts about suicide are just thoughts. They do not mean you have to act on them.

No matter how overwhelming the thoughts are or how often you have them, they don't mean that you will always have those thoughts.

Everyone goes through tough times and experiences times when things seem hopeless. It is possible to get through these times by creating your own 'tool kit' of coping strategies, which you can use when you're feeling suicidal or when things feel hopeless.

Some suggestions include:

Postpone any decision to end your life

While it may feel like you have to act now on your thoughts of suicide, try to postpone that decision. Keep a list of other things you can do to distract yourself.

This might include:
- watching a DVD
- going to the movies
- playing a game
- ringing a friend
- chatting on msn

- doing some exercise
- reading a book
- listening to music.

You can then put this into action when the suicidal feeling starts to surface. Many people report that by postponing a decision to die, they found that their life did change. They were able to get the support they needed and could move on to a better, happier place.

Although it may seem hard to reach out to someone and ask for help, and may seem like a bigger challenge than taking steps to commit suicide, it's important to reach out to others who might help you to see alternative ways of solving or thinking about a problem, and to help you to realise what is important to you, allowing you to have a more positive outlook.

You could tell a family member or friend, counsellor or any person that you feel comfortable with (this might also be a teacher or religious leader). If they don't believe you or don't want to listen, keep trying until someone else does. Sometimes people don't react well at first because they don't know how. This is not your fault, and although it may feel hard, don't give up!

If you are having difficulty speaking about what you're going through, you might start with sentences such as 'Right now, I'm feeling...', 'I think it started when...', 'I've been feeling this for...', 'My sleep has been...', 'Lately school/work/uni has been...'.

Or try writing something down and giving the paper to the other person if you're having real difficulty speaking.

If you are having difficulty talking to people you know, phone a crisis line.

Writing down your feelings, or keeping a journal, can be a great way of understanding your feelings and a particular situation. It can also help you think about alternative solutions to problems.

Sometimes people set goals which are almost unachievable and then feel worse when they cannot reach them. Try to set goals that are achievable for you, even if it's on a day by day, or hour by hour, basis. And remember to reward yourself too.

Psychiatrists are health workers who have special training in mental illnesses, including depression and suicide. Clinical psychologists have a similar training, but do not administer medication. You may be able to find them through your GP, your local community health centre, or through colleges of psychiatry and psychology. Some GPs and other allied health staff also do counselling. You may be able to obtain details through divisions of general practice in your area, and/or through your community health centre.

Secrets can be dangerous. It is important to tell someone in your offline life who can help you and can help you keep safe.

Remember that thoughts about taking your life are just thoughts. They do not mean you have to act on them - no matter how overwhelming the thoughts are or how often you have them. They also don't mean that you will always have those thoughts.

B3: GRANDMOTHER CAUSED BDD

Female-Initial Post: It's been ages since I posted on here, but I still come lurk sometimes. After a particularly triggering episode last night, I'm feeling the need for some advice/support.

Long story short, I was diagnosed with BDD a couple years ago, have been suffering with it almost all my life. Work with my therapist made it pretty clear to understand that a lot of my body issues started as a result of my Nana's constant comment and judgement of my looks when I was a child. She was extremely loving, but also, always telling me to suck in, "suck in that gut" etc. when I was a kid, despite the face that I was very scrawny as a child (underweight, by doctors). Twenty-some years later I'm still hearing her commentary in my mind, but I've done a lot of work to make a lot of improvements.

Last night while I was hanging out with Nana and my mom, Nana started in on something she's been going on about lately, which is her belief that my niece is overweight. My niece (we'll call her Jess, not real name) is not at all overweight, but she IS ten years old, which means of course she has the body of a ten year old, chubby cheeks, soft, belly the same size as her chest and hips, totally totally normal. But Nana keeps haranguing my mom to mention to my sister (Jess' mom) that she needs to put her on a diet, or maybe take her to the doctor and find out what he can do. Nana thinks Jess should quit ballet because she's too fat to be seen in a leotard. I tried to point out that she is NOT at all, and that even if she were overweight, as long as she enjoys ballet of course she should keep doing it, no matter what she looks like.

After another comment about how if maybe Jess could do some exercises so she didn't have such a "huge belly" I had to just leave, so I made an excuse about the playoffs starting, changed the subject and went into the other room to watch the NHL. But later when I went home, I had a full blown panic attack, spent most of the night crying, lost my no-cutting streak, and am still this morning fighting back tears. I refuse to let Nana do to my niece what she did to me. I don't want my niece to ever spend a night as a 29-year-old woman sobbing over pains that were instilled in her as a child by the ignorance of a grandmother (or in her case, great-grandma). Does anyone have any advice for handling this situation?

I realize that Nana's thinking on bodies and figures is as distorted as some of us; she's an extreme perfectionist and expects perfection is other people's physiques, to the point of being completely irrational. But just like me when I was a child, my niece doesn't know this, so she'll think that what Nana says is truth. What can I do to break the cycle?

B4: THE MOST BEAUTIFUL WOMAN

Female-Initial Post: Hi everyone.

I'm just looking for some support, because I'm tired of feeling alone all the time. I'm 22, and I was diagnosed with BDD about a 1-1/2 years ago.

Anyways, I hate myself. I have had an exceptionally low self esteem for as long as I can remember. I grew up with an overweight mother who was abused by my father and her boyfriend, and in turn, I was a witness to it. She's still overweight today. I'm about 5 pounds overweight technically- But I feel like a whale. One day I'll hate myself, the next I'm okay with myself until I see someone pretty, then it all goes to hell and I break down again. I constantly compare myself to every other woman, and I'm tired of it. I'm always on an emotional rollercoaster and I just can't stop it. 😢

I had an eating disorder when I was 16, and ended up extremely sick. My dad encouraged it by telling me "You'd be so much prettier if you weren't so chubby" and similar things. And when I finally started losing a ton of weight (I was 125 originally mind you) My dad would tell me how I was so pretty etc. The positive attention caused me to continue and get worse.

Then at 19, I had my daughter, and my BDD has just gotten worse. I remember when my daughter was a few weeks old and we flew out to visit family, I saw this 6 foot tall, blonde, perfect skinny, tanned woman, and I just broke down and cried right there. Things like this happen to me so often...And I just hate myself because of it. I have this horrible fascination with being "The most beautiful woman in the world" and since I'm not, I feel like I'm not worth anything...And I know everything I feel is totally illogical, but I can't stop. I get compliments all the time about my looks, and my first thought is "he must be lying to make me feel better"....And because of this mental insecurity, every relationship I have is a struggle. My ex husband and I argued constantly over my looks- he'd tell me how beautiful I was, and I would call him a liar....And of course the porn thing- I can't handle that like a normal woman...I see that as the guy needing to look at other naked women because I'm ugly.... And as unrealistic as it is, I've always wanted so badly to be the most beautiful woman my guy has ever seen...and I know I'm not, so it kills me inside.

I'm sorry I'm rambling...I've just never had to explain this before, and I just need some support....I hate hating myself...but even if I could stop, I don't think I would- I'd be too afraid....I just hate being so screwed up, because I obsess over every little thing and I can't stop...Please tell me I'm not alone....

Female-Reply: Your text really struck a cord with me, because you've expressed very well what it's like. Isn't it weird how a person, probably on the other side of the world, can express exactly how you feel yourself?

I have the same problem in my relationship right now (it's my first and I'm 24). With wanting to be the most beautiful girl in the world for my boyfriend, completely crashing down as soon as you see a beautiful women leaving you feeling completely worthless, and the porn thing. The problem is my boyfriend is quite a good looking guy with lots of money, who's had a model ex (6ft tall, blonde, skinny) and who once told me that my body wash't up to scratch (weighing 114 pounds). He's changed a lot but can still be a complete asshole (I'm certainly no angel, growing up in a verbally abusive home where it was a routine to try to hurt each other as much as possible, and when hurting I still resort to this and have told him some absolutely horrible things during our time together).

I've asked my boyfriend to help, to give me compliments even if he does't mean them, just to make me feel good when I'm feeling very,

very bad about myself but he just says that he's not that sort of person. Never spontaneous you look nice, you're beautiful etc. He only tells me that I'm good enough when we've had a big fight and he wants to make up. And because I love him I don't want to disappoint him. But I disappoint myself every day by waking up looking the same as I did the day before.

And then the porn thing, I sorta get it, I really do, when it applies to other people. I would never tell another women that it's because there is something wrong with her, for him it's probably just a form of foreplay. But when my boyfriend does it it makes me feel so $#%^ about myself. Because the women in those movies are not beautiful, they're trashy and usually not even fit. But then again, he has cheated on me with a prostitute once (as I know of, could be many more times). Even though, at that time, I has sex with him up to 6 times a day whenever we met, all just to please him and make him not stray (my father destroyed my family and left me after having cheated on my mother, and after that didn't want any contact with me).

I don't really know what to say to you, just that you're obviously very intelligent being able to express yourself the way you've done. And I know that it seems that in this world that counts for nothing, but for some people it does. For me it does. Just not when it comes to myself.

B5: How to Cope with a Bad Day

Female-Initial Post: Today I'm having a bad day. I am depressed and I'm thinking nonstop about my appearance. I look in the mirror and see an ugly face. When I'm having good days, I always tell myself to ignore everything I see and think when I'm having a bad day because it's not real. It's really hard to do that though when I look in the mirror and actually see a horrible face. I hate not knowing who the "real me" is. I try my best to ignore my thoughts and especially mirrors, but it's hard. How do you deal with it?

Fran-Reply 1: I'm sorry you had a bad day... you started a thread I was intending to start, how to manage these such bad days that erases all hope. Today I am having one of those also. When my boyfriend was here, I had him close to talk to, and he we would try to joke and get my mind off of things, he got me hoping of the future, and telling me all the nice things we will do and have then.

When we are on our own, there are more efforts to make, and I will share mine.

Here are just some personal things I use to do to manage a bad day:

1. Occupy yourself with house tasks - cleaning, laundry and cleaning places that never seen sunshine before. Diverging your mind onto something else. You can also do something creative that you know can capture your attention for some hours, drawing, writing, playing games.

2. Perform physical activity - Get your running shoes on and go for a jog, or even a walk. Slow pace, breathe deeply, observe the yellow leaves, listen to their crunching below your feet. Look how the sun looks like diamonds in the water reflection. As you know there are several positive functions in doing this: the light has a positive influence, endorphins influences our well-being, relaxation, focusing on the beauty that naturally exists there, and realizing what a tiny part in all this we are. Be in it, not outside of this beauty. As much as its mine, it's all yours.

3. Drawing attention onto somebody else - since i live far away from family I try email them in my hard moments to tell them how much I appreciate them. I cuddle and play more with my cat, give her extra love and extra good food.

4. Avoid to always take out the load on somebody - like today, i avoided speaking about my sadness to my boyfriend, because I don't want it to occupy too much place in our relationship, I think I already do it too much. It is hard when he insists on how I am feeling, but after its done, I feel that I can be strong to handle my problem myself also.

5. Do take your load off on somebody - if the person is somebody that loves you and wants you to share your problems with, then speak openly. They can make you smile, do activities with you to take your mind off the hard day.

6. Make plans for tomorrow/next week - Make a diet or exercise plan, something for yourself to feel better. Maybe book in a day to go to the psychiatrist. Even if the plans are hard to follow through, making the plans gives a hope in itself.

7. Create a nice environment around yourself - My way of handling a really bad day right now:

• I lid 3 candles, I put on relaxing music, I make a cup of tea and dress in a cozy bathrobe. I sit, lonely and let thoughts come to me... i let them sweep over like a wind that I know comes in circles. And notice that it is here...again. I just let it come.

• Make a hot bubble bath for yourself, and intend to stay there min 1 hour, in candle light of course.

• If you're a girl, paint your nails, these small things.. can help, if only a microliter.

• I made a proper diet and exercise plan, and prepared portions of food, protein drinks, etc for a whole week.

• I supercuddled the cat the poor thing.

• Eventually I will fall asleep.

What will happen next day, is a Russian Roulette. And if you have planned your day on a manageable level, use positive thinking, self encouragement and a little self-pressure yourself, the ball might land on your number.

We have the power to influence our minds. Remember what you are worth in this life, what you want from it, and keep fighting, you will get there one day.

Fran-Reply 2: I wanted to add something to my answer that I thought about today jogging.

While outside, what really helps me to get my thoughts away from negativity such as "people looks funny at me", "i think it was me they laughed about" etc etc paranoid behavior, I bring my little ipod with my encouraging music, I place the headphones deep into the ears, I put on loud sound, I put on my sunglasses (without works ok also) and I walk on the streets looking only at the beauty around me. I don't look at any person, or car. I live into the music and i sing along (not too loud). You will never meet somebody's look or hear a laughter or feel strangely perceived, because you just walk there and you just don't care. I feel so good in those moments, because I got no clue whatsoever what happens around me. Just check out for cars when you cross the road and so on.

Usually I do this when I go out and run. People here has it as a national sport to comment on every people jogging by them, not necessarily something negative, mostly sexistic, but they catch your attention when you just want to be left alone and do your workout. So this works perfectly for me. I can run and breath as loud as I want and need because I can't hear myself how loud it is = not feeling self-conscious = no need to hold back. I don't look at the people I run by, I don't see if they talk to me or whatever they do. And when I am home I am fully at peace, plus feel wonderful after a tough run.

I am not encouraging these methods of avoidance as a cure, but as management, so that you don't feel scared of going out taking a jog or walk which feels so good.

B6: RECOVERY TO ADVOCACY STORY

Male-Initial Post: I have been living with BDD since a young age. The thoughts and irrational beliefs about my appearance intensified from middle school to high school and then throughout college. I have had girlfriends and friends tell me that I am attractive. I have also had people make seemingly harmless remarks about certain characteristics of my appearance like my nose, scars on my back from acne, and other aspects that are slightly different than the norm. I remember those comments more than any compliment I have ever received. I was co-captain of my football team in high school, had attractive girlfriends, joined a popular fraternity at the University of Miami, traveled Europe with friends, and had everything one could ask for in young adult life. Nearly every single experience and memory has been tainted by persistent thoughts that I am extremely unattractive and my life would be significantly better if I didn't have my flaws. I constantly checked mirrors at home and when in public. I was never fully in the moment during all of my experiences.

I sought counseling at school in Miami and subsequently wrote a book about living with BDD. I plan to use a portion of the proceeds to start a counseling center for people with BDD. My ultimate goal is to have support groups on every college campus and in other settings like 12 step programs have throughout the country. One of the major challenges with most sufferers of BDD, like myself, is the secretive nature of the disorder. The thought of even one person knowing how I thought was mortifying and kept me away from counseling for years. When life became unbearable I mustered the courage to enter counseling still withholding many specifics from my counselor. I then eventually told a close friend. I still have only told a few people, but with the publication of my book I am ready to come out with my story. I want to help fellow BDD sufferers and know that all of my pain and suffering can serve some greater purpose. I want to start an awareness campaign to help people not only realize they may have BDD, but to seek treatment when they do. I never knew I had BDD, but was typing in the symptoms of my obsessive thoughts a few years back and came across the Wikipedia page on BDD. I felt a piano sized weight come off my back when I found out I wasn't the only one suffering with these symptoms. Learning that I had an actual disorder that affects millions of Americans made me feel much less alone.

I hope you read my story and feel less alone. Maybe it will inspire you to enter counseling and no longer be ashamed of your thoughts. Maybe it will inspire you to help others who may be suffering.

Below is an excerpt from something I wrote to help me deal with BDD. I hope it will help you, too.

Mirrors are everywhere. I know where each one is in every house, school, and office I have ever spent a considerable amount of time in.

I had a teacher who said something interesting about the mirror. She said, "Everyone must pay homage to it when they walk by. It sort of pulls you in like some magnetic force." I nodded my head in agreement. I always had to look. The mirror truly was my friend and my enemy. I needed to see myself as often as possible. I would sit in my room and look for long periods of time. I would go to the bathroom every chance I had when in public. I could feel perfectly fine, but had to go check that mirror and subject myself to all the emotions that came with it. The urge was so powerful.

I always tried to leave the bathroom on a good note, look at myself from an angle that pleased me so I could leave happy. Most of the time, I didn't even know what I was checking in the first place. Sometimes I would see my reflection and say, "Phew, everything looks OK." Other times I would see my reflection and feel pain- an inescapable feeling that I am stuck with this body for the rest of my life, stuck with this face for the rest of my life, stuck with this skin for the rest of my life. What an overwhelming feeling! I could barely take one day in this body. How would I ever manage to live an entire life in it?

I hated and loved when someone else was washing their hands in the bathroom. I loved that I couldn't look at myself in the mirror to go through the rollercoaster of thoughts and emotions involved in that experience. I couldn't let someone else see me stare at myself. But that was often why I went to the bathroom in the first place- to ride that rollercoaster. I hated that they stood in the way of that.

I would often think how great it must have been to live thousands of years ago before there were mirrors everywhere. What a glorious life it must have been. I noticed I felt much better on days I spent less time looking in the mirror.

I would try tactics I later learned are called "mirror avoidance" for a whole day. And they worked wonderfully. It's strange how well they worked. Even though I still had all those insecurities in there somewhere, they stayed away from the surface of my thinking when I avoided the mirror. But what kind of life would that be if I never was able to feel comfortable looking at a mirror? I knew I couldn't go on like that forever. More importantly though, I wasn't strong enough to avoid mirrors on a regular basis. Eventually my overwhelming urge to check the mirror at every chance would return. It would start out harmlessly and then turn into longer and more frequent trips. I learned which mirrors had the best lighting, which ones I could usually look at the longest before someone came in, and eventually which ones to avoid altogether because of atrocious lighting, unless of course I felt like subjecting myself to that pain. Sometimes I would go to the mirrors with bad lighting knowing it would bring me down. It was masochistic. What a waste of time and energy I would think in a brief moment of clarity. Clarity was rare.

Female-Reply: Thanks for sharing this. It's a truly great thing you're doing, spreading awareness of a not-well-known (yet probably very common) disorder, and helping people who are suffering/those who may not be able to attribute any kind of 'label' to their severe body image issue.

The piece was really well written. I could really relate to the parts about the mirrors, having 'good days' where you wouldn't mind the mirror but still obsessively checking anyway to ascertain that nothing had changed physically. Then of course, the days when you just want to tear your hair out when you look in the mirror, feeling like you're trapped looking so ugly. It's sheer agony to look at yourself and realise you're stuck looking like this, that this is **really** you.

I also have phases of 'mirror obsession' and 'mirror avoidance.' I have periods where I deliberately don't look in mirrors or any reflective surface because I know I'll be sucked into that whole cycle of mirror checking, and I can't take it. But of course sometimes I'll catch sight of myself, be really shocked by how ugly my body is (or legs, in particular) and it'll send me spiralling into 'manic depressive' episodes where I'm just sobbing all day long about how I look, the pain of living in this body, and usually my life in general and how $#%^ it is, for instance being too afraid to leave the house, yet feeling even more depressed if I stay in all day).

Sorry, I'm just ranting now.

Anyway, yeah, thanks for sharing. That extract was excellent and really well written. It's nice to know someone else experiences almost exactly what you do when they look in the mirror.

B7: Beating BDD Story

Male-Initial Post: I have been suffering from BDD for as long as i could think of, I'm now 27 and have lost alot of my 20's being isolated, housebound, and depressed. Thanks to the help of professionals and my own initiative, I've managed to minimise the presence of its manifestation these days. I'm always aware that BDD is a "mode" i could always slip back into, and manage my attention and focus to prevent this happening.

If any of you were to see me, I know you'd point flaws in me physically. I'm not the best weight because of my medication either but I'm willing to take the punches of weight gain for mental clarity any day.

In the early days when i was hospitalized and put into a BDD group, pretty much the whole group used to analyze me and put me down physically!... it took me a long time to realize their opinion didn't matter... What did matter for me in the end was the firm core belief that my sum of worth as a whole Human being is so much more than what BDD told me it was.

These days i don't think about myself as an aesthetic object or use comparative and hierarchical analyses anymore to value myself on. I just let it be, call me ugly, call me handsome, or even the elephant man, I know my own worth and know that its more than my mere exterior.

I'm back at university and this has helped my BDD about 500%. Being around people who are normal in the sense they don't judge you on your appearance or don't consider appearance important has helped lots. When i was hospitalized it was about 50 times worse because everyone in there who had BDD would scrutinize you head to toe. And because you knew they were doing it, you'd ruminate and thus would unravel the disorder at it's worst.

I'm still not 100% free of challenges, I consider most women my age group to be daunting and have been single for 3 years, I don't have many friends due to the fact im a different age group to my peers at Uni, and the isolation gets me down. But it's not half as bad as what BDD puts you through.

The reason i wrote here was to create a perception for you all on what it's like "post" BDD. I know alot of you won't believe it's possible to reach this level, but i urge you to keep pushing and pushing... I want you to know it's possible. I've done stupid things, lost friends family and partners cus of my BDD fuelled behaviour. I know what it's like, but i urge you to keep going, you will get there, and when you do you'll feel complete. That feeling of completeness is so much more than anything you might be looking for.

Kathy-Reply 1: Thanks for your post 😄 it's really inspiring and motivating. It's great to hear from someone who is beating BDD! I often wonder if it is truly beatable, but you prove that it is 😄

Male-Reply 2: I thank you also for this great post. What you've put here is very encouraging. I think you've hit the nail on the head focusing on management rather than cure. I'm come to realize the same in regards to my own Bdd - questing for complete freedom from it I've found to be futile at best, counterproductive and damaging at worst.

I'm at the stage where I'm thinking this stuff, similar to what you've outlined in your best, but not yet applying it. I can't seem to move beyond the theory into actual real life practice. Can you give me some specifics as to how you did it, as in the actual application of your new outlook/thought processes?

All the best with continued recovery.

Male-Reply 3 (OP): Thank you for your replies it's great to meet people who are going through the same battle as me, sometimes you can feel so alone but it's great to know there are people out there that share the same problems as me, and have felt the same as me.

Regardless of whatever ways we may put ourselves down by, we exist on this planet and we are all trying to be happy in this life, and i really really hope that one day we can all come out of this fully recovered and look back on it as a thing of the past .

Thank you Kathy for finding my post inspiring:) It is indeed beatable and i hope you beat it soon for you deserve alot more in you're life than what BDD brings you. It will be hard and it's always a mode you can slip back into. But I promise you though it is beatable, and you will beat it, keep going and hold your head high, avoid all the traps BDD puts you into, and you'll feel free 😄

Thank you Male 2 also for your response 😄 You're absolutely right focus on managing the BDD and it'll become so minimal that you won't notice it being there at all. Then the trick is to become so unconcerned with appearance (even more than the average person on the street) that a relapse becomes very small probability wise.

You're absolutely right it's nothing but futile, counterproductive, and damaging. I'm so glad you realize this as it's one step to winning the battle.

Ok there are a few answers I've got to give you and i hope it's not too long to read but i wish you nothing but well so i guess I'd rather type more rather than less just so i can cover everything for you 😄

my new outlook/thought processes come from long practise of exposure, attention refocus, and the resultant improved metacognition that comes with it. Metacognition is a big theme for us, it basically means how you think about you're thinking. I notice my thoughts, and then decide whether they are helpful/maximize my chances of being happy/well, and then choose whether to buy into them or not. 100% of the time BDD is wrong/unhelpful! Believe me, it'll try and tell you that it's right and you're wrong, but i firmly assure you, we are all human and we all deserve happiness, we all deserve good mental health and not what BDD puts us through.

For example if i walk down the street and see a beautiful girl, and then think she thinks i'm ugly, i notice and literally "watch" the thought, then i focus on something that is sensory (like the feel of wind on my face or the feeling of the footpath on my feet) and this helps me engage with the outside world to such an extent that the thought does not follow through with an irrational emotion (usually would be fear/anxiety for me).

On top of this i do attention training every morning an this helps me get into the correct mindset of functioning. I still avoid some situations and still find them hard, but remember, the less you avoid the less BDD/problems you have in general 😀

Additionally, I couldn't help notice that you said something very similar to what i said to my therapist today! you said you can't seem to put the theory into real life and practise. This is a very very interesting statement for both of us! For example i know im avoiding going to a sports club to try and find friends at the moment because im overweight due to my medication. I want to go but the fear of being overweight is stopping me literally putting the theory of exposure into practise. The answer is simple for both of us: We must put the theory into practise. we owe it to ourselves and deserve better than what BDD tells us. We deserve happiness and we will get this if we put the theory into practise and expose ourselves to places and situations that our BDD makes us anxious in.

So there are ways to manage the BDD, but it will be hard at first to put the theory into practise (not just for you but also for me and this darn sports club thing 😀). Luckily i can tell you that once you start within days it gets easier and easier, i'm at a place now where i can go anywhere (apart from fitness/sports places) and you'll notice when you start doing it how wrong your BDD was and how right mental freedom and happiness is 😀

so in summary :

1) do attention training every morning (designed by Adrian Wells from the University of Manchester)

2) regular exposure and use the attention refocus and metacognitive ability to fight the BDD during exposure.

3) spot your avoidances and target them immediately,

4) positive data logging (this really helps me !):- with a therapist, find out you're core beliefs that cause your BDD. These core beliefs are split into 3 categories: self, world, and others (e.g mine was that i was defective/ugly for self, the world is a hostile place for world, and other people are out to taunt me as others). Then what you do is every day for each belief, write down a piece of evidence that disputes it that happened during your exposure. try really hard to find at least the tiniest bit of evidence and you'll help yourself immensely 😄

5) trauma work. most people with BDD believe it or not have had a history of social anxiety and trauma (myself included). addressing these traumas with your therapist using specific techniques they give you can help massively. At the root of BDD is trauma, and if the trauma is not resolved by the brain it will always resurface in one way or another. Most of us think we're ugly because we've been traumatized into thinking so. So, by treating BDD like a post trauma occurrence, we can resolve it and dampen it loads by emotionally resolving and coming to terms with what happened in our childhood/early life.

For example, i was bullied massively about my appearance from the ages of 0-12. Then puberty hit and hormones kicked in and i found myself dating and being dumped by girls one after another! this didnt help either! especially when my so called best mates ran off with the women i was dating 😢 But what i've done is address these traumas with a skilled therapist, and worked out that anyone in my position would end up thinking they're ugly if they had what happened to me happen to them (I'm even hedging my bets that Brad Pitt would consider himself to be not very attractive if he was bullied and traumatized like i was).

So i really hope this helps dude, Remember BDD is a multifaceted problem, but at its root lies our trauma. Addressing these traumas will help you massively.

I really really wish you the best as you sound like a nice person and you don't deserve what you're going through. I really hope I've covered everything, but please if there is anything you'd like me to help with please ask. I hate BDD and i hate it that lovely people always seem to end up the one's getting it, I really want sufferers to be free from it and will help as much as i can within my ability.

B8: FEELING TOO UGLY TO LIVE

Female-Initial Post: Hi there. I'm new and have not posted in this forum before. First off, my sympathy to anyone who has or may have BDD. I'm sending you all good thoughts.

I think I have Body Dysmporphic Disorder. I am at the point where it is making me think about killing myself. If my family or friends knew what I was thinking they would hit the roof. I believe that I am ugly, fat and revolting, and will never be anything more than that.

People tell me I am pretty. My boyfriend (god help him) tells me I am beautiful every day. He might as well be telling me the sky is red, not blue - it means absolutely nothing to me. Every time someone tells me I look nice, or I am pretty, I want to punch them, kick them, scream at them and call them liars, because I know it isn't true. When I look at myself in the mirror, I want to punch it. I spend hours each day focusing on how I look - doing my hair, putting on make up, fake tan, you name it. Nothing works. I take a step back and all I can see is an ugly, ugly, fat girl with a load of make up slapped on her face. It doesn't matter what I do.

I had an eating disorder that messed up my body and how I look - I was severely bulimic for about 2 and a half years and when I came out of it, I looked horrible. I lost teeth and hair and my already-bad cystic acne got much much worse. I wanted to die then too. I got through that because I fell in love with a boy who was nice enough to see through that to what I was like inside. We are still together and I love him.

I have had my rotting teeth removed, although some are still crumbling and rotting in my head. I have had hair extensions to hide the feathery, matted pieces of hair I had left. I have gone through every trick in the book to address my cystic acne, yet it persists in flaring up and leaving me with blotchy, lumpy skin all over my face and back.

I feel like crying all the time. I see so many beautiful, beautiful girls around me everywhere I go, and I will never ever ever be as beautiful or thin as them. One of my closest friends is beautiful. She has perfect skin, perfect teeth, and a perfect body. She is everything I will never ever be. She is successful too, in her career. I feel it is her looks that have made her that way, because I am also well-qualified and experienced, yet I never seem to succeed, career-wise. I feel that the way I look is dragging every other part of my life down with it. Everywhere I go, I see gorgeous people and it frightens me, because I know what they think when they look at me. They look at me and see my terrible skin, my sunken cheeks, my wobbly fat thighs, my disgusting fat stomach, my huge nose and ears, my dry hair and my disgusting teeth, and they think "why can't this girl just get it together and look nice? if not for herself then for the people around her?"

I am sure that my boyfriend sees me as a girl he loves, but who has let herself go. He has had girlfriends before me who are so beautiful and look like something I could only dream of being. But yet he decided to stay with me. He says he wants to marry me. I can't imagine why. I feel like I am the laughing stock of wherever I find myself. I don't trust anyone, and when they say "you look nice"/ "you're pretty" / etc, I look at them, then myself and think - are you f***ing kidding me? Why are you lying to me? Why are you trying to make me feel worse?

My boyfriend is coming to the end of his rope with me. He says I used to be so happy, and it's true, I was. I was used to being thinner than my friends, and now that I don't have an eating disorder anymore, they are thinner than me. I am left looking disgusting and ugly and fat, and they look beautiful. It isn't fair.

I wish I could look in the mirror and love what I see. All I can see is disgusting skin with acne and more acne about to erupt. Some days I just can't look at myself because it makes me so sad. Other days I need to look at myself, and study the mirror, every couple of minutes. I have to constantly run my hands through my hair because it looks bad. I feel my skin for new spots. I have to constantly run off somewhere private to lift up my top and look at my stomach because it is so fat. I pinch the fat on my thighs to remind myself it is still there, blobby and disgusting. I feel my nose and pinch it and wish and wish it was smaller. I bare my teeth at myself in the mirror and see how ugly and yellow and horrible and chipped they are. I hate the way I look, and I am starting to hate myself for looking this way. I don't hide away all the time. Although sometimes I do. I will lie to my friends and say I'm not around when they want to meet up, because I can't handle what seeing them does to my self-esteem on a given day. Whenever I see them, however I might be feeling that day, my self-esteem will always shoot down 100% because I am reminded that they are beautiful, I am ugly, and that is how it will always be. I rue the day I joined Facebook, because now my stupid face and body are there for the world to see. I feel like an idiot for saying what I have just said, because I have studied psychology, philosophy and education in quite a bit of detail, and I know that there is so much more to our existence than what we look like. I am going to die someday, so why am I wasting my life feeling like this? The problem is that I feel too ugly to live.

I don't know what to do. I am frightened, sad and I feel very alone about this problem. I know that society has bred insecurity in girls, but this is something much much worse. I want to get help but I am 1) embarrassed and 2) unsure as to what help I could even get.

Thank you if you happened to read this. I feel better for even having typed it out. But I can't ever, ever say that to anyone.

Male-Reply 1: If you are fat, you shouldn't have BDD about it, since it is easily fixable with the right diet and exercise.

Flamer-Reply 2: If you have a boyfriend who wants to marry you, then you probably aren't ugly. Also if people compliment your looks often, that's another sign.

If you were truly ugly, you wouldn't have friends, much less a boyfriend, and you wouldn't receive compliments on your looks.

Kathy-Reply 3: Hi, welcome to the forum 😄 I'm so sorry that you are going through all of this! Thanks for sharing your story, I can relate with some of the things you have said and it's awful.

Are you receiving any treatment for this? I hope you like the forum, feel free to join any discussions or message me if you ever need to talk about anything.

Female-Reply 4 (OP): Thanks for your replies, I appreciate the time you all took to write them.

In response to Male 1 and Flamer, while I'm thankful for your suggestions, I should probably have been more specific. I am clinically just above underweight for my height, so while it shouldn't ring true that I am fat (i.e a medical professional would tell me I am near-underweight, not fat) all I can see is a fat girl with rolls of fat on every part of her body. This is most likely some warped sense of perception left over from bulimia. I will not go any further with that because I will be going into eating disorder territory and this is not a forum for that kind of thing.

Thank you for the suggestions on having my teeth fixed, however, this is an ongoing problem and I unfortunately spend a lot of time having dental surgery to fix it. I have had many root canals, extractions and fillings in the last two years, and will need to stabilize the decay situation in my mouth before cosmetic dentistry can even be considered. I feel that your argument that "ugly people do not have friends or boyfriends" is a bit flawed. I think that the people I am friends with enjoy have someone uglier than them as a friend because it makes them look even better and more beautiful by comparison. But that's just how I feel.

Kathy, thank you for your reply - I hope you are at some level of feeling okay with yourself, and hopefully not too much like me because I don't feel very good about myself at the moment, I'm sending you good thoughts.

I am not seeking any treatment at the moment, because I am not even sure about what it is that is wrong with me. Are you? And if you don't mind me asking, how does a person go about this? Does a GP make a diagnosis and refer you to someone? Are GPs even knowledgeable about this kind of thing? I have no idea, so please excuse my ignorance.

This may sound ridiculous, but I am pretty convinced that people say nice things to me to make me feel better, or worse, to make me look stupid - i.e. if I ask my boyfriend or friend if i look okay twenty times a day, and each time they say yes, I have to check, and look at myself, and ask them again, because I am convinced they are lying to me and want to make me look silly.

Good thoughts to you all 😄

Kathy-Reply 5: I'm not at the best place just now but I'm working on getting there 😄 yeah you just go and speak to your GP and they will refer you. I actually just went to see my GP today. She was very helpful and very knowledgeable about it, im getting referred to someone else but she said it could take a while as therapy etc isnt very good on the NHS.

I also think people just say things to be nice or because they feel sorry me 😔 it's incredibly hard to believe people.

Female-Reply 6 (OP): Congratulations, that must have taken a lot for you to go and seek help 😄 I'm sure it will be a very positive experience for you once you are able to talk to someone professional about this. I think I might try and do the same. I live in Ireland and have health insurance but for some reason, it doesn't cover me for therapy I don't think. Crazy world 😨 I'd be really interested to hear how you get on with the specialist you are referred to, even if it takes you some time, do drop me a PM and let me know what happens as I am trying to decide what the best option is for myself at the moment.

I completely understand about the hard time you have believing people, I actually can't take what anyone says to me seriously anymore. I also think that people are saying things like that to me to make me angry, I get so angry sometimes at my boyfriend or my mum, just because they might say "you look nice today" - I have totally flown on the handle at them sometimes, swore at them, and worse 😣 so yes I think this is something I'm going to need help with.

Best of luck with getting treatment! I hope it goes really well for you.

B9: FRAN LEAVING FORUM

Fran-Initial Post: To moderators/administrators:

I have read in the FAQ that you cannot delete your own posts. I cannot even delete anything in the blog as it seems.

Do you mean that once I have written my story here it must be online here forever?

Because I would like to remove my posts, all of them, and also delete the account. Can moderators/administrators help with that?

Fran-Reply 1 (OP): I have made the decision of leavening this forum, including having all my posts deleted. There are several reasons.

I came here because I was in a very low mood, needed some support from someone who understands my condition. Also, if I was able to help anyone, that meant a lot. Helping others will also help yourself.

263

But it kind of ends there. Perhaps it was me, my way of writing that was incorrect, i am open to change, but it has left a bad after taste this whole experience. I may have expected something different, more of a community to talk about normal things in life, than somewhere were people just left their load off and get replied "everything will be fine". It is nothing wrong with saying that, it is very important to say that, but maybe I was expecting to make closer connections. And again, I can take the blame on myself. I also understand that living with BDD or any other mental disorder can depress you to a state of not being able to properly take in other peoples information. As we get very depressed, we stop caring for our selves, and in all areas interest is lost, maybe also in other members. I notice in most of the topics, when a person is in need of support, there is very seldom found a reply based on real concrete help facts, but mostly those klishé words, and always bringing back the topic to your own self. I have noticed I can do that too. But it is not a strange thing, we are so very preoccupied with our selves, so how can we dedicate proper support to a stranger?

With those facts, I had hoped to finding people with my problems, but who were also able to speak about normal and good daily days, and not get offensive reactions about talking about something awesome happening once in 30-100-365 days, be proud of it without negative word feed-back. I am a sensitive person, an I take offense also. I feel that on this forum I was not allowed to feel well, to feel beautiful, even though for me it happens so seldom. I have days, many days, each week of wishing I didnt have to do this anymore, that I am disappointed for having a family and a wonderful boyfriend living that will be devastated if i just dissapeard (died), which is what I want to do most of the days. But I dont mention that, I try to be positive with you people. Life is very hard to live, for me it is. I have tried to be as positive as I have could, helped as much as I have could, within the range of my knowledge. And when you notice it is not received well, then I feel no point in continuing.

Posting a very personal drawing that I have spent a lot of time on, out of all people who saw the thread, there were two wonderful reactions, I thank you for those.

But honestly it was then, than I realized, that on this forum, I am not allowed to be good, talented, or successful. Posted a wonderful drawing which I am very proud of, but it seems like it was too much, and nobody wanted to give complements...why?? I cannot have BDD and be talented and successful and smart? I am, but I am also often in suicidal thoughts, I am fighting with them on a daily basis.

I wanted friends, people with BDD, but who can forget also their problems for a moment and see the beauty in life. Maybe in this way I might have come a long way in my progress. I dont feel I have progressed. I feel terribly uncomfortable every single day I go out, to school or to pay my bills or food shopping. Standing in a line is a very very hard thing. Standing, being observed, get looks, which you dont know how to interpret because you are paranoid, ALL THE TIME. It is truly exhausting. Exhausting........

And when I am home I can relax, and I come in here to write a bit of the day, trying not to let the bad experiences take too much space, because I intentionally want to focus on the good aspects, the hope and the future. Maybe I kept away the negativity too much, to the extent that people here thought that my problems were minor. And maybe I came off arrogant? Thats not how I am.

Next year I am graduating as a Medical Doctor, which I am enormously proud of, just beacause of the fact of that every day is a true struggle, every minute of it.

In this forum though I have found it hard to relate to others, except in the beginning when I saw there were more with BDD. Thats as far as it reached.

In the end we have two questions to ask:

1. Is my contribution here making other feeling better?

2. Is my membership here making ME feel better?

I think in my case both answers are NO. Therefore I have to go where I can do use.

I hope that this forum will continue to be a very useful page for those who seek support, comfort and answers. It was just now right for me, it kind of hurt me more than it helped. I was seeking a normality within this chaos. Just some understanding.

I hope that anyone at all has had any kind of use in what ever I have written, I have always good intentions, I really wanted to help.

But I am leaving now, to take care of my last very hard year, trying to survive by myself from now on (boyfriend went away a long time).

It is hard, but I am fighting for my boyfriend and our life together, for our future child. I know it will be fine in the end.

Best of luck to you all, and hope that you all find your own ways of dealing with BDD and have an improved life quality.

I will continue on my thesis on BDD, it is very exiting and who knows, maybe one day I will choose to specialize within psychiatry. Some of your have indeed fascinated me.

Much love and understanding, keep your fight alive.

I hope that a moderator/administrator can please take my wish seriously.

Female-Reply 2: i don't know if i should say this.

But what i noticed that regarding such self help forums, many people i noticed face the similar problems including myself. We find out that such forums are not helpful or not helping us at all including myself i have such thoughts too. But why am i staying here? Sometimes i feel i am worst off by staying in such places but would i be better if i left.

Why? This is a mental forum for people of all problems so it so calls add the the air of depression and gloominess. I do feel a bit fed up as some of the post in other sections, i see people with problems so minor who thinks that it is the end of the world. while what i faced was worst of than them but i am still around which makes me sadder.

Also although we are facing the same problem BDD but due to our different environment and character and our different ways in solving things. We may disagree. So it may end up this forum is not helping you.

What i would like to say is just hang on, don't be quick to delete your posts as now you are still facing problems. Just keep your posts as references to help you sort out your feelings.

I don't know are the people you mentioned am i one of them? If yes i am sorry just that we have to find our solutions. One solution may not fit all.

At least you are a medical doctor, looks fade. You have a bright career ahead. 😊 i am just a good for nothing girl who is unemployed. If i had your brains i would not feel half as sad as i am. You have a chance to succeed while my future seems bleak.

Undetermined-Reply 3: Your reasons for leaving are exactly the reasons I had for leaving BDD central forums: positivity doesn't seem to be welcome. I think that's just how forums for people with certain mental issues work. They serve as an outlet for people to be like "omg,

I'm in the same sucky situation, I feel less alone now", but they don't focus enough on finding concrete solutions to get out of that paralyzing mindset. People who are enthusiastic and try to bring some positivity quickly get dragged down by everyone else's negativity.

I won't lie, I see why your attitude might rub some people the wrong way. From my experience, most people with BDD also have self-esteem issues that go beyond looks. I don't; I think I'm kind of awesome. And I'm completely aware of how arrogant and annoying this claim makes me sound. I don't think I'm better than anyone, but that's how people are going to interpret it, and that's why it's hard to form connections or make friends with people who are self-assured on a forum where most people have major confidence issues. I've always hoped to make friends on BDD central, but that's never happened. I've reached out, but I guess people just hate me.

Maybe that's because I'm really proud of myself for not letting these BDD symptoms destroy me. I've confronted my fear of people, I've traveled, I've spent a year studying abroad, I tackled my issues face-on and had surgery done, I let myself fall in love, and I grew as a person. In 6 months, I'm going to graduate in philosophy and I'm ######6 proud of that. It's been a long journey full of obstacles, but I did pretty good for someone this hideous. It's not bragging by any means, I'm just happy about myself, but I've learned that I can't show any pride on BDD forums or I'm going to be judged and disliked.

Was this an inappropriate reply? I haven't seen your drawing btw, and I'd like to.

Fran-Reply 4 (OP): Firstly, thank you both for your understanding and great replies. I was honestly expecting an attack from various places, I am really grateful that somebody can relate to this.

And to answer you individually:

Female 2 - 😄 I am really surprised and very happy to see you post such a positive and helping post, because I know yourself is struggling a lot.... It means a lot to me, thank you. I am thinking of the things you said, and you are right in that maybe we still need this forum in one way or the other, and we should throw it away just because our expectations were not fulfilled. I was wondering where you had gone, if I was to harsh on you last time, and look here you are helping my butt out. 😉

Undetermined 3 - It seems as if you know precisely what I am feeling about this forum. Our similarities are many also regarding life and accomplishments. The first days I went on here I felt that something I had very different from many others was that I felt far from inferior to others or insecure in myself. That I have, like you, very high thoughts of myself. Maybe that is one of the mistakes to make entering this kind of forum. We are all on different levels, different ages, different backgrounds, educational level and life experience. I am 28, and I think I may be among the older ones (just my appreciation), with a lot of things behind me. Travels, education, fails, learning, and growing, improving from there. It was maybe wrong of thinking I could find friends here that can relate. I am in my life now, where I am able to go out on most days (despite feeling like $#%^), i am able to talk to people, but more importantly: I PUSH MYSELF to improve a lot. And I try concrete solutions to overcome this. But that doesnt mean I am well, or anywhere close to it. I just know how to smile or laugh at this $#%^ of a BDD that is inhibiting me in my otherwise normal life. I know who to turn to to give me hope for yet another day. And I have these two big factors career and life partner which I cannot let down.

Also, thank you for the encouragement, even confident persons like us needs it aloooot. <3   Your answers really had a huge positive impact on me. <3

B10: Roger (Moderator) Updated Rules

We have updated the rules now. As well as the forum general rules we have addressed one or two things that are to be specifically enforced in the BDD sub-forum. The following is now applicable...

[1] Photographs.

This is a BDD support forum and, just like in all the other forums, we value the privacy of our members. Due to the sensitive nature of BDD though it is necessary to clarify this rule in addition to the general rules which can be found at the end of this post. You must understand that a person's true intentions cannot always be so easily seen and it is our duty to make this a safe place for people to post freely without the temptation of asking for visual approval from people whose intentions could possibly be malicious. Therefore we must stress that under no circumstances are members allowed to:

(1a) request another member to share their picture.

(1b) post a picture of themselves or offer to share a picture of themselves to other members.

(1c) critique another member who has attempted to share their photo without express consent from the site owners.

[2] Cosmetic surgery

In keeping with the principles of the forum rules and the purpose of the forum as a support forum, we wish to clarify what is acceptable with regards to mentioning cosmetic surgery on the forum. Cosmetic surgery is universally regarded as a bad treatment plan for people suffering with Body Dysmorphic Disorder. Medical professionals/psychologists etc strictly advise against cosmetic surgery as a method of combating the symptoms of BDD. Offering treatment advice that is contrary to professional opinion is strictly against the rules. Therefore we must stress that under no circumstances are members allowed to:

(2a) advise another member with BDD that cosmetic surgery is a viable treatment option.

(2b) generally imply that cosmetic surgery is a good treatment option for patients with BDD.

(2c) promote individual cosmetic surgeons and clinics.

However, please note that discussing personal experience under the knife or the general ideology of cosmetic surgery is fine so long as it does not break (2a),(2b) or (2c)

We want this forum to be a pleasant experience for all, where members can discuss their experience with BDD without the more unpleasant aspect of malicious intent from anyone who may have an agenda which does not involve the betterment of yourself and people around you. If you see anything unpleasant, anything you feel is not beneficial to the treatment of others or anything that breaks these rules then please feel free to use the report function in the top right hand corner of a post or contact a moderator.

Thanks for your co-operation and understanding.

The Mod Team

APPENDIX C:
RESEARCH RESULTS

The BDD forum had more than 4,000 messages posted during 2012 by 218 members and two moderators. The number included 280 initial posts and 3,728 replies. The median number of replies to initial posts were three; half of the posts contained fewer than three replies, and half had more than three replies. Most excerpts in the book are taken from the 280 initial posts and first three replies (a total of 911 messages).[1] Additional replies (after the first three) have been taken from threads where extended conversations took place between the original poster and other members.

The message posts and replies contained multiple comments primarily disclosing one's personal experiences with BDD and then seeking or providing support to other members. Comments within messages could contain one sentence or multiple consecutive sentences. Forum messages contained similar amounts of personal disclosure (76.9 percent) and social support (76.8 percent) since messages often contained both. However, more comments contained social support (62 percent) than personal disclosure (38 percent). Of the total of 2,278 comments, 857 were labeled as personal disclosure and 1,421 as social support.[2]

PERSONAL DISCLOSURE

The personal experiences requested and disclosed in the forum were focused on three broad areas: peoples' appearance-related feelings, thoughts, and behaviors (impact on self); BDD symptoms and social relationships (impact on family, friends, dating/relationships, job/career); and recovery from BDD (diagnosis, treatment, coping, overcoming symptoms). Comments about one's appearance were more prevalent in the study (360) than those about the impact of symptoms on one's social relationships (197) and about recovery from BDD (300). These findings indicate that most individuals who disclosed personal experiences were still struggling with BDD symptoms. The forum was used more by individuals who wanted to share their problems with BDD and less by those who had received a clinical diagnosis and treatment for the disorder.

SOCIAL SUPPORT

Social support comments were classified into three categories: informational support, emotional support, and network support. Informational support was defined as advice and opinions directed to others on the forum about actions to take or taken to help the person solve a problem causing stress. Emotional support comments contained expressions of empathy/understanding, caring/concern, gratitude, encouragement, sympathy, compliments, and validation meant to comfort or console another person without trying to solve the problem.[3] Network support comments contained references about the BDD forum as a community of people with similar interests and concerns.

There were more informational (652) and emotional (559) than network support (186) comments. Only 9 percent of the social support comments by forum leaders involved seeking social support, while 91 percent consisted of providing support to others. The five emergent leaders and two moderators accounted for 51 percent of the comments providing social support to other members, but only 17 percent of the comments asking for support.[4]

There were also a small number of comments that were considered unsupportive (24). Some forum members disagreed on topics such as whether beauty is objective or subjective, whether getting plastic surgery is helpful for people with BDD, and how to raise awareness outside the forum. Unsupportive comments contained expressions of disagreement or disapproval with another person's opinions and advice, sarcasm/criticism directed toward other members, and comments that were considered offensive or hurtful (flaming). Only a small percentage (1.1 percent) of the comments posted during the year were considered unsupportive to other members.[5]

Please refer to *"Am I ugly or do I have BDD?": Personal disclosure and social support on a body dysmorphic disorder online forum*[6] for more information about the study research questions, methodology, coding guide, results, and discussion.

ENDNOTES

1. My Road to Recovery

1. Brody, 1997

2. Learning about BDD

1. Brody, 1997
2. Phillips, 1996/2005
3. Phillips, 1996/2005
4. Hartmann & Buhlmann, 2017
5. Koran et al., 2008
6. Fawcett et al., 2020
7. Statistics and Research on Eating Disorders, 2019
8. Personal Correspondence, Roberto Olivardia, July 15, 2022: The OCD graph is in line with general prevalence research. However, studies show that males have higher prevalence in childhood and earlier age of onset, whereas females have higher prevalence in adolescence and adulthood. Some research also points to some gender differences on the manifestation of OCD symptoms. According to Mathes et al., (2019), men are said to have more intrusive thoughts, while women more commonly struggle with contamination concerns.

   It's important to consider and understand how gender and symptom manifestation can impact reporting, self-identification, and treatment seeking. For example, popular notions of OCD involve contamination concerns, so people who struggle with that form of OCD are more likely to recognize it as OCD and possibly seek help. If women are more likely to have that, they may be more willing to seek help (in addition to many studies that show males have more shame and resistance to seeking treatment).

   Research on BDD in the late 1990s showed a slightly higher prevalence in males versus females (51 percent to 49 percent). Current research has shown BDD slightly more common in women than men (60 percent to 40 percent). I would challenge that, since BDD is underreported with males. Clinically, I see more males, but they may know I specialize in working with men with BDD, muscle dysmorphia, and eating disorders.

   The graph on Anorexia Nervosa (AN) is about right: 25 percent of people with AN are male. The Bulimia Nervosa (BN) statistics displayed on the graph are also aligned with what current research says, although I think BN is vastly underreported in males. Most research studies are geared toward women. I'm speaking from a clinical lens, where I see many men with BN who never report it to anyone. It is a common experience in my practice with men with BN that I am the ONLY person they have disclosed this to, and some of these men are married.

   See also: Mathes, B. M., Morabito, D. M., & Schmidt, N. B. (2019).

Epidemiological and clinical gender differences in OCD. Current psychiatry reports, 21(5), 1–7.

9. Hartmann & Buhlmann, 2017
10. Rosenblum & Lewis, 1999
11. Hart & Niemiec, 2017
12. Phillips, 1996/2005
13. Phillips, 2009
14. Phillips, 2009
15. Crerand et al., 2017; Tignol et al., 2007
16. Phillips, 2017b
17. Brody, 1997
18. Veale et al., 2002
19. Schnackenberg & Petro, 2016
20. Brody, 1997
21. Wilhelm, 2006
22. Psychology and Mental Health Forum, 2012
23. Fisher, 2016
24. Balkundi & Kilduff, 2006
25. Fisher, 2016
26. Fisher, 2016
27. Fisher, 2016

3. BDD Peer Support

1. Thoits, 2011
2. Marques, Weingarden, LeBlanc, Siev, & Wilhelm, 2011
3. Cohen & Wills, 1985
4. Albrecht, 1987
5. Barak et al., 2008
6. Alcoholics Anonymous, 2001
7. Arminen, 2004
8. Walther & Boyd, 2002
9. van Uden-Kraan, Drossaert, Taal, Seydel, & van de Laar, 2008
10. Wright et al., 2013
11. Walther & Boyd, 2002
12. Winograd, 2017
13. Greene et al, 2006
14. Tidwell & Walther, 2002
15. Pennebaker & Seagal, 1999
16. Fisher, 2016

4. Seeking and Providing Support

1. Chung, 2013
2. Kim et al., 2012
3. Phillips, 1996/2005
4. Van Noppen & Sassano-Higgens, 2017

5. BDD Forum Leaders

1. Benne & Sheats, 2007
2. Benne & Sheats, 2007
3. Benne & Sheats, 2007
4. Phillips, 2009

6. Looking for Causes

1. Feusner et al., 2010
2. Wolke & Sapouna, 2008
3. Buhlmann et al., 2007
4. Malcolm et al., 2021
5. Rytina, 2008
6. Veale et al., 2002
7. Malcolm et al., 2021
8. Winograd, 2017
9. Phillips, 2017a
10. Phillips et al., 1993
11. Allen & Hollander, 2004
12. Neziroglu & Barile, 2017
13. Feusner et al., 2010
14. Phillips, 2009
15. Phillips, 2017e
16. McCurdy-McKinnon & Feusner, 2017
17. McCurdy-McKinnon & Feusner, 2017

7. Painful Appearance Obsessions

1. Phillips, 2009
2. Simmons & Phillips, 2017
3. Phillips, 2017d
4. Simmons & Phillips, 2017
5. Phillips, 2009
6. Phillips, 2009
7. Phillips, 2009
8. Phillips, 2009
9. Kelly & Kent, 2017
10. Simmons & Phillips, 2017
11. Phillips, 2009
12. Winograd, 2017
13. Phillips, 2009
14. Phillips, 2017b
15. Phillips, 2009
16. Winograd, 2017

8. BDD-Related Behaviors

1. Crerand et al., 2017
2. Winograd, 2017
3. Winograd, 2017
4. Crerand et al., 2017
5. Marques, Weingarden, LeBlanc, & Wilhelm, 2011
6. Winograd, 2017
7. Simmons & Phillips, 2017
8. Simmons & Phillips, 2017
9. Simmons & Phillips, 2017
10. Simmons & Phillips, 2017
11. Simmons & Phillips, 2017
12. Festinger, 1962
13. Phillips, 2009
14. American Psychiatric Association, 2013
15. Phillips, 2009
16. Phillips, 2009
17. Simmons & Phillips, 2017
18. Festinger, 1954
19. Phillips, 2009
20. Feinstein et al., 2013
21. Dove, 2020

9. Impact on Relationships and Career

1. Greenberg et al., 2017
2. Simmons & Phillips, 2017

10. Getting Diagnosed

1. Brody, 1997
2. Giles & Newbold, 2011
3. Marques, Weingarden, LeBlanc, & Wilhelm, 2011
4. Phillips, 2009
5. Bandura, 1986
6. Brody, 1997
7. American Psychiatric Association, 2013
8. Phillips, 2017a
9. American Psychiatric Association, 2013
10. American Psychiatric Association, 2013
11. Veale et al., 2017
12. Giles & Newbold, 2013
13. American Psychiatric Association, 2000
14. American Psychiatric Association, 2022
15. American Psychiatric Association, 2000
16. American Psychiatric Association, 2013

17. Phillips, 1996/2005
18. American Psychiatric Association, 2013

11. TREATMENT EXPERIENCES

1. Phillips et al., 2008
2. Phillips, 2017c
3. Greenberg et al., 2017
4. Phillips, 2009
5. Phillips, 2009
6. American Psychiatric Association, 2013
7. Phillips, 2017c
8. Phillips, 2009
9. Phillips, 2009
10. Phillips, 2017c
11. Buhlmann, 2011
12. Marques, Weingarden, LeBlanc, & Wilhelm, 2011
13. Phillips, 2009
14. Veale et al., 2017
15. Vidourek et al., 2014
16. Marques, Weingarden, LeBlanc, & Wilhelm, 2011
17. Body Dysmorphic Disorder Foundation, n.d.
18. Phillips, 2009
19. Phillips, 2009
20. Phillips, 1996/2005
21. Phillips, 2009
22. Phillips, 2009
23. Phillips, 2009
24. Veale et al., 2009

12. COPING WITH BDD SYMPTOMS

1. Phillips, 2017c
2. Barak et al., 2008
3. Barak et al., 2008
4. Tichon & Shapiro, 2003
5. Goffman, 1963

13. RECOVERY STORIES

1. Substance Abuse and Mental Health Services Administration, 2011
2. Bandura, 2004

14. Emotional Support

1. van Uden-Kraan, Drossaert, Taal, Shaw et al., 2008

15. Network Support

1. Bambina, 2007
2. van Uden-Kraan, Drossaert, Taal, Shaw et al., 2008
3. Graham & Wright, 2014
4. Kim et al., 2012

16. Conflicts between Members

1. Benne & Sheats, 2007
2. Nyeyk, 2017
3. Hardaker, 2015
4. Freitas, 2017
5. American Psychiatric Association, 2013
6. Phillips, 2017e
7. Phillips, 2009
8. Benne & Sheats, 2007
9. Drebing, 2016
10. Graham & Wright, 2014

17. Support Group Pros and Cons

1. Kelly et al., 2017
2. Dickerson, 1998
3. Barak et al., 2008
4. Aardoom et al., 2014
5. Kral, 2006
6. Mo & Coulson, 2014
7. van Uden-Kraan, Drossaert, Taal, Shaw et al., 2008
8. Wright et al., 2013
9. Freitas, 2017
10. Newman et al., 2011
11. Tanis, 2008
12. Winograd, 2017
13. van Uden-Kraan et al., 2009
14. Buchanan & Coulson, 2007
15. Chang & Bazarova, 2016
16. Mo & Coulson, 2014
17. Phillips, 2009

APPENDIX C: RESEARCH RESULTS

1. Fisher, 2016
2. Fisher, 2016
3. Cutrona & Suhr, 1992
4. Fisher, 2016
5. Fisher, 2016
6. Fisher, 2016

Bibliography

Aardoom, J. J., Dingemans, A. E., Boogaard, L. H., & Van Furth, E. F. (2014). Internet and patient empowerment in individuals with symptoms of an eating disorder: A cross-sectional investigation of a pro-recovery focused e-community. *Eating Behaviors, 15*(3), 350–356. https://doi.org/10.1016/j.eatbeh.2014.04.003

Albrecht, T. L. (1987). *Communicating social support*. Sage.

Alcoholics Anonymous. (2001). *Alcoholics Anonymous. The story of how many thousands of men and women have recovered from alcoholism* (4th ed.). Alcoholics Anonymous World Services.

Allen, A., & Hollander, E. (2004). Similarities and differences between body dysmorphic disorder and other disorders. *Psychiatric Annals, 34*, 927–933.

American Psychiatric Association. (2000). *Diagnostic and statistical manual of mental disorders (DSM-IV-TR)* (4th ed.). American Psychiatric Publishing.

American Psychiatric Association. (2013). *Diagnostic and statistical manual of mental disorders (DSM-5)* (5th ed.). American Psychiatric Publishing.

American Psychiatric Association. (2022). APA Dictionary of Psychology. Somatoform disorder. https://dictionary.apa.org/somatoform-disorder

Arminen, I. (2004). Second stories: The salience of interpersonal communication for mutual help in Alcoholics Anonymous. *Journal of Pragmatics, 36*(2), 319–347.

Balkundi, P., & Kilduff, M. (2006). The ties that lead: A social network approach to leadership. *The Leadership Quarterly 17*, 419–439.

Bandura, A. (1986). *Social foundations of thought and action: A social cognitive theory*. Prentice Hall.

Bandura, A. (2004). Health promotion by social cognitive means. *Health Education & Behavior, 31*, 143–164.

Bambina, A. (2007). *Online social support: The interplay of social networks and computer-mediated communication*. Cambria Press.

Barak, A., Boniel-Nissim, M., & Suler, J. (2008). Fostering empowerment in online support groups. *Computers in Human Behavior, 24*(5), 1867–1883.

Benne, K. D., & Sheats, P. (2007). Functional roles of group members. *Group Facilitation: A Research & Applications Journal, 8*, 30–35

Body Dysmorphic Disorder Foundation. (n.d.). *NHS services for BDD*. https://bddfoundation.org/support/support-in-the-uk/nhs-services-for-bdd/

Brody, L. (1997, May). When the mirror lies. *Shape*, 144–149.

Buchanan, H., & Coulson, N. S. (2007). Accessing dental anxiety online support groups: An exploratory qualitative study of motives and experiences. *Patient Education and Counseling, 66*(3), 263–269.

Buhlmann, U. (2011). Treatment barriers for individuals with body dysmorphic disorder: An internet survey. *Journal of Nervous and Mental Disease, 199*(4), 268–271.

Buhlmann, U., Cook, L., Fama, J., & Wilhelm, S. (2007). Perceived teasing experiences in body dysmorphic disorder. *Body Image, 4*(4), 381–385. https://doi.org/10.1016/j. bodyim.2007.06.004

Chang, P. F., & Bazarova, N. N. (2016). Managing stigma: Disclosure-response communication patterns in pro-anorexia websites. *Health Communication, 31*(2), 217–229. https://doi.org/10.1080/10410236.2014.946218

Chung, J. E. (2013). Social networking in online support groups for health: How online social networking benefits patients. *Journal of Health Communication, 19*(6), 1–21. https://doi.org/10.1080/10810730.2012.757396

Cohen, S., & Wills, T. A. (1985). Stress, social support, and the buffering hypothesis. *Psychological Bulletin, 98,* 310–357.

Crerand, C. E., Sarwer, D. B., & Ryan, M. (2017). Cosmetic medical and surgical treatments and body dysmorphic disorder. In Katharine A. Phillips, M.D. (Ed.), *Body dysmorphic disorder: Advances in research and clinical practice* (pp. 431-448). Oxford University Press.

Cutrona, C. E., & Suhr, J. A. (1992). Controllability of stressful events and satisfaction with spouse support behaviors. *Communication Research, 19*(2), 154–174.

Dickerson, F. B. (1998). Strategies that foster empowerment. *Cognitive and Behavioral Practice, 5,* 255–275.

Dove. (2020). The evolution film: Digital distortion in the media. https://www.dove.-com/uk/dove-self-esteem-project/help-for-parents/talking-about-appearance/the-evolution-video.html

Drebing, C. (2016). *Leading peer support and self-help groups: A pocket reference.* Alderson Press.

Fawcett, E., Power, H., & Fawcett, J. M. (2020). Women are at greater risk of OCD than men: A meta-analytic review of OCD prevalence worldwide. *The Journal of Clinical Psychiatry, 81* (4). https://doi.org/10.4088/JCP.19r13085

Feinstein, B. A., Hershenberg, R., Bhatia, V., Latack, J. A., Meuwly, N., & Davila, J. (2013). Negative social comparison on Facebook and depressive symptoms: Rumination as a mechanism. *Psychology of Popular Media Culture, 2*(3), 161–170. https://doi.org/10.1037/a0033111

Festinger, L. (1954). A theory of social comparison processes. *Human Relations, 7,* 117–140.

Festinger, L. (1962). *A theory of cognitive dissonance.* Stanford University Press.

Feusner, J. D., Neziroglu, F., Wilhelm, S., Mancusi, L., & Bohon, C. (2010). What causes BDD: Research findings and a proposed model. *Psychiatric Annals, 40*(7), 349–355.

Fisher, E. E. (2016). *Am I ugly or do I have BDD?: Personal disclosure and social support on a body dysmorphic disorder online forum.* [Doctoral dissertation, Colorado State University]. ProQuest Dissertations Publishing.

Freitas, D. (2017). *The happiness effect.* Oxford University Press.

Giles, D. C., & Newbold, J. (2011). Self- and other-diagnosis in user-led mental health online communities. *Qualitative Health Research, 21*(3), 419–428. https://doi.org/10.1177/1049732310381388

Giles, D. C., & Newbold, J. (2013). 'Is this normal?' The role of category predicates in constructing mental illness online. *Journal of Computer-Mediated Communication, 18,* 476–490.

Goffman, E. (1963). *Stigma: Notes on the management of spoiled identity.* Penguin Books.

Graham, T., & Wright, S. (2014). Discursive equality and everyday talk online: The impact of 'super participants'. *Journal of Computer-Mediated Communication, 19*(3), 625–642.

Greenberg, J. L., Limoncelli, K. E., & Wilhelm, S. (2017). Body dysmorphic disorder by proxy. In Katharine A. Phillips, M.D. (Ed.), *Body dysmorphic disorder: Advances in research and clinical practice* (pp. 95-101). Oxford University Press.

Greene, K., Derlega, V. J., & Mathews, A. (2006). Self-disclosure in personal relationships. In A. L. Vangelisti & D. Perlman (Eds.), *The Cambridge handbook of personal relationships.* (pp. 409-427). Cambridge University Press.

Hardaker, C. (2015). "I refuse to respond to this obvious troll": An overview of responses to (perceived) trolling. *Corpora, 10*(2), 201–229. https://doi.org/10.3366/cor.2015.0074

Hart, A. S., & Niemiec, M. A. (2017). Comorbidity and personality in body dysmorphic disorder. In Katharine A. Phillips, M.D. (Ed.), *Body dysmorphic disorder: Advances in research and clinical practice* (pp. 125-136). Oxford University Press.

Hartmann, A.S., & Buhlmann, U. (2017). Prevalence and underrecognition of body dysmorphic disorder. In Katharine A. Phillips, M.D. (Ed.), *Body dysmorphic disorder: Advances in research and clinical practice* (pp. 49-60). Oxford University Press.

Kelly, M. M., Brault, M. E., & Didie, E. R. (2017). Psychosocial functioning and quality of life in body dysmorphic disorder. In Katharine A. Phillips, M.D. (Ed.), *Body dysmorphic disorder: Advances in research and clinical practice* (pp. 139-153). Oxford University Press.

Kelly, M. M., & Kent, M. (2017). The relationship between body dysmorphic disorder and social anxiety disorder. In Katharine A. Phillips, M.D. (Ed.), *Body dysmorphic disorder: Advances in research and clinical practice* (pp. 493-502). Oxford University Press.

Kim, E., Han, J., Moon, T., Shaw, B., Shah, D. V., McTavish, F. M., & Gustafson, D. H. (2012). The process and effect of supportive message expression and reception in online breast cancer support groups. *Psycho-Oncology, 21*(5), 531–540. https://doi.org/10.1002/pon.1942

Koran, L. M., Abujaoude, E., Large, M. D., & Serpe, R. T. (2008). The prevalence of body dysmorphic disorder in the United States adult population. *CNS Spectrums, 13*, pp. 316–22.

Kral, G. (2006). Online communities for mutual help: Fears, fiction, and facts. In M. Murero & R. E. Rice (Eds.), *The internet and health care: Theory, research, and practice* (pp. 215-232). Lawrence Erlbaum Associates.

Malcolm, A., Pikoos, T. D., Grace, S. A., Castle, D. J., & Rossell, S. L. (2021). Childhood maltreatment and trauma is common and severe in body dysmorphic disorder. *Comprehensive Psychiatry, 109*. https://doi.org/10.1016/j.comppsych.2021.152256

Marques, L., Weingarden, H. M., LeBlanc, N. J., & Wilhelm, S. (2011). Treatment utilization and barriers to treatment engagement among people with body dysmorphic symptoms. *Journal of Psychosomatic Research, 70*(3), 286–293.

Marques, L., Weingarden, H. M., LeBlanc, N. J., Siev, J., & Wilhelm, S. (2011). The relationship between perceived social support and severity of body dysmorphic disorder symptoms: The role of gender. *Revista Brasileira De Psiquiatria, 33*(3), 238–244.

McCurdy-McKinnon, D., & Feusner, J. D. (2017). Neurobiology of body dysmorphic disorder: Heritability/genetics, brain circuitry, and visual processing. In Katharine A. Phillips, M.D. (Ed.), *Body dysmorphic disorder: Advances in research and clinical practice* (pp. 253-276). Oxford University Press.

Mo, P. K. H., & Coulson, N. S. (2014). Are online support groups always beneficial? A qualitative exploration of the empowering and disempowering processes of participation within HIV/AIDS-related online support groups. *International Journal of Nursing Studies*, *51*(7), 983–993. https://doi.org/10.1016/j.ijnurstu.2013.11.006

Newman, M., Lauterbach, D., Munson, S., Resnick, P., & Morris, M. (2011). "It's not that I don't have problems, I'm just not putting them on Facebook": Challenges and opportunities in using online social networks for health. Proceedings of the ACM 2011 conference on computer supported cooperative work, 341–350.

Neziroglu, F., & Barile, N. (2017). Environmental factors in body dysmorphic disorder. In Katharine A. Phillips, M.D. (Ed.), *Body dysmorphic disorder: Advances in research and clinical practice* (pp. 277-284). Oxford University Press.

Nyeyk, M. (2017). *Trolls and trolling: An exploration of those that live under the internet bridge.* Michael Nyeyk Publishing.

Pennebaker, J. W., & Seagal, J. D. (1999). Forming a story: The health benefits of narrative. *Journal of Clinical Psychology*, *55*(10), 1243–1254.

Phillips, K. A. (1996/2005). *The broken mirror: Understanding and treating body dysmorphic disorder.* Oxford University Press.

Phillips, K. A. (2009). *Understanding body dysmorphic disorder: An essential guide.* Oxford University Press.

Phillips, K. A. (2017a). Classification of body dysmorphic disorder and relevance for patient care. In Katharine A. Phillips, M.D. (Ed.), *Body dysmorphic disorder: Advances in research and clinical practice* (pp. 33-45). Oxford University Press.

Phillips, K. A. (2017b). Suicidality and aggressive behavior in body dysmorphic disorder. In Katharine A. Phillips, M.D. (Ed.), *Body dysmorphic disorder: Advances in research and clinical practice* (pp. 155-170). Oxford University Press.

Phillips, K. A. (2017c). Pharmacotherapy and other somatic treatments for body dysmorphic disorder. In Katharine A. Phillips, M.D. (Ed.), *Body dysmorphic disorder: Advances in research and clinical practice* (pp. 333-355). Oxford University Press.

Phillips, K. A. (2017d). Insight and delusional beliefs in body dysmorphic disorder. In Katharine A. Phillips, M.D. (Ed.), *Body dysmorphic disorder: Advances in research and clinical practice* (pp. 103-113). Oxford University Press.

Phillips, K. A. (2017e). Differentiating body dysmorphic disorder from normal appearance concerns and other mental disorders. In Katharine A. Phillips, M.D. (Ed.), *Body dysmorphic disorder: Advances in research and clinical practice* (pp. 227-239). Oxford University Press.

Phillips, K. A., Didie, E., Feusner, J., & Wilhelm, S. (2008). Body dysmorphic disorder: Treating an underrecognized disorder. *American Journal of Psychiatry*, *165*(9), 1111–1118.

Phillips, K. A., McElroy, S. L., Keck, P. E. Jr., Pope, H. G. Jr., & Hudson, J. I. (1993). Body dysmorphic disorder: 30 cases of imagined ugliness. *American Journal of Psychiatry*, *150*, 302–308.

Psychology and Mental Health Forum. (2012). *Body dysmorphic disorder.* https://www.psychforums.com/body-dysmorphic-disorder/

Rosenblum, G. D., & Lewis, M. (1999). The relations among body image, physical attractiveness, and body mass in adolescence. *Child Development*, *70*(1), 50–64.

Rytina, S. (2008). Imagined ugliness. *Scientific American Mind*, *19*(6), 72.

Schnackenberg, N., & Petro, S. (Eds.) (2016). *Reflections on body dysmorphic disorder.* Body Dysmorphic Disorder Foundation.

Simmons, R. A., & Phillips, K.A. (2017). Core clinical features of body dysmorphic disorder: Appearance preoccupations, negative emotions, core beliefs, and repetitive and avoidance behaviors. In Katharine A. Phillips, M.D. (Ed.), *Body dysmorphic disorder: Advances in research and clinical practice* (pp. 61-80). Oxford University Press.

Statistics & Research on Eating Disorders. (2019). https://www.nationaleatingdisorders.org/statistics-research-eating-disorders

Substance Abuse and Mental Health Services Administration. (2011). *SAMSHA announces a working definition of recovery from mental disorders.* http://www.samhsa.gov/newsroom/advisories/1112223420.aspx

Tanis, M. (2008). Health-related on-line forums: What's the big attraction? *Journal of Health Communication, 13*(7), 698–714. https://doi.org/10.1080/10810730802415316

Thoits, P. A. (2011). Mechanisms linking social ties and support to physical and mental health. *Journal of Health and Social Behavior, 52*(2), 145–161. https://doi.org/10.1177/0022146510395592

Tichon, J. G., & Shapiro, M. (2003). The process of sharing social support in cyberspace. *Cyberpsychology & Behavior, 6*(2), 161–170. https://doi.org/10.1089/109493103321640356

Tidwell, L., & Walther, J. (2002). Computer-mediated communication effects on disclosure, impressions, and interpersonal evaluations: Getting to know one another a bit at a time. *Human Communication Research, 28*(3), 317–348.

Tignol, J., Biraben-Gotzamanis, L., Martin-Guehl, C., Grabot, D., & Aouizerate, B. (2007). Body dysmorphic disorder and cosmetic surgery: Evolution of 24 subjects with a minimal defect in appearance 5 years after their request for cosmetic surgery. *European Psychiatry, 22*(8), 520–524.

Van Noppen, B., & Sassano-Higgens, S. (2017). The family and body dysmorphic disorder: Impact, responses, and a suggested family-based treatment approach. In Katharine A. Phillips, M.D. (Ed.), *Body dysmorphic disorder: Advances in research and clinical practice* (pp. 411-427). Oxford University Press.

van Uden-Kraan, C. F., Drossaert, C. H. C., Taal, E., Shaw, B. R., Seydel, E. R., & van de Laar, M. A. F. J. (2008). Empowering processes and outcomes of participation in online support groups for patients with breast cancer, arthritis and fibromyalgia. *Qualitative Health Research, 18*, 405–417.

van Uden-Kraan, C. F., Drossaert, C. H. C., Taal, E., Seydel, E. R., & van de Laar, M. A. F. J. (2008). Self-reported differences in empowerment between lurkers and posters in online patient support groups. *Journal of Medical Internet Research, 10*(2), e18. https://doi.org/10.2196/jmir.992

van Uden-Kraan, C. F., Drossaert, C. H. C., Taal, E., Seydel, E. R., & van de Laar, M. A. F. J. (2009). Participation in online patient support groups endorses patients' empowerment. *Patient Education and Counseling, 74*(1), 61–69.

Veale, D., Ennis, M., & Lambrou, C. (2002). Possible association of body dysmorphic disorder with an occupation or education in art and design. *American Journal of Psychiatry, 159*(10), 1788–1790.

Veale, D., Willson, R., & Clarke, A. (2009). *Overcoming body image problems including body dysmorphic disorder (overcoming books).* Constable & Robinson, LTD.

Veale, D., Phillips, K.A., & Nezioglu, F. (2017). Challenges in assessing and treating patients with body dysmorphic disorder and recommended approaches. In Katharine A. Phillips, M.D. (Ed.), *Body dysmorphic disorder: Advances in research and clinical practice* (pp. 313-332). Oxford University Press.

Vidourek, R. A., King, K. A., Nabors, L. A., & Merianos, A. L. (2014). Students' benefits and barriers to mental health help-seeking. *Health Psychology and Behavioral Medicine, 2*(1), 1009–1022. https://doi.org/10.1080/21642850.2014.963586

Walther, J. B., & Boyd, S. (2002). Attraction to computer-mediated social support. In C. A. Lin & D. Atkin (Eds.), *Communication technology and society: Audience adoption and uses* (pp.153-188). Hampton Press.

Wilhelm, S. (2006). *Feeling good about the way you look: A program for overcoming body image problems.* The Guilford Press.

Winograd, A. M. (2017). *Face to face with body dysmorphic disorder.* Taylor & Francis Group.

Wolke, D., & Sapouna, M. (2008). Big men feeling small: Childhood bullying experience, muscle dysmorphia and other mental health problems in bodybuilders. *Psychology of Sport and Exercise, 9*(5), 595–604. https://doi.org/10.1016/j.psychsport.2007.10.002

Wright, K. B., Sparks, L., & O'Hair, H. D. (2013). *Health communication in the 21st century.* Wiley-Blackwell.

Acknowledgments

I know how important it is (and how difficult it can be) to find people who are supportive when you are struggling with BDD symptoms. a.

I am grateful to my friend Stephanie Ehret, who responded with curiosity and compassion after hearing about my diagnosis, and to my counselor Ann Hazen, who aided in my recovery. Many thanks are also due to my partner, Doug Stansberry, for his love and support during the dissertation and book-writing process. The dissertation took eight years to complete and the book another year.

This book is based upon the results of my doctoral research about online peer support for BDD. My research was guided by my advisor Kirk Hallahan and the members of my dissertation committee at Colorado State University: Donna Rouner, Marilee Long, Jennifer Ogle, and Elizabeth Williams. Thank you all for your support during the research, writing, and revision process.

My recovery was made possible because of the resources provided by dedicated BDD researchers and clinicians. First, I want to express my gratitude to Katharine Phillips. Her seminal research on BDD, books about the disorder, and most of all, the decades she has spent treating people with BDD symptoms have made her a hero to me and many others who struggle with this disorder.

My heartfelt gratitude also goes out to the BDD researchers and therapists who are members of the International OCD Foundation BDD Special Interest Group (SIG). Your contributions to the BDD community are greatly appreciated. I want to acknowledge the following clinicians who provided treatment resources for the Appendix: Katharine Phillips, Sabine Wilhelm, Fugen Neziroglu, Roberto Olivardia, Scott Granet, Arie Winograd, Steven Poskar, Eric

Hollander, Chris Trondsen, Robyn Leigh Stern, and Tania Borda. In addition, thank you to the team at the International OCD Foundation in the United States and the BDD Foundation in the United Kingdom. These organizations provide grants, resources, and support to BDD researchers, clinicians, patients, and their families.

My vision to transform my dissertation into a book was made possible due to the valuable feedback and assistance I received from my publishing team, including my editor Alexandra O'Connell, proofreader Jennifer Jas, layout designer Bryan Canter, and project manager Polly Letofsky. Finally, I wish to thank my parents, who passed away in 2000, for providing guidance and support for my academic and career pursuits. I know by overcoming BDD and publishing this book, I would have made them both proud.

ABOUT THE AUTHOR

Eva Fisher, PhD, is a communication faculty member at Colorado State University Global. Eva received her PhD from Colorado State University in 2016. She has presented her research at the National Communication Association Convention and her recovery story at the International OCD Foundation Convention. She facilitates peer support groups for therapists and people with body dysmorphic disorder (BDD). More information about her virtual support groups can be found on the International OCD Foundation website and the BDD Foundation website.

Eva is a member of the International OCD Foundation BDD Special Interest Group and has authored multiple blogs about coping with and recovery from BDD. She is a professional communication consultant and founder of Fear to Courage, LLC. Eva empowers her clients to overcome their communication challenges and accelerate their business, career, and personal success. She resides in Colorado with her partner, Doug, and her cat, Misti. She can be reached at eva@feartocourage.com.

BECOME PART OF THE GLOBAL BDD FAMILY

Become part of the global BDD family!

Contact Eva at eva@feartocourage.com to learn more about her recovery from BDD and to book her for podcasts and speaking engagements.

Visit Eva's website now to access the many resources provided throughout her book and to join her Recovery from BDD peer support group: feartocourage.com/bdd-resources/

Connect with Eva on social media via LinkedIn: linkedin.com/in/evafisherphd/

Follow the Recovery from BDD Facebook page and join the private group here: facebook.com/recoveryfrombdd/

Made in the USA
Las Vegas, NV
23 March 2023

69603512R00174